# CLOTH AND CULTUF
## EDITED BY LESLEY

# CREDITS

| | |
|---|---|
| Published by | University College for the Creative Arts at Canterbury, Epsom, Farnham, Maidstone and Rochester |
| Editor | Lesley Millar |
| Essays | Astrida Berzina, Keiko Fujimoto, Jennifer Harris, Kai Lobjakas, Lesley Millar, Leena Svinhufvud, Virginija Vitkienė |
| Translation | Marianna Auliciema (A. Berzina text); Mary Murata (K. Fujimoto text); Michael Haagensen (K. Lobjakas text); Mike Garner (L. Svinhufvud text); UAB Metropolio Vertimai ed. Michael Haagensen (V. Vitkienė text) |
| Copy Editor | John Pym |
| Editorial assistance | Celia Pym, June Hill |
| Photographic Editor | Damian Chapman |
| Art Director | Gerry Diebel |
| Designers | Anders Fagerhus, Laurie King, Ed Walker, Phil Chandler |
| Design & Production | Direct Design – www.directdesign.co.uk |
| Printing | Windsor Print Production Limited – www.windsor-print.co.uk |
| Website | www.site-designs.co.uk |
| Project Co-ordinator Japan | Keiko Kawashima |
| Project Co-ordinator Latvia | Astrida Berzina |

**WORLD ART
COLLECTIONS
EXHIBITIONS**
SAINSBURY CENTRE
for Visual Arts

The book Cloth & Culture Now has been published December 2007 in support of the exhibition 'Cloth & Culture Now' curated by Lesley Millar, opening at the Sainsbury Centre for Visual Arts, University of East Anglia, January 2008.

All credits for photographs of artists work are with the images. Studio images supplied by Lesley Millar except Michael Brennand-Wood, Maxine Bristow, Shelly Goldsmith, Diana Harrison, Una Laukmane, Kadri Viires, Mare Kelpman, Krista Leesi.

University College for the Creative Arts at Canterbury, Epsom, Farnham, Maidstone and Rochester
Epsom College, Ashley Road, Epsom, Surrey KT18 5BE

# CONTENTS

WEBSITE

For the full text of the statements by all the
participating artists and further information
about Cloth & Culture Now please visit
www.clothandculturenow.com

# CLOTH AND CULTURE NOW

ESTONIA
FINLAND
JAPAN
LATVIA
LITHUANIA
UNITED KINGDOM

# FOREWORD

PROFESSOR ELAINE THOMAS

As Rector of the University College for the Creative Arts, at Canterbury, Epsom, Farnham, Maidstone and Rochester, I am delighted to have the opportunity to acknowledge the achievements of Professor Lesley Millar. The research project documented in this publication is one of several which Lesley has pioneered with support from the University College, and it exemplifies our commitment to working with partners worldwide to contribute to cultural understanding. Exposure to and dissemination of the work of artists from a range of cultural contexts enhances our understanding and fosters creativity, which is at the heart of what we do. Cross cultural communication and exchange requires real collaboration and when it involves the creative processes employed by makers, it results in tangible and accessible outputs.

The University College for the Creative Arts is proud of its own origins and artistic heritage, particularly relating to textiles and crafts and seeks to build upon this foundation of traditional making skills while embracing new technologies, celebrating innovation and pushing the boundaries of contemporary practice.

In initiating and leading this project, Lesley Millar has fostered understanding of the links between traditional and contemporary practice and the importance of acknowledging and understanding origins and influences. She has also created a means of effecting real cross-cultural communication at an international level, which furthers the aspirations and values of the University College and contributes to a better understanding of cultural context and creative practice for participants and audience.

# TRANSITION AND INFLUENCE

LESLEY MILLAR

Professor of Textile Culture,
University College for the Creative Arts
at Canterbury, Epsom, Farnham,
Maidstone and Rochester

'Cloth is the universal free element. It doesn't have to explain itself. It performs.'[1]

I have been told that there is a mountain tribe in China who, maybe a thousand years ago, migrated to the Mayo region from the country's lowland rice fields. Their traditional embroidered wedding cloaks are created from triangles of yellow, brown and green silk: the pattern of the rice fields they left behind so long ago. Although they have forgotten the fields, the cloth keeps the memory.[2] In this, and many other ways, cloth holds the memory of our time and connects us with memories of other times and other places. In Cloth and Human Experience, Jane Schneider and Annette B Weiner, describe the range of symbolic and economic roles attributed to cloth as reflecting more than the labour invested in its production, citing: 'The connections of its threads and weaving patterns with ancestral or mythical knowledge' (Weiner and Schneider 1989:25).

From the traditional to the contemporary. My work with textile practitioners in the UK and Japan has resulted in my increasing interest in the way that contemporary practitioners see their work in relation to traditional practice. (For the purpose of this project, the term 'traditional practice' describes textile practice and competencies that have demonstrably transcended generations.) My intention with this project has been to explore that transition from the repetition of traditional practice,

to the development of a contemporary language of making, and the factors that influence that development. Within the project I sought to identify where there is a conscious connection between innovatory contemporary practice and the recognised 'authority of customary traditional practice' (Bhabha 1994:254).

As the research progressed, the investigation focused on those geographical locations where contemporary practice draws on the traditional expression of cultural particularity through textiles, whilst also engaging with cross-cultural and trans-national influences. The thirty-five artists in 'Cloth & Culture Now' have been selected from six different countries: Estonia, Latvia, Lithuania, Finland, Japan, and the UK. In each of these countries textiles have traditionally played a central role, both economically and also as a carrier of the narrative of place. And in each of these countries contemporary textile artists are using that embedded narrative of traditional practice within the discourse surrounding their practice.

In the highly contemporary work of these artists it is possible to identify a continuum from specific traditional practice. It is also possible to identify approaches that link across countries and individual cultural backgrounds. These links reflect the natural progression of cross-cultural exchange and absorption that has been a continuous influence on the production, use and understanding of textiles. The links can also be seen to reflect the disintegration of traditional geographical borders brought about either by migration or globalisation.

It is now possible for cultural groupings to be located in multiple centres: no longer defined by national boundaries, or by how nations perceive themselves, or believe they are perceived by others – that interrogation of the 'internal and external gaze' (Isozaki 2006:57). There is a movement away from a national culture of memory, defined by the history and tradition of nationhood, towards a model based on individual memory, made up from complex fragments, which can be understood trans-nationally. (Bagnall 2003:) Such tendencies mean that identifying 'The natural(ized), unifying discourse of "nation", "peoples", or authentic "folk" tradition, those embedded myths of culture's particularity' (Bhabha 1994:247) becomes more and more difficult.

Cloth and Communication. Within these shifting reference points, where demarcation is in a state of flux, cloth and the making of cloth provide a continuous undercurrent between cultures: a shared understanding which is both universal and culture-specific. Many contemporary practitioner's, including those taking part in 'Cloth & Culture Now', are combining the language of materiality with specific social, political and utilitarian histories. In this way they are reflecting both their own cultural particularity, and establishing narratives for the new cultural groupings, characterized by the architect and writer Arata Isozaki as 'the space-in-between communities'. These narratives are ones of connection, to the past and to the future, located in the present – the 'now' of making. It is important to emphasize that the bringing together of these different levels of engagement is not about 'here and there, now and then', but rather could be represented as 'simultaneous modes of embodiment' (Bell 2007:26). The act of

making enables different sets of relationships to take place simultaneously: between the artist and tradition, the translation of that tradition, and the development of a personal narrative – all of which are inherent within the process and evidenced in the work.

Today, when globalisation and mass media have become such diffusing and permeating forces, posing significant threat to cultural particularity, are there indications that textiles have a role as a possible means of subversive communication in the renegotiation of cultural boundaries? If we look to recent as well as historical precedents: over the last thirty-five years contemporary practitioners have used the cultural space presented by the domestic history of the making and use of textiles, to move between the personal and the political.

More specifically, over a period of more than forty years, the Soviet occupation of the Baltic countries created an additional, precise focus for textile artists. From the interviews with the artists, from their web statements and from the country related essays within this book, we understand that textiles, and in particular pattern, were consciously used by textile artists in Estonia, Latvia and Lithuania, during the Soviet occupation, as a powerful and subversive element, an implicit sign of national and cultural particularity. Working with textiles in this way, the artists were connecting to the historic use of pattern as an overt and covert language in the form of:

'codified cultural texts in the form of symbols and patterns which speak of the specific local culture, relationships with the surrounding natural environment, the skills of the maker, as well as the status and taste of the wearer' (Viires 2006).[3]

Several of the artists in this exhibition have continued to reference and develop this

understanding of pattern and language, including Kadri Viires, Mare Kelpman, Krista Leesi, Lina Jonikė, Severija Inčirauskaitė-Kriaunevičienė and Peteris Sidars. Japanese artist, Mitsuo Toyazaki, cites the importance of the Jōmon aesthetic, which is most present in its use of pattern, within his own work.[4] In the context of pattern as 'codified text', it is interesting to note that, according to Arata Isozaki, in the period following the Second World War, during the occupation of Japan by American forces, the Jōmon aesthetic became a 'secretly nurtured native dynamism opposing the gaze of the occupier'. The use of the Jōmon aesthetic in this manner could be seen as a response to the appropriation of the more refined Yayoi aesthetic of space, which had been taken to New York and integrated into the American Modernist aesthetic (Isozaki 2006:39).

Narrative. All the artists in 'Cloth & Culture Now' are concerned with narrative in one form or another. Although stories traditionally play a significant role in the continuity of embedded knowledge, they can also be renegotiated as social situations change (Tilly 2002), and open to subjective editing. Such intervention does not render the story untrue, only that the context of the telling is a powerful element in the construct of the story (Bell 2007). The fact, for example, that Severija Inčirauskaitė-Kriaunevičienė embroiders ersatz folk patterns on pan lids, or rusty garden tools as a comment on the 'bogus' folk art used to construct new national identity, extends rather than negates the original use of embroidered pattern.

As stories shift in shape, so too the approach to narrative within cloth and the making of cloth takes many forms, as demonstrated by those taking part in 'Cloth & Culture Now'. Artists Eglė Ganda

Bogdanienė, Auste Jurgelionyte and Ieva Krumina are pure storytellers, the images serving the story, the unravelling of which is at the heart of the work. However, stories can also be vehicles for the covert transfer of information, suggesting the possibility that things may be other than the status quo. This approach can be seen in the work of Jun Mitsuhashi and Silja Puranen who are also storytellers, allowing the images to form the story, creating worlds where nothing is as it seems.

For some textile artists, the narrative is carried through their interrogation of surface, material or structure. In the work of Shelly Goldsmith the story is told as much through the material and technique as through the imagery, while the cultural narratives described by Merja Winqvist, Sue Lawty and Hideaki Kizaki are embedded in material and structure. Winqvist's archetypal forms, recognisable across all cultures, and linked directly to specific cultural experience, create a narrative that is universal and also culture specific. Lawty is much concerned with the physicality of the landscape, its stones and rocks. She is relating the embodiment of time within the strata of the earth to the time taken to make, which is embedded within the work. For Kizaki the material itself, jute, has become a metaphor for integrity, being associated with hard work and nature in its rawest form. Diana Harrison and Masaaki Tate engage in an internal discourse about the ways in which their extensive vocabulary of making is revealed in the surface of the work. The mark making that informs that surface – either the pulled thread in the dyed cloth or the 'drawn' line across the surface of the cloth - represent the narrative of their personal aesthetic and the process of making.

Continuum. The material or technical approaches of Tate, Harrison, Kizaki, Lawty and Goldsmith reflect the continuum from tradition to contemporary in a direct manner. This is also true of, for example, Freddie Robins with her knitted work, or Krista Leesi with her patchwork. Other artists, however, may not always engage directly with textile, having chosen to apply their textile vocabulary in the development of a personal iconography. This second approach is particularly apparent in those whose work is concerned with the mapping of space, as can be seen in Michael Brennand-Wood's referencing of lace and the structure of lace as a key factor in his work. Lace and space – the shape and the space between the shape take on equal significance, the spatial properties within and around the work are interdependent. His installations move out from the wall, causing the viewer to renegotiate his or her relationship to the surrounding space.

Jun Mitsuhashi and Mitsuo Toyazaki are both trained dyers, Toyazaki also trained in traditional stencil printing. Each has developed particular vocabularies based on that training. The spatial tension that Mitsuhashi evokes between the batik surface of the cloth, and the objects both on and in the cloth, functions as an entrance point for a magical other world. In his wish to transform our understanding of mundane objects, he brings to his work the processes of alchemy that are inherent in the act of dyeing. In Toyazaki's work the overall patterns create distinct forms which, through the relationship of the pattern's constituent elements – buttons, paper clips, tiny burnt holes – develop the sense of the affinities between the micro and macro cosmos. His detailed patterning of space clearly references his deep understanding of stencil technique, which is embedded in the textile tradition of Japan.

Connection and difference. The constructive articulation or intuitive uses of space are aesthetic concerns for artists from all backgrounds. In previous projects[5] I have investigated the relationship between Japanese textile artists and 'the expressions of space inherent in Japanese culture' (Isozaki 2006:68). This relationship is inextricably influenced by the artists' experience of nature, a relationship that is also evident in the approaches of the artists from Finland.

Finland is a country subject to extreme seasonal contrast of light and darkness as reflected in Helena Hietanen's use of brilliant white light, throwing the surrounding space into deepest shadow, reminding the viewer of endless day and everlasting night. Many of the Finnish artists describe the importance of experiencing both the dark time and the light time, and their resulting heightened awareness of the nuances of light and shadow. Agneta Hobin speaks of Finnish light 'strained and filtered through clouds, foliage or blades of grass',[6] and both her work and that of Japanese artist Shoko Nomura allow the passage of light to soften our sense of those lines of demarcation formed by their work. Through her references to both the traditions of papermaking and wider cultural traditions,[7] Nomura can be seen to represent 'the Japanese aesthetic of modesty, symbolism, tradition and darkness' (Hara 2007:10).

As certain approaches to space and nature reside within specific countries, it is also possible to identify other particularities that denote a textile language peculiar to a localised culture. For example, to return to the Japanese, there is an unmediated engagement with objecthood, a commitment to understanding the intention of the cloth through the act of making. By way of contrast, textile artists working in Lithuania often employ a dynamic use of performance as a means of direct communication through ritual enactments, as evidenced in this exhibition by Eglė Ganda Bogdanienė and Laura Pavilonyte. Here in the UK, many artists, including most in this exhibition, have chosen to reference, rather than embody, the relationship to the traditional, often engaging with a wider, fine art discourse.

However, it is also clear that, while intrinsically distinct, there are also overlapping influences that can be seen to emerge from national comparisons. For example, many of the artists in this exhibition are, in some form or another, responding to the body; tracing a journey from the body present to the body absent. In some cases, they are describing the body through the body, for example Eglė Ganda Bogdanienė's use of her own body as *tabula rasa*, or Laima Oržekauskienė's use of human hair to model the body within the cloth. In other cases, for example Shelly Goldsmith, the reference is through allusion to bodily fluids; or through trace elements, as in the 'Skin Stories' of Zane Berzina's empirical studies of skin patterns as the basis for her textile 'specimens'. Some artists create an awareness of the body through its 'absence'. As Maxine Bristow puts it: the cloth acts as silent witness to its many encounters with the body.[8] Bristow's

work also provides a secondary narrative of 'body', that of the body of the maker, and through the maker connecting to the history of the method of making.

All the artists documented in this project are very aware of and so deeply grounded in traditional practice that it has become a part of their makeup. However, as discussed in this essay and throughout the book, and as evidenced by their work, each has been in a position to make choices about their individual relationship to that tradition. In their ability to imagine that the outcome may be 'other', their work embodies past practice in ways that can shape future practice. They have all inherited a form of cultural capital, which is mediated through personal narrative and life history that is not necessarily bounded by cultural particularity. These factors afford the opportunity for each of the artists to translate their individual pool of cultural reference through the re-negotiation brought about by shifting connections within the 'space-in-between communities'. This fluidity enables the artists to re-present traditional practice in new contexts, outside restrictive structures, and through this regenerative process offer tradition the best hope for its survival. As participating artist Mitsuo Toyazaki has written in his web statement: 'within the unexpected you can find the inevitable'. [9] ■

References:

Bagnall, Gaynor. (2003). 'Performance and Performativity at Heritage Sites'. Museums and Society. 1(2) pp 87–103.

Bell, Vikki. (2007). Culture & Performance. Oxford. Berg.

Bhabha, Homi K. (1994). The Location of Culture. London. Routledge.

Hara, Kenya. (2007). Designing Design. Baden. Lars-Muller.

Isozaki, Arata. (2006). Japan-ness in Architecture. Cambridge, MA. MIT Press.

Tilly, Charles. (2002). Stories, Identities and Political Change. London. Rowman & Littlefield.

Weiner, Annette B, and Schneider, Jane (eds). (1989).Cloth and Human Experience. Washington, DC. Smithsonian Institution Press.

1. Lubbock, Tom. 'The secret life of cloth.' The Independent. 18 June 2002.
2. Taken from the video interviews 'What is cloth to me?' Becker and Millar. 2005.
3. Taken from web statement www.clothandculturenow.com.
4. In interview with Lesley Millar, published in this book .
5. Textural Space and Through the Surface.
6. Taken from web statement www.clothandculturenow.com.
7. For example the traditional door used to enter tea ceremony houses, which is very low, causing every person who enters, of no matter what rank, to bow.
8. In interview with Lesley Millar, published in this book.
9. Taken from web statement www.clothandculturenow.com.

# ESTONIA

MARE KELPMAN
KRISTA LEESI
KATRIN PERE
AUNE TAAMAL
KADRI VIIRES

# INTERPRETATIONS OF TRADITION IN ESTONIAN TEXTILE DESIGN

KAI LOBJAKAS

Tradition and traditionalism in Estonian textile design are principally associated with notions of folk art and nationalism. Delve a little deeper, and we see that the manner in which folk art and nationalism have been interpreted is definitely more interesting than the different techniques and materials involved. Interpretations of what is or is not national are just as important in the formulation of a tradition as is the existence of tapestries and rugs over the decades. At the same time, from the perspective of tradition, Estonian professional textile design itself fits into a relatively short period.

We can start to talk about applied art as a professional cultural field in Estonia from the 1920s or 30s. Alongside the emergence of a national awareness, it arose from local peasant culture and the Baltic-German handicraft tradition, and paved a clear direction for itself with successes both locally and in international exhibitions. From the different periods of Estonian textile design several interesting and clearly defined examples of 'the national' as a recurring theme can be found. My purpose here is to investigate some of the more significant concepts and expressions of tradition.

Tradition as opportunity. Working with textiles has always been an essential part of folk art traditions, and it was also the first subject to be taught at the first Estonian art university. The subject of women's handicraft was included as the first applied art subject in the curriculum of the Tallinn School of Applied Art, which opened in 1914 as the forerunner to the State School of Applied Art. Until then, opportunities to study textile design had been offered by various private handicraft schools for women, handicraft courses and home economics schools in Estonia and neighbouring areas – for example in Helsinki, but also in Berlin, Stockholm and Copenhagen.

The new school set out to be different from these many needlework and private sewing schools, and also to give the students a good general education in art along with some technical skills. In the early years, the main subjects were embroidery and lace work but, by the beginning of the 1920s, the teachers wanted to extend their activities by opening a knitting workshop and ordering handlooms. Sufficient funds, however, were unavailable.

As was a common practice, the designs and motifs used were often based on ethnic floral patterns and stylisations of them. The rising national awareness at the beginning of the 20th century and attempts to preserve 'one's own' culture caused makers to look for material from local folk art traditions. A few years later, in the publication Handicraft, which first appeared in 1906, we can see draft designs of tapestries based on ethnic motifs and made by the first Estonian professional applied artists to have returned from study abroad.

Finnish national romantic tapestry from the 19th century became an important example and influenced a young Estonian painter named Oskar Kallis who created tapestry designs inspired by folk mythology between 1915 and 1917 (Image 1a). This is usually considered the beginning of the development of professional Estonian tapestry art. These early days were characterised by a close adherence to folk art, even to the point of copying directly from it. During the 1920s, the style became more constructivist and geometric in the style of Art Deco. A relationship between the modern and the traditional began to take place simultaneously – a connection with the contemporary, while at the same time a return to the past.

Tradition as obligation. With the end of the Second World War came the end of Estonia's first period of independence and a change in our relationship with traditions and national inheritance. In opposition to Western modernism, the Soviet regime chose Traditionalism as its 'style'. Under the slogan 'socialist in content, national in form' a large number of art works using mandatory patterns were produced. The stylistic aim of these works was to be 'nationalist', which was initially difficult to comprehend and caused fear, while the broader aim was for the works to be visually clear, portraying realistic imagery.

In textiles this meant rugs made using a wide range of techniques, but employing the same designs. Ornamentation originated from local folk art as well as that of other countries in the Soviet Union, and was typified by a high degree of stylisation (Image

2a). Constant use of certain specific images resulted in a steady stream of uninteresting works, which were all similar and in retrospect are typical examples of the period.

The second half of the 1950s was marked by the post-Stalin 'thaw' for both Estonian society and the art world – a period when the propagation of ideology began to relax and desired aims were changing or being changed. In November 1955, the Central Committee of the Soviet Communist Party passed a regulation 'About the elimination of exaggerations in the field of design and building activities'. This affected the applied arts and its canons and parade-like compositions of the Stalinist era were abandoned, although, it must be said, ideological control was definitely not as strict in this field as it had been in the fine arts.

Nevertheless, national themes also played an important role in the applied arts in the late 50s, and this was especially apparent in the gifts presented to neighbouring Soviet republics. These items were to carry the giver's seal of approval when the two republics' slogan-like characteristics were united. The folk art tradition was also dealt with on a wider scale, continuing to force national themes into increasingly modern geometric forms, and this occurred in one-off tapestries as well as serial production.

Tradition as an expression of being modern. Towards the end of the 1950s a relatively rapid development of modernist styles took place. The 'modern style', actively promoted at the time, had an unambiguous content: stylised forms, clarity and occasional asymmetry. In addition, simple materials and colour became an important element. Bruno Tomberg was successful in connecting the key words modernity and traditionalism in an unconventional manner. A good example is his tapestry series 'Perspectives' I–IV (Image 3a).

Tomberg is known as the cornerstone of Estonian applied art. It was under his instruction that the department of applied art was created in the art institute; and in 1969 he produced a significant series of works for exhibition that experimented with space and form. The 'Perspectives' series can be considered the result of a manly, rational and designer-like approach in an otherwise gentle and picturesque world of tapestry art. Tomberg refers to the dominance of this approach, but he also emphasises that his focus on folk art – in particular the striped skirts of Estonian folk costumes – has received little attention. So it is in this series of rugs that he combines his undoubted interest in geometry and the unmistakable stripes of folk costume.

In a constructivist and heavily stylised manner similar to that used by Tomberg, albeit via mere suggestion, Nette Liivak and Lea Valter (Images 4a) have also addressed Estonian folk art. Both developed motifs of the traditional obliquely striped tapestries originating from folk art. Nette Liivak has also boldly stylised flower motifs, while Lea Valter often uses the flame motif, which through the process of contemporising has become a powerful independent geometric detail. In the works of both of these artists, a use of colour is even more definitive than their references to folk art motifs.

Tradition in memory. In the 1950s and 60s, Elgi Reemets worked with folk art from a completely different point of view, an approach which was nostalgic and sometimes naive. She is like some kind of polyglot with craft techniques, working equally with textiles, ceramics, leather and metal. Folk art developed into one of the central themes in her work and it all started during the furore stemming from the post-war slogan – socialist content and nationalist form. Her chosen motifs, which continued

1a. OSKAR KALLIS (1892-1918)
"Siurulind". Designed 1915, executed 1997. Wool, woven

2a. GALINA LEŠKINA (1925)
"Friendship of the Soviet People".
1951. Wool, woven

3a. BRUNO TOMBERG (1925)
From series "Perspectives". IV 1968.
Wool, woven

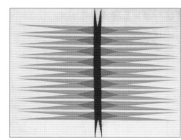

4a. LEA VALTER (1926)
"Pink". 1978
Wool, woven

to inspire her for many decades, included stories and tales, the gentle appreciation of simple people, humorous representations of everyday life and stylisation.

Alongside folk art themes, other important elements were the handling of colour and an abundance of detail. The details, ranging from flower chains to kerosene lamps, also derived from folk art and emphasised the spirit and traditions of the past. The importance of Reemets' work is that alongside ornament, verbal and written inheritance – motifs from folklore, figurative compositions, historical events – find their way into her work in textile form.

In the mid-1970s, Anu Raud began to work intensively on traditional themes, successfully uniting past and present and the connections between them. She bases her work on folk art, mostly making tapestries with themes closely connected with a love of the home (Image 5a). By pondering on the past and present in the creation of her compositions, she employs patterns from belts and gloves and stripes from skirts and fashions completely new national images based on folk ornament.

In a society where the need to recognise one's national identity and appreciate regional traditions is acute, nationalist themes in art lost their relevance in the early 1990s when independence was restored, but rose again through the new generation of artists.

New interpretations of tradition.
Understandably, nationalist themes and exaggerated nationalism lost its impetus for some time after the regaining of independence. Progress, catching up and making new discoveries were the most challenging tasks for the future. A reworking of traditions (or 'local heritage') and bold interpretations arising from this has only recently re-emerged on the scene. This has been a breath of fresh air and caused us to rethink many clichéd notions and assessments from the past.

One of the first to revisit this theme was Signe Kivi. She combined two histories by printing an embroidery pattern originating from the early 20th century over floral chintz fabric from the Soviet period (Image 6a). Annike Laigo has taken an even more confrontational approach to tradition with her greatly enlarged image of a fragment of lace pattern applied to industrial felt with rivets (Images 7a). The contrast between the idea and the materials used (although they also suit one another surprisingly well) justifies this approach.

Krista Leesi has also sought traditions from the recent past with her pattern sheets, printed on to simple cotton fabric, and aimed at the soviet woman, and her loosely crocheted lace covers over car inner tubes. Piret Valk, with her special interest in the opportunities offered by various exotic techniques, has endeavoured to amalgamate them with various traditional techniques, for example delicate lace work with felting.

Being contemporary has been a predominant theme in the treatment of tradition in Estonian textile design. Traditions are free for interpretation and even await reinterpretation, thus providing the opportunity to think about the past and add new versions to an understanding of it. ∎

5a. ANU RAUD (1943)
"City Night". 1977
Wool, woven

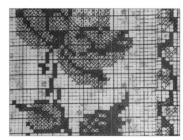

6a. SIGNE KIVI (1957)
"Routine". 1998-9.
Cotton fabric, printed

7a. ANNIKE LAIGO (1972)
"ba rocco". 2004
Felt, rivets

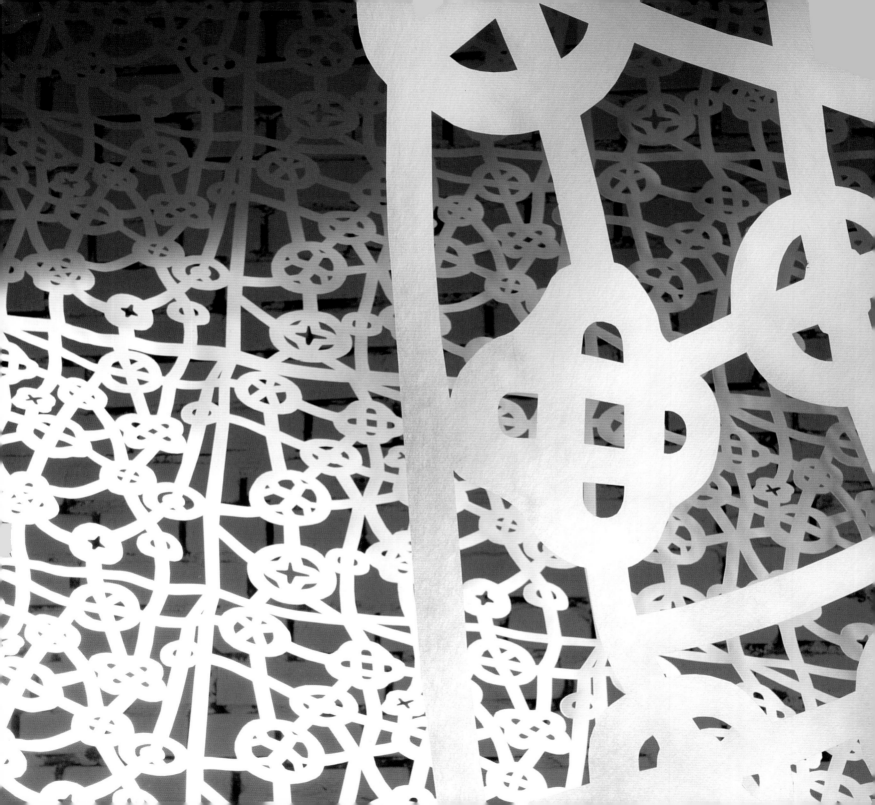

■ Edited extracts from interview with Mare Kelpman, Tallinn, May 2007, with Lesley Millar

Could you talk about the work for the exhibition? I am very interested in patterns and for this work I will use Estonian national patterns, but in a totally different way, using new technology. My interest is to build up new possibilities with traditional patterns. Estonia has quite a large handicraft tradition, and people who make handicrafts use older embroidery patterns. It is not too artistic and it feels old. I want to show people that you can use old patterns in a new way. It also interests me how there are many patterns being used in Estonia manufacture and sold in Estonian shops that are not Estonian patterns.

The idea of taking traditional Estonian decorative motifs and demonstrating that they can look very modern has important design implications. Do you think the Estonia design industry would be interested? Hopefully, yes. Usually in Estonia designers make their work themselves by hand.

So the idea came from looking at traditional Estonian embroidery? Yes, we ran a project called 'Remembering the Future'. The idea was to collect something from the past that nobody remembered. Preparing for this project, I visited the Isle of Kihnu with my students. It is a very small island with a closed community and it is totally normal for everyone to wear traditional costume. Schoolgirls wear these traditional skirts everyday and it is normal. I had visited this island before, but my students hadn't and they were very shocked.

I started to think about this island and what kind of meaning the wearing of traditional costume had. There were so many beautiful things. Even, for example, if you make coffee – it is elegantly done and suddenly, playing with ornamentation had new meaning for me. I started to think how I could use what I had seen and the new ideas I was having. I started to collect ornaments to see what I could use. These are very old, and with sun markings.

Is it important that the viewer understands the history behind your work? Yes. I mean our Estonian culture is very mixed, we have influences from Russia and Germany and the Nordic countries and these ornaments are a reflection of this. I look for patterns and think that baroque patterns are not typically Estonian because at that time we started to make our own patterns.

What materials are you using? Here is a sample that I made in Holland. It looks like typical cross stitch but it is in fact laser cut. This is also polyester, but it looks like old material with stripes. I design it on the computer, I create a file and then I put it in machine and the machine cuts it. The machine does have limits and cannot cut very big areas. It is a stable fabric, and for softer material I have a slightly different approach to make it stable. I also use a material from Finland – I use a resist technique, and then I wash and felt it to make it soft. This is my own technique.
You know it is not interesting to me if I already know how to do a technique. I know everything about it – I am always interested in learning something new. The learning and making the experiments are what excite

METHODS OF MAKING
**Design process, construction of cloth and technical understanding and innovation, all supported by rigorous research, these are the elements that are central to Mare Kelpman's practice.**

NARRATIVE OF MAKING
**Kelpman's study of Estonian national patterns and craft practice provides the cultural narrative linking new technologies and tradition.**

SUGGESTED LINKS
**New technology: see Freddie Robins, Outi Martikainen.**

Lesley Millar

ESTONIAN NATIONAL
EMBROIDERY, 9TH & 10TH
9th: 1.19 x 2.70 m, 10th: 1.27 x 2.70 m
Lasercut polyamid
Photograph: Tiit Rammul

MARE KELPMAN

**15**

me, and I am quite happy to share my ideas – I am a teacher, that's the point, I have to share my ideas. My interest is not so much maybe artistic value. I spend a lot of time working out my designs on the computer. Scanning many images and selecting them and working out many drawings. This is the way I work.

All the time you are doing that, you are not touching the material. Do you miss feeling the material? Yes. For me the material is very important. I spend a lot of time choosing materials. Also how to touch textiles – and skill – are both very important to me. Students must learn to do it by hand. Weaving is our language, so you understand what comes out before you make it. ■

WEBSITE STATEMENT EXTRACT
www.clothandculturenow.com

'I am in awe of every yarn producer, knitter, maker of knitting machines, dyers, printers and all the other technicians, who put their heart and soul into their work.

I usually enjoy a wonderful textile produced by a factory more than a unique piece created by a textile artist.'

MARE KELPMAN

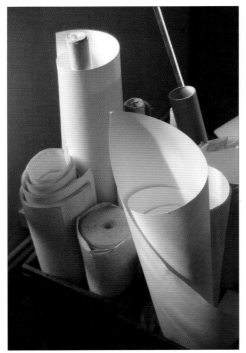

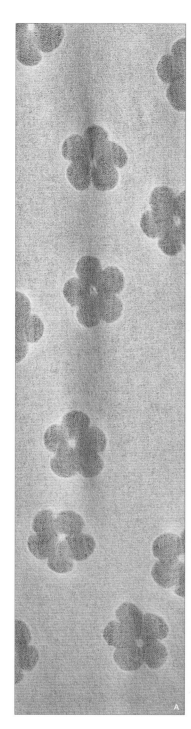

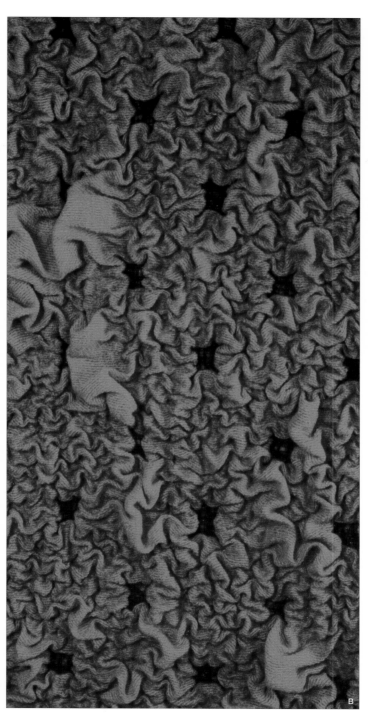

A: FLOWERY (in Estonian language
   – LILLELINE). 2004
   1.2 x 3.9 m
   Wool (technique resist-felting)
   Photograph: Albert Truuväärt

B: FESTIVE 1 (in Estonian language
   – PIDULIK 1). 2003
   0.85 x 1.22 m
   Wool, cotton (technique
   doubleweaving, felting)
   Photograph: Albert Truuväärt

C: ESTONIAN NATIONAL EMBROIDERY 1
   (in Estonian language – EESTI
   RAHVUSLIK TIKAND 1). 2007
   1.8 x 3 m
   Polyester (technique lasercutting)
   Photograph: Albert Truuväärt

■ Edited extracts from interview with Krista Leesi, Tallinn, May 2007; and by email, September 2007 with Lesley Millar

Most of the materials you use in your work normally have another use. I don't think about this question if I am working. In earlier work, usually the idea came first, now if I have an idea for a piece I just decide which material and which technique to use. With the work 'Black Magic' both materials and idea came together at the same time, one did not lead the other. I wanted to make something simply beautiful, just a nice piece.

I wanted to make a work out of crochet and was undecided about the material to use. I looked around and found bin liners. With crochet, the work often gets heavy, but this material – bin liner – stays light. I also tried shopping bags, I was interested in their different colours – and the possibility of using different materials. I am thinking about crocheting with transparent material. Maybe one black and one transparent piece. The problem with working with bin liners is it causes static and attracts dust.

What attracts you to crochet and lace work? It is just a technique that I use. I don't remember where the pattern comes from because I have used it in many of my pieces. But it is not very Estonian design. I don't know why crochet is not used more widely in art. In the past, of course, it was a female handicraft and crochet is a traditional craft in Estonia – we learnt it in school. Old techniques are again popular, which is

good for me because I have known these techniques since childhood – I actually thought I would ask my mother to help.

Were you thinking about recycling? Yes, of course. Because these are not materials that we wear, that are used for clothing, I thought I could make something interesting from it. But I wasn't thinking so much about petroleum and linking the black plastic bags with tyres. In my work I don't want to say something directly, but it should reflect my core – the core reason for making the work.

I don't think it's important to call my work 'textile' – it's just art, there is no difference because it is textile. Aune Taamal and I had an exhibition in which we used materials that were not textiles at all, and recently I made a piece that is like wallpaper with images from political parties. However, as I come from textiles, I put the images together in a textile pattern.

Would people be angry with you for using these political images in this way? I thought about it and, yes, I think people might not think it is right to use these images in this way.

I notice that playing with images, placing them in different context, is a way of working that you often use. For example the work you propose for the exhibition. I thought a lot, which image it should be, so that everyone could recognized it. Then as the project started in England I thought that James Bond would be nice. Also I like the idea to combine such a masculine iconic character with this feminine feeling from the quilting technique and typical small scale pattern printed textile.

METHODS OF MAKING
Krista Leesi subverts traditional skills: crochet, embroidery, etc through the use of disposable or everyday materials. Language, written words that surround a particular idea, form the impetus for the work.

NARRATIVE OF MAKING
Leesi wishes to retain a degree of ambiguity about the identity of individual works although there is a core personal narrative that runs through her work, much of which has been related to the body.

SUGGESTED LINKS
Subverting traditional techniques: see Severija Inčirauskaitė-Kriaunevičienė.

Lesley Millar

FOR YOUR EYES ONLY (detail)
1.60 x 3.84 m
Cotton fabric, thread
Photograph: Krista Leesi

Word play also features in your work, I am thinking about the book you made. Do you draw or paint? Not any more. I do make sketches of my work – not drawings. First, I just write some words about the idea and sometimes I can't find the paper on which I wrote the ideas, but I do remember that I wrote something down. I have always been interested in playing with words and for me the name of the work is very important – more than longer speeches, I think. Sometimes I don't think it's so easy for the viewer to understand the narrative in my work, but why not have viewers make up stories that are different from the one I have in mind, when they see the work? I really think that works must talk for themselves – and I do want people to find the work amusing and smile, though not always… ∎

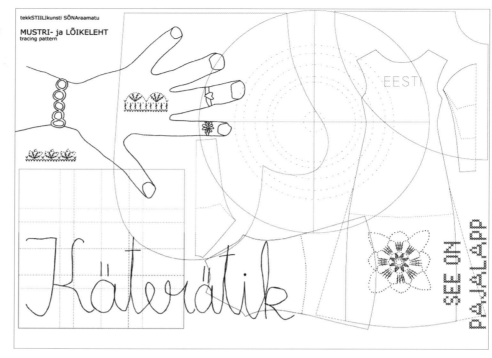

WEBSITE STATEMENT EXTRACT
www.clothandculturenow.com

'The significance of Estonian culture in textile art suggests first and foremost ethnographic influences… There is, however, much more to culture than just ethnography.

The cultural environment of the Estonian language has allowed quite a lot of room for playing around with words. The word tekstiilikunst means textile art, but if we deconstruct it into its constituent parts it becomes blanket (tekk), style (style) and art (kunst).'

KRISTA LEESI

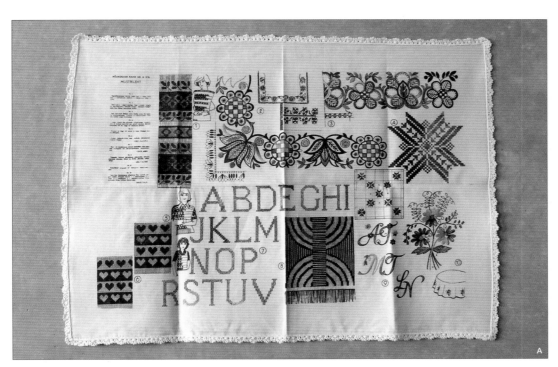

A: TRACING PATTERN. 2003
0.79 x 0.9 m
Fabric
Photograph: Krista Leesi

B: NETWHEELS. 2007
0.66 x 0.66 x 0.16 m (x 4)
Car inner tyre, polypropylene
Photograph: Heino Prunsvelt

C: SOFT MESSAGES. 2004–5
0.3 x 0.8 x 0.15 m (x 12)
Cotton, wool
Photograph: Heino Prunsvelt

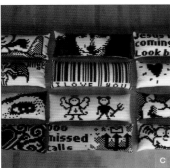

■ Edited extracts from interview with
Katrin Pere, Tallinn, May 2007, with Lesley Millar

**The work you have proposed for the exhibition is in the form of a triptych, why did you choose this form?** This work was a result of a long time of thinking and observing, about colour and about relationships. I have been thinking about relationships, people from my past, in the present and in the future. I wanted to show the line of living. The piece for the exhibition is a triptych because the work represents past, present and future. We don't always make the connection between these three elements of our lives, so perhaps a triptych can communicate this. Also as a composition I think it works better this way.

**One of the first things I noticed about your work was the colour. Do particular colours have specific meanings?** I have been interested in working with a combination of gold and blue. Gold for me is something very special, but it has to stay in the background. The desire to work with gold and blue was inspired by my trips to Italy, in particular the Arena Chapel frescos in Padua. Since that time the combination of gold and blue has been in the back of my mind. Blue is related to feelings I have in springtime, particularly in early spring, when the sky has many different blues, and is full of light after all the grey of winter.

**A time of optimism…** There are so many colours to depict negative feelings and sadness. When you are really happy it is

BEFORE NOW AND EVER MORE (detail)
2 x 1.55 m (x 3)
Silk, cotton, synthetics
Photograph: Tarvo-Hanno Varres

difficult to depict that. I discovered that perhaps gold matches the golden feeling of happiness, and I have been thinking about images of a particular state of mind. How can I depict the state of mind of being happy? When you are younger you are full of energy, and struggling, and your work can comment on this. When you have some years behind you, you understand that people enjoy just normal, ordinary life – and this is very hard to express as art – it can become kitsch. Sometimes it's important to express struggle within the work, but at other times you may wish to express that you are happy and healthy, and that's difficult to put into art.

It is strange how I am beginning to like the very extreme colours, because there were times when I used only black and white and I was very happy with those colours. Now I feel I can use any colour next to another, because the colour is a symbol of something I feel at a particular time, I don't ask myself why, I don't question my work verbally, I use my intuition. Later on I can explain it, but before and during the making my concern is to express the feeling.

**Is there a sense of autobiography in your work?** You always express yourself in your work and the more you express yourself the more vulnerable you are. On the one hand I want to say something in my work, and on the other I don't want to be too open. The making is the fixing of a moment. Ideas live somewhere in my deep subconscious, co-existing in the mind – I might not be aware of them, but it is like a cupboard, you open the drawer and take out an idea and then put it back. There are so many highways in your mind it is difficult to know when images will emerge. All experiences in life you put somewhere, they stay somewhere. When you need them, they are there.

METHODS OF MAKING
**Katrin Pere works with stitch in a responsive, direct and intuitive manner, allowing specific materials, their transparency and opacity to determine her approach.**

NARRATIVE OF MAKING
**While Pere works in an immediate manner when making, the personal narrative embodied within the work has been developed over a much longer period of time, the colour and worked surface of the cloth reflecting and evoking particular states of mind.**

SUGGESTED LINKS
**Personal narrative and materials: see Peteris Sidars.**

Lesley Millar

The surface of your work has a real dynamism… I chose to work in stitch because I think it expresses the moment. I like the dynamic quality of the stitch in my work. I think of myself as more of a drawing person than a painting person and I use pencil and stitch in exactly the same way, the stitch is like the drawn line. Every stitch communicates something unique, the last word is added at the very end of the process. I almost never make a very exact design or even preliminary sketches, only sometimes technical drawings when I need to work out the proportion of a figure, or if I might damage the fabric by doing and undoing a particular detail.

Working in this direct way, I can think and work at the same time. Sometimes I start with an idea of moving to the right side of the work and then work tells that I have to move to the left hand side. I have to follow the logic of the work. When I feel the surface dying somehow, it is because I have worked it too much, it is essential to know when to stop. The moment I feel I can't do it in the way I want to, then I must stop because this is not the way the work wants it to be.

Your material of choice at the moment is one that has associations with dancing and parties – a frothiness… I have tried to use materials that are both transparent and reflect light, so that in the day they are one colour and in the evening another. I use tulle a lot in my work; it gives a certain lightness, playfulness. I first discovered this material by accident, I was buying thread and I saw a huge container full of every kind of tulle – neon colours – and I thought they were really vibrant and beautiful, and I just had to use it. I realised that not everything has to be gold or silver, or silk, it can just be this transparent material that enables me to mix colour in a very different way, by layering. The first piece I made was tulle roses, transparent pink with

neon yellow – quite crazy. I realised nothing is forbidden.

I have now found a way of working that suits me, I sometimes think I have to find a new way of working, and when I turn back to my stitching I realise that this is the way I am happiest working, this is what I can do and is best for the work. ■

WEBSITE STATEMENT EXTRACT
www.clothandculturenow.com

'What is the place, time and space that we call home? What does it embody? It is such a lot of things that you remember and experience again and again, which have filled minds before you and will continue doing so after you are gone. Most important is that there are people around you who feel and speak the same language, live to see and recognise the same signs, reacting to a common understanding of things.

I suppose my work is about living, very simple things, things that I care about, and not all simple things are primitive.'

KATRIN PERE

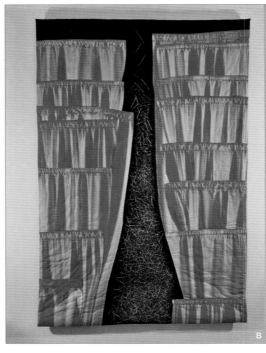

A: WITHOUT NAMES (detail). 2004
2.2 x 1.45 m
Synthetic, silk, cotton, wool
Photograph: Vera Kikas

B: SECRETS. 2004
2.4 x 1.4 m
Silk, synthetics
Photograph: Vera Kikas

C: CARES NOT. 2004
1.6 x 0.9 m
Stainless steel, steel, feathers, glue
Photograph: Vera Kikas

■ Edited extracts from interview withAune Taamal, Tallinn, May 2007, with Lesley Millar

What was the starting point for the work you are proposing for the exhibition? The work represents something about the greed that is surfacing around the world, we want more and more, but we are not giving back.

There is a very strong underlying narrative to your work, is it important that those looking at the work understand that narrative? I want people to experience good feelings, good emotions from my work but they should also know my belief that we, humans, have damaged the earth and I wonder how can we help the planet? Whether we are textile artists, businessmen, whatever, the only purpose we have must be to raise our consciousness and we must help the planet. Our experiences are only what we think. This is how the world exists in our collective thinking – it is hard to believe, but for me I can't do my work without such thinking.

For me, also, light is so important, the light within our bodies and the light of the universe. We consist of light and if we can bring more light into ourselves then our cells become radiant. This is also tied into the sacred geometry – I am very interested in this – especially the meditation of the kabbala.

We are all connected to each other and to nature. In our hearts there is a very sacred place and in this place we are connected to each other and to nature. Sometimes I feel

this connection which is a wonderful feeling, I feel that I am everywhere, then I don't feel my body.

Making for you is part of your meditative journey. How do you feel when you are making? The working process is very important. Sometimes I like and sometimes I don't like the finished work. I find the weaving process very meditative. I also play piano and find that meditative too. I have perfect pitch, but I cannot practise or play as much when I am weaving. The notes represent colour to me – in fact I can see colours when I hear music. I have been this way since I was very little – I could always hear colours.

Both use a language expressed through the fingers. Yes, the language of music and the language of art are very close.

Have you ever tried to play one of your textiles? Yes, I have. Sometimes I improvise. Music gives me inspiration. I always meditate before starting work, otherwise I would not be able to work. I see my work as a complete piece before I begin, and then sometimes I am a little disappointed with what I actually make. I do make sketches but ideas change and I don't like to be fixed by a design or a sketch. I like to respond to changing ideas.

You have found a material now that you are very happy to work with? All the time I change materials and techniques. I like to always try new things. It is very interesting, but also sometimes very problematic. My inspiration does not come from the material. I always have the idea first and then find the material. I use water soluble fabric as well and then you are left with just the stitch.

THE GOLDEN AGE (detail)
1.10 x 1.70 m
Non-woven fabrics, organza, silk thread
Photograph: Aune Taamal

METHODS OF MAKING
Aune Taamal improvises, using a variety of techniques from simple embroidery on soluble fabric to the complex technology of computer looms; concepts always govern the choice of material and technique.

NARRATIVE OF MAKING
Aune Taamal's work is dictated by her inner journey, her ideas are envisioned as a totality and her desire is to make clear to the viewer the underlying beliefs at the centre of the narrative within her work.

SUGGESTED LINKS
Ecological concerns: see Shelly Goldsmith, Laura Pavilonyte.

Lesley Millar

I also work with double weave, and on my computer loom for more complex designs. I weave and I embroider and sometimes I print on the warp before I put it on the loom. It is difficult because I don't see the whole work all at once. Often I take the work off the loom and I'm surprised by it. If the idea is not quiet right or the work does not work maybe I won't change it immediately – instead I will go and do something else and then come back to it.

I was surprised when you said you have been using a computer loom, because your work looks so done by hand. Yes, I have a computer loom with 16 shafts. For complicated designs I use all 16, but that is often not necessary. Even better would be to use a Jacquard loom.

A lot of your work contains references to angels. Angels are very important to me. I made one work recently, 'Duality', based on the tale of the two angels Michael and Lucifer who were brothers. I am interested in the idea of duality, the whole world has this black and white grading, our reality consists of opposites. If we could move away from such a judgmental attitude and just accept what is good and what is bad – that that is just the way it is, I think if we could see this we would solve a lot of problems. ∎

WEBSITE STATEMENT EXTRACT
www.clothandculturenow.com

'The significance and influence of Estonian culture in my work cannot be undervalued. I was born and raised in this cultural space, and so it could be said that I breathed this air.

I have been inspired by Estonian ethnographic motifs, Finno-Ugric ornamentation, medieval stained glass windows and oriental mandala's.

Combining traditional patterns and techniques with the latest technological inventions and materials and contemporary approaches ensures the permanence and continuity of culture.'

AUNE TAAMAL

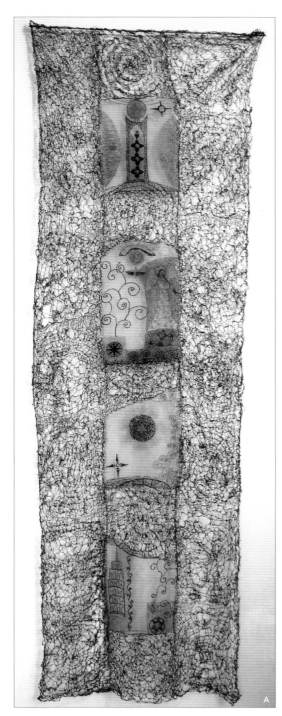

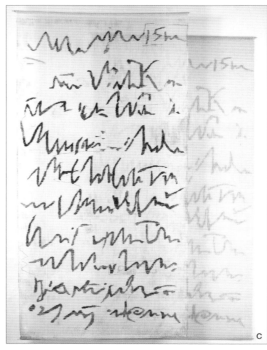

A: AIRCASTLE. 2004
   1.8 x 0.8 m
   Cotton, silk, organza,
   embroidery, (author's technique)
   Photograph: A.Taamal

B: MEDITATION. 2005
   1.16 x 0.87 m
   Wool, cotton, embroidery,
   (author's technique)
   Photograph: A. Taamal

C: WRITINGS. 2001
   1.1 x 2.3 m (x 2)
   Linen, wool, cotton,
   weaving, printing on warp
   Photograph: T. Veermäe

■ Edited extracts from interview with Kadri Viires, Tallinn, May 2007, with Lesley Millar

Could you tell me about the work you are planning to make for the exhibition? This collection starts with my research work. I was fascinated by the decoration on these tiny wooden grey houses, decoration that was only on the windows. I thought it looked very nice. The owner wants to show beauty and they usually make the decoration themselves on the outside of the house. One of my first discoveries was looking at the frames of the windows and the symbols that they used and then seeing the same ornaments in textiles. It is a kind of wooden embroidery.

These beautifully decorated windows inspired me. First I took a lot of photographs, maybe over 100 different windows. It is possible to follow the stylistic progress, from simple geometrical cuts or engravings to more rich – and nowadays new rich people make very colourful windows. Baroque Renaissance windows were brought by traders from the larger cities – what traders saw in Saint Petersburg they brought with them and influenced villages.

The rich people used this as a kind of sample and of course they influenced others. And so it goes. These pictures have a life story, but the end is not very funny, because there are broken windows and then finally some totally closed windows. As globalisation and architectural modernism and contemporary influences infiltrate the villages this kind of decoration doesn't survive.

DUNGEON
1.15 x 0.75 m
Felt, wood, print
Photograph: Kadri Viires

As you say they are almost embroideries in wood. But the work also links beautifully to your point in your Statement about pattern being symbols and signifiers, and that if they are seen out of place they mean something different. Yes, if you can see or imagine the story or make the connection between the stories and beliefs and decorations, it is interesting to see.

Why have you chosen to make these pieces in felt? Yes, exactly – Why felt? Particularly as I am using felt to make a window, and you cannot see through felt. I think because of its thickness it gives the form. Also maybe because it is very similar to wood and decoration of many layers. I will combine both hand felt and industrial felt. I will hand felt – not needle felt the pieces I make. I think with hand felting it is possible to encase something in the work. But I wanted to combine these two techniques.

Most of my works are not very colourful. First, I hoped that it would be different tones of white – very natural maybe adding some natural materials, maybe linen. Hand made felt is a completely different structure to industrial felt. All those works for me start from the photo, for me it also starts from story.

You have used the word story several times, is it important that your work has a story? Yes, it must say something. For me it is a story I want to read more – a kind of background. It is like a short extract of the thoughts behind the work. I don't think that the viewer can follow my thoughts completely and of course it is not necessary. Why not make their own stories? That's not bad.

Also I think that the story of making is important for students. They start by admiring the textiles, but quite soon have to think about how you make the textiles.

METHODS OF MAKING
Kadri Viires works in a variety of techniques: tapestry, felt, wax resist dyeing, the concept determining the appropriate technique. Her Finno-Ugric academic research and fieldwork have been central to the work in this exhibition.

NARRATIVE OF MAKING
The iconic imagery, which is a fundamental result of Viires research into fenestration, has become the underlying motif in her exploration of cultural narrative and mapping of place evidenced in her felt pieces.

SUGGESTED LINKS
Mapping of place: see Lina Jonikė.

Lesley Millar

Knowing how to make opens the doors. The stories in textiles very strongly exist. Textile stories are a bit like a camera. They go into society and tell stories. And it works well.

I can see that your Finno-Ugric research influences your textiles, but does your textile practice influence the way you approach your research? I think that knowing more about materials and handwork – and of course crafts – gives a wider focus to my research. I have a better understanding of techniques and materials. And if you know the materials, for instance, you can understand the living style of people. What are they doing, how are they living. In most cultures textile is a very important thing – symbolically, for instance, at a wedding. A lot of people have kept hold of those textiles. If the people really are proud of their culture most of them keep their textiles and jewellery.

Can you talk a little bit about your work based on your hand print? It started from the title of the exhibition: 'Possession' – and I thought that your fingerprint is what belongs to you, absolutely. If you have touched it, it's something that is yours. It is quite personal. Also it is about being in close contact with things. In my mind, it is something about our future and decisions being in our hands, of course that is quite illustrative – but anyway that is what I was thinking.

Hands are a very common subject, but I don't think I have thought too much about the idea being embedded in the textiles. For me it was about making the image. But it is important to feel that it is in the cloth.

How important is it that you are working in textiles – and not in photography, for instance? It is strange, but it is really important. When I started my studies I was absolutely clear that I would become an industrial designer, but after two years I couldn't explain myself and I found myself one day in the textiles department and I went to the textile dean and said I would like to change my profession, my studies – and she agreed. I was very happy that they took me. ∎

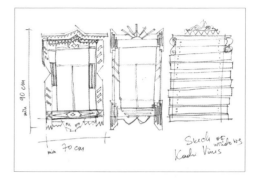

WEBSITE STATEMENT EXTRACT
www.clothandculturenow.com

'For me, knowledge of the existing wealth of folk traditions and the preserved heritage of folk art is very important. In my textiles I have not interpreted specific, recognisable traditional symbols, but have been inspired by nature, colours, and the world view and folklore familiar to Estonians and our distant linguistic relatives – the people who speak Finno-Ugric languages. In my work this tends to be expressed in the form of an abstract connection with the heritage of the culture of the natural world as well as with the spirituality of folk traditions.'

KADRI VIIRES

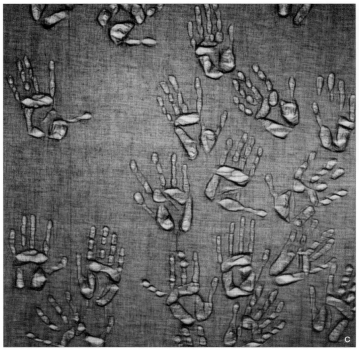

A: THROUGH THE STONE. 2003
0.03 x 0.04 x 0.08 m each
Stones, polyester fibre
Photograph: Kadri Viires

B: CODA. 2007
9 x 2 m
Print on canvas
Photograph: Kadri Viires

C: THE VOTERS. 2004
1.16 x 0.9 m
Cotton, needle
Photograph: Tiit Rammul

# FINLAND

HELENA HIETANEN
AGNETA HOBIN
OUTI MARTIKAINEN
SILJA PURANEN
KRISTIINA WIHERHEIMO
MERJA WINQVIST

# FINNISH TEXTILE ART AND THE INTRICACIES OF TRADITION

LEENA SVINHUFVUD

'I am a small dot
At the crossroads of ages.
With history behind me, on this planetary
sphere, hundreds of thousands of weavers.
Tying the knots with me.'

Katri Haahti, 2006[1]

The role of the textile as a means of interpreting history prompts respect, but it also restricts the gaze. The precious textiles in the oldest museum collections are message bearers from ancient civilisations in various parts of the world and also represent the cultural history of the European nation states. As a distinctively aesthetic category these museum textiles present a selective image of 'the tradition'.

The social and economic history of textiles is no less significant. The roots of all modern mechanical industry lie in fabric weaving, and the textile industry has been of special significance for the processes of modernisation. In Finland, too, cotton and linen factories long represented the only industrial production and, even at the start of the 20th century, produced most of the country's exports. On the other hand, in the slowly industrialising north, hand weaving was the primary cottage industry; home-woven fabrics were an important source of income for women right up to the Second World War. The cheap, skilled workforce also gave textile artists a chance to engage in commercial serial production.

The rya rug. The rya rug, or 'ryijy', has often appeared as a symbol of Finnish textile art.[2] This successful export article represents Finnish exoticism, while also being the most important link with the folk-textile tradition. From the beginning of the 20th century, the rya rug became a Finnish textile in a special way, as a part of the national project whose main premise was admission to the western cultural sphere.

In the creation of the textile-art tradition it was significant that rya rugs woven by anonymous peasant women from the 18th and 19th centuries were collectors' objects early on, and were displayed in exhibitions in Finland and abroad. Nevertheless, it would hardly have become such a vital textile if it had not had a counterpart in the handwoven designer carpet canonised in the European decorative art of the 1920s and 30s.[3]

During the inter-war years, the rya rug was reintroduced into Finnish homes. Women in both town and countryside wove or sewed rya rugs for their own homes. The artist-designed rya rug has been a cherished piece of handiwork ever since. The popular culture of the rya rug made it banal, but at the same time laid the foundations for the development of a unique rya-rug art alongside and above its handiwork aspect.

In the 1950s, Finnish rya rugs once again toured Europe, one venue being the Victoria and Albert Museum, London. From the 1970s on, Finnish state funds were used to acquire a national collection of designer rya rugs, which were shown abroad alongside ultramodern design. The latest items in this collection were purchased in 1999, one of them a unique work by Johanna Vuorinen woven with tie-dyed yarns and optical fibres in the tuft.

Over the years, parallel discourses embedded in the rya rug include the national narrative, the drawing of the demarcation line between art and handicraft, and a modern 'folkish-ness' realised via handicraft designs. Thus, when taking up 'the rya rug', a contemporary textile artist is not latching on to some ancient, unchanging, ossified textile tradition, but embracing this entire package.

Art. The pioneering age in Finnish textile art occurred between the world wars, at a time when Finland was also politically and culturally on the fringes of Europe. Finland gained its independence from the Soviet Union in 1917, and subsequently descended into bloody civil war. The nation's image of the art of textiles was built on this framework. It had a job to do in the national project, in the creation of internal unity, and in establishing links with western cultural circles.

Teaching of textile art began in 1929, in what is now the University of Art and Design Helsinki. Professional training at first specifically meant mastering weaving techniques, while other modes of textile expression were long absent from the curriculum,[4] and the textile faculty became specifically the women's department. The Textile Department (the Weaving Workshop) at the German Bauhaus was also set up in that same decade, its creation and activities reflecting a desire to limit the scope of the work of women students.[5]

In Finnish social discourse the place allocated to female designers was the 'natural' one. The popular magazine Kotiliesi (The Hearth), published from 1923 on, frequently showed women at their looms. The idea of textile artists busying themselves with traditional women's work, often at home or in their own weaving workshops, with women working together, was an idealised image, too.

For the critics, textile art was a modern art form, but one whose traditional method made it easy to understand. The results were intimate and heart-warming '…as if it were a matter of the ryijy and "raanu" woven by the women who were our Finnish ancestors,' as Professor of Art History Onni Okkonen described Maija Kansanen's textiles in 1930.[6] Reviews linked modern textile art with the tradition of women's handicraft. This was the accepted way of harnessing textile art to the service of the national project. It was also a way of rhetorically taming this new art form with its new found economic and cultural power – and its makers – in a spirit of cultural conservatism.

Nevertheless, the bond between modern textile art and the textile tradition is not, and never has been, self-evident. For the pioneers, renunciation of tradition was an important statement: they were modern professionals.

Talk. 'The modern industrial arts are, however, founded on old traditions and on folk art. It is from this soil that our contemporary art textiles have grown into their own unique flourishing at this historical juncture, when all values are being created anew and when the new is bursting out of its shell at the speed of an express train. The creation of a new

style is the combined outcome of all these circumstances. Every creative textile artist unconsciously makes her own contribution to the creation of textile style.' Eva Anttila, 1933[7]

In her writings around the turn of the 1930s, Eva Anttila, who is ranked among the 'pioneer' generation in textile art, commented on the status of the new profession in relation to contemporary discussions about serial production and social design.

At that time, modernism in design was mirrored against the history of style and the decorative-art tradition. In this sense, the folk tradition in textiles was a more neutral reference point. The modernisation of design has often been described as a battle between functionalism and traditionalism. Anttila's writings occupied a position somewhere between the two 'mainstreams': defending textile artists' freedom of expression and expressive skills; and conversely their desire to act as all-round textile designers in the service of the consumer.

In the inter-war period, textile artists had a high public profile in Finland. They were featured in magazines, and their works found their way into Finnish homes – perhaps in greater numbers than ever before. In exhibition reviews, however, their image is restricted to that of a maker of art: criticism painted a picture of an expressive colour artist, who weaves poems or paints with yarn. Their multifaceted involvement in society and the economy (in everyday life) was left out of the picture, and still is. Eva Anttila, who was a businesswoman, teacher and active member of several organisations, is remembered for her tapestries, which she concentrated on from the 1940s until her death in 1994.

The textile artist Kirsti Rantanen was the first person from the field of design to be a government-appointed 'artist professor', in

1981. In her own career, she has shattered the image of a technically and materially 'pure' textile art. As a writer and in her public activities she has burst the bubble of the artist who speaks 'only through her works' (or is silent).

'The demands of pure Finnishness present the textile artist with difficult choices. A redefined feeling for materials, appropriate, aesthetically correct decisions, and a humility that serves functionality are the fundamental elements by which Finnish applied arts is recognised. And we must not stray from this path.' Kirsti Rantanen, 1981[8]

Women. Textiles continue to be very much a women's cultural symbol, a medium that is loved or loathed, one that simultaneously gives energy and imposes restrictions. It is both an arena and a reservation, as the Swedish researchers Birgitta Svensson and Louise Waldén have described. The boundaries of this reservation also extend to research on textiles and textile art, and as the discussion becomes more profound, it also becomes more closed.[9]

The gendered tradition in textiles has left its stamp on the making of art in this 'women's domain'. Seen from within the field, this has affected the degree of respect accorded to textiles in design and art. Nevertheless, it would be wrong to maintain that textile art has been marginalised; here in Finland it has consistently occupied a strong position, and also currently receives recognition and public funding.

In Finland's officially egalitarian culture feminism has been a difficult issue and a theme long left undiscussed in design.[10] Textile artists have been cautious about raising the question of gender, and artworks openly referring to women's history only became common in the 1990s.

The appearance of textiles in feminist art

has reinforced their status as a craft and accentuated the traditional view of textiles as an unprofessional women's culture. This view has been put forward by the English artist Janis Jefferies and others.[11] In the education of designers, textiles and that other women's domain, ceramic art, were long hallmarked by discussions about amateurism: middle-class girls took them up to pass the time before they got married. Here, too, it has taken a lot of effort to establish a career as an independent artist, and the existence of a public strategy is crucial.

Tradition. 'Textiles preserve the human touch. Old folk textiles are highly vulnerable everywhere and you cannot help loving them… Textiles are signs of their times, and nor does time pass without leaving its mark, which is both a good and a bad quality, yet, simultaneously, it adds a physical dimension and evokes mental images and a sense of connection with people and events.' Ritva Puotila, 2004.

Ritva Puotila's diary entry indicates what an abundant, wide-ranging source old textiles and the textile tradition are for a designer. In her career she has represented both the Finnish and the international. In the 1960s, Puotila made her name as a rya-rug designer, revelled in crackling colours and abstractions, in the manner of painting that was being done in various countries at that time. At the same time, as a colourist and designer of woven tabletop textiles, she brought 'Finnishness' into the product range of the US company Dansk Designs, which aimed to evoke a Scandinavian impression, right down to its name.[12]

As we enter the new millennium, clichéd Finnishness is to the fore. A culture tempered by nature and set apart from the big city is producing authentic artists increasingly useful to the internationalised design economy At the same time, the contradiction between discursive Finnishness and multinational reality is becoming increasingly evident.

The opening quotation from textile artist Katri Haahti illustrates how the timeless tradition of textile making constitutes a global community in which textile artists do their work. The relationships between Finnish textile artists and the Finnish tradition is more complex.

Discussion about textile art has shifted from 'pure' textile expression to the identity of the maker. This creates a climate in which the history of textiles can be viewed differently. In contemporary works of textile art, tradition has extended to include women's handicraft culture and references to popular culture. At the same time, its degree of presence in society has increased.

The 'continuation' of a tradition is never linear, and the choice of textiles as a medium for art is not an innocent one. Over the last two decades, the boundary between visual art and textile art has become increasingly transparent, and opting to work with textiles as an artist has become an increasingly clear statement of a point of view. Although the form and the means contain allusions to the past, the significance of the works emerges here and now, as Outi Martikainen and Silja Puranen bring out in their statements for the Transition and Influence website. It has become increasingly important to ask what the word 'tradition' means in any particular instance – Whose tradition are we talking about, and why? ∎

1. Castrén, Hannu, and Svinhufvud, Leena (eds). (2006). Kädet ja kaikki (Hands and All). 7th Finnish Textile Triennial, the Amos Anderson Art Museum Textile and Artists TEXO, Helsinki.

2. See Svinhufvud, Leena. (1998). 'Finnish Textiles en route to Modernity' in Marianne Aav and Nina Stritzler-Levine, Finnish Modern Design: Utopian Ideals and Everyday Realities, 1930–1997. Bard Graduate Center for Studies in the Decorative Arts, NY, and Yale University Press.

3. See Day, Susan. (2002). Art Deco and Modernist Carpets. San Francisco. Chronicle Books.

4. Wiberg, Marjo. (1996). The Textile Designers and the Art of Design. On the Formation of a Profession in Finland. University of Art and Design Helsinki.

5. Droste, Magdalena, and Ludewig, Rolf (Hrsg). (1998). Das Bauhaus webt. Die Textilwerkstatt des Bauhauses. Berlin. G & H Verlag. Particularly the article by Anja Baumhoff.

6. Okkonen, Onni. (1930). 'Maija Kansasen kudontataiteesta'. Domus 1930/1. pp 1-6.

7. Anttila, Eva. (1933). 'Uusia suuntaviivoja taidetekstiilissämme'. Koristetaiteilijoiden liitto Ornamon vuosikirja. VI, p 62.

8. Rantanen, Kirsti. (1981). Ajatuksia tekstiilitaiteilijan työkentästä Tekstiilitaiteilijat TEXO 25 1956–81, Forssa.

9. Svensson, Birgitta, and Waldén, Louise. (2005). Den feminina textilen. Makt och mönster. Stockholm. Nordiska museets förlag.

10. Aav, Marianne (ed). (2006). 'Naisen muoto – Female Form' exhibition at the Design Museum, Helsinki.

11. Jefferies, Janis (1995). 'Text and textiles; weaving across the borderlines' in Katy Deepwell (ed) New feminist art criticism. Critical strategies. Manchester and NY. Manchester University Press. pp 164–73.

12. Svinhufvud, Leena. (2003). Ritva Puotila. Helsinki. Designmuseo & Woodnotes Oy.

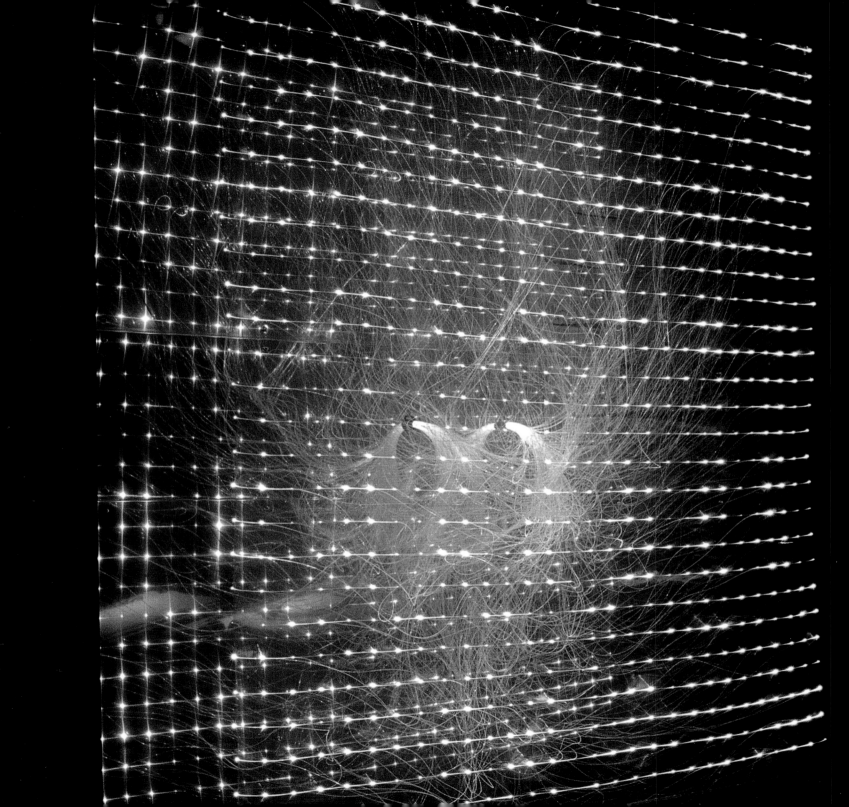

■ Edited extracts from interview with Helena Hietanen, Helsinki, April 2007, with Lesley Millar

Light and Lace, they fit together very well. In the beginning, working with optical fibres, came about through curiosity and accident. Previously I had been making a kind of lace out of silicone. I put a transparent silicone on tulle with the idea that, because the tulle is so fine, what you see is the shadow. At that point I saw that I could work with optical fibre. But then I discovered that the optical fibre was totally different and could not be used the same way and everything changed.

I needed to make bigger surfaces, with more light and I had to start using stronger materials. In 2002 I began to weave with steel and iron work, which does not have such a clear reference to the lace making tradition. When you weave optical fibres they break very easily and that is a problem – but with special hydraulic looms, developed by a Finnish woman, we figured out a system in which she could weave the fibres into the steel. In this way I was able to make huge public works with her.

Do you have any training in electronics? I have just done a lighting design course, and it has made me think about my point of view in relation to light. This point of view is not just electrical and technical, not just electrical light, but light reflections – the materials that reflect light and light as a material.

What I first liked about fibre optics was the possibility that you could work with light and form the light. I then started to think about how these works and objects interact with the surrounding light. Now I prefer to think about how I can work with light in a certain space. The issues that concern me now are light and space.

These works are concerned with architectural space. However, you do have another body of work that is much more personal, more intimate. Those works made from human hair are very different in approach and content from the light pieces. The content can be quiet heavy. The hair looks beautiful, but it's also divisive – some people like it and some are disgusted. I like this hair work because the material is so strong, so meaningful.

I was making it when I was very critically ill and it deals with this time of sickness and cancer and death. I always feel that these hair works are close to the soul. Every time I have had some trouble with this cancer I have come back to this work. So sometimes it is so delicate and also powerful that I don't want to touch it.

When I became sick, I saw the meaning of my light works differently. Up until that point I had just been playing around, curious about the light and experimenting with it. During the first two weeks when I was waiting for results from the doctor – at that time I had a really terrible fear of death. The only thing I could do to relax myself was lay down and try and visualise relaxing images.

One day, I don't remember if I was sleeping or just on the edge of sleep, I could see this dark vision – I am in the middle experiencing this, then suddenly from above is a really strong pillar of light which comes straight to me. I am standing there and I heard this voice that says hold your hands to the pillar and you will survive. This image gave me peace.

METHODS OF MAKING
**Helena Hietanen works with optical fibres, either as a lace construction, or woven by a technician on specially developed hydraulic looms, combining the optical fibres with steel thread.**

NARRATIVE OF MAKING
**Although Hietanen is concerned with the mapping of space, her work also contains a highly personal narrative, which includes the mapping of the body. Light is both a material and the carrier of the narrative.**

SUGGESTED LINKS
**Use of new technologies: see Zane Berzina.**

Lesley Millar

REFLECTIVE SURFACE. 2003
3 x 3 x 2 m
Optical fibres woven into steel and plastic, aluminium and reflective steel construction
Photograph: Helena Hietanen

After that I deliberately imagined that image over and over again and even years after when I became sick again, second time, third time, I still remembered this image. I feel this vision showed me my meaning of light and for me it represented God. After that the quality of light in my work started to change – I wanted to work more and more with light that was so intense, so bright, that it almost breaks your eyes, like ultra-violet light.

You now create work in collaboration with your husband, artist Jaakko Niemalä. Last year we made a wall from video projected light, there was a fog machine in the room and so the rays of light penetrated the fog and there was a noisy rhythm. Some people said they were almost afraid to go there because it was so bright, and many people said they wondered what was hidden, what lay behind the wall. Since then I have been working with my husband, trying to use this light as a metaphor for the 'other side'.

Last year in Stockholm he was also making a wall, but he changed it a little bit, using text. Inside the room you see the text – the word he used was 'unfinished'. Then on the other side of the wall you see a video projection of text falling – a little bit unclear – from the Bible, Genesis Chapter 1. And the light is moving inside the room.

We called it 'Genesis on the Inside'. I am religious but my husband is not. People liked the work and because of the religious dimension it raised a lot of questions and discussion. You know these things can be a little taboo, Christianity is not very easy to write about.

The Japanese are very poetic about light and shadow. Yes, I have just been working in Japan and I really liked working there and the Japanese way of doing things. In Japan a great many people can speak Finnish, and said to me that they feel a connection with Finland. I found many things were familiar – the simplicity of design – the wooden floors in building, it felt very natural to me.

I read Junichiro Tanizaki's In Praise of Shadows, and that book really spoke to me. When he talked about the Japanese old houses and how they are dark, and they don't want to light them up because they want to keep the secrets of the shadows. This appreciation for the shadows is so beautiful. ∎

WEBSITE STATEMENT EXTRACT
www.clothandculturenow.com

'I have noticed that the images that I have perceived and captured with photographs are memorised in my mind, and they influence my work this way. When working I have this material in my mind. When the actual technique or structure of the artwork has to be planned I then remember the experience and bring the feeling of it to my work. This is not a process of thinking about the material but rather feeling it. It is an intuitive process.'

HELENA HIETANEN

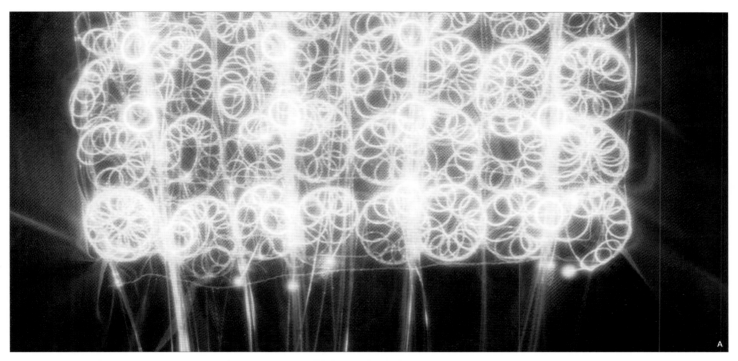

A: TECHNOLACE / FROM SERIES OF
SMALL LACES. 1997
0.5 x 0.5 m
Optical fibre sewn into tulle, light
projector, acrylic shelf
Photograph: M. Alatalo

B: TECHNOLACE. 1999
3.5 x 3.5 x 3.5 m
Optical fibres, reflective steel/glass,
aluminium construction, light projectors
Photograph: P. Simon

C: TECHNOLACE. 1997
3.2 x 2 x 2 m
Optical fibres, reflective steel/glass,
aluminium construction, light projectors
Photograph: M. Alatalo

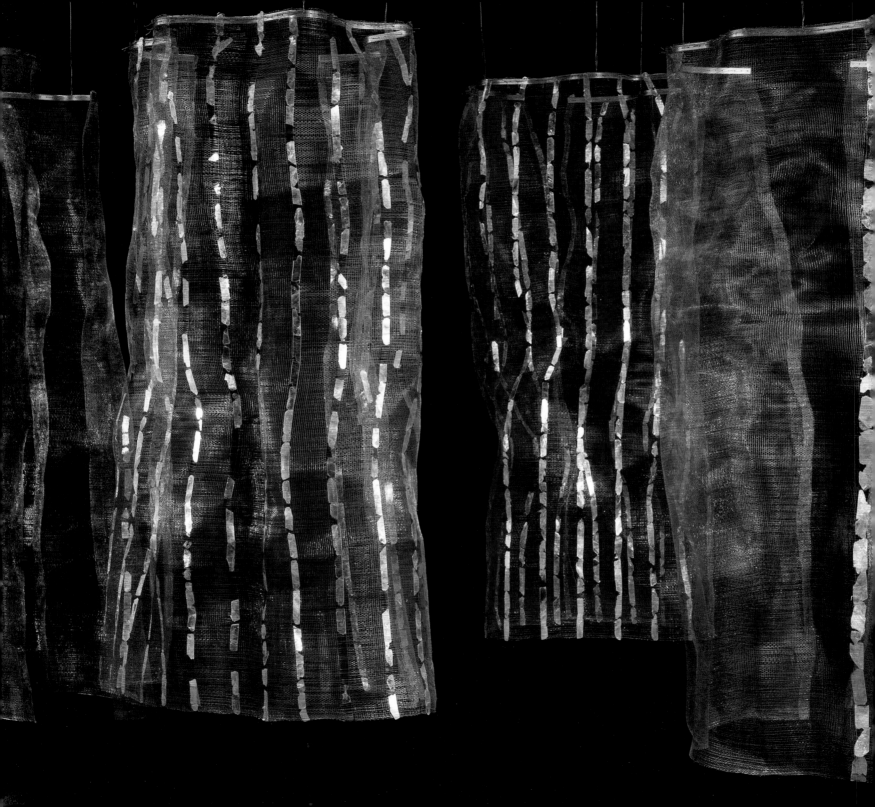

**The work for this exhibition has quite an intimate feel to it. What was the starting point for this shape?** I have an idea and then I draw sometimes – but very quickly after I have made initial drawings and worked out starting ideas, I want to try out the ideas. I want to see the pieces in the right proportions, proportions are really important to me, so I make maquettes. I have been making relief work for a long time and for this exhibition I wanted to make something more three-dimensional and to create a space that was both inside and outside. I wanted them to hang in space. When I first hung the finished pieces I was disappointed, I thought there was something wrong with them but I did not know what.

I was upset because the material is good and the principle of the work was a good idea, but there was something wrong. After a week, I thought the form was too regular, the structures were too straight and it was too tidy, so I started to wrinkle it, to break it and now I think it has a voice. Even if I use different materials (like wood, for example), there is something that makes it like soft textile – whether they are made of fibres or not. They are soft-wavy, like textiles would be and they use a textile language.

**What is your textile background?** When I studied to become a textile artist, I did a lot of hand printing and that was the technique I was most fond of. At the beginning of my career I was a designer of prints for industry. Then slowly, after ten years or so, I started to look for something else. At that point I began to work with ecclesiastical textiles and this became a kind of bridge from design to another world.

**As you trained in printed textiles, what triggered the move into weave?** The way I work involves a lot of joint work. I don't weave, ever. I'm not a good weaver and my work is always woven by someone working with me. Over the years I have had fifteen different apprentices, all weavers, so if I want to do something together with them, that helps both of us, it must be weaving. The first apprentice I had, in around 1989, and when she asked if I would take her, I said, yes, what is your strongest technique? – and she said, weaving. So I said, OK, I'll think about how we can combine our interests in some way. And I thought maybe we will use metal thread, because one can weave metal thread on the looms, then afterwards shape it – and I was interested in relief and 3D forms. Now I've been working with this metal thread and wire for a while. Somehow it still seems to have many possibilities – so I am not finished with it. I still feel there is a lot to try out with it.

**Your work is very concerned with space, light and shadow.** Whatever I'm doing, I'm doing it for a specific space. I ask myself why someone wants a piece for this space and from me. Is it to soften the space? Is it to bring it some colour? I have actually described my works as architectural art space, I think it is often quite difficult to describe my works as art, they are more like parts of architecture.

My work is not so far away from how architects deal with spaces, so I often feel that we understand each other. Architects have a lot of feeling and understanding of

METHODS OF MAKING
**Agneta Hobin's work always has architectural intention, she is designing for specific spaces and for specific purposes. Although she controls the making process, there is no imperative for her to weave the cloth herself.**

NARRATIVE OF MAKING
**Through her textile knowledge and background, Hobin brings her particular understanding of texture and light to architectural space. In partnership with architects, she provides a material sensitivity to the built environment.**

SUGGESTED LINKS
**Architectural space: see Shoko Nomura.**

Lesley Millar

AIR (detail)
Height: 1 m
Diameter: 2.5 m
Mica, bronze
Photograph: Rauno Träskelin

WEBSITE STATEMENT EXTRACT
www.clothandculturenow.com

'I am a Finnish-born artist living in Finland. Thanks to my Swedish mother and Norwegian grandmother, I also contain a generous dose of Scandinavianness. It seems natural that all this will be visible in my work.

My art textiles, or my 'works', are, for me, recognisably Finnish-Nordic. The need for simplification is rooted in this tradition. The attempt at subtle use of colour is linked with this, too. I am also intensely aware of the importance of quality, of the authenticity of the materials.'

AGNETA HOBIN

space, but not always for materials – the way artists have. I think it's very good when architects and artists work on projects together.

Lightness is such an important part of the work, the play of light is very subtle, and of course, shadows are very important in transparent work. They become part of the work. Also, when you make transparent work, you have to be very aware of how you mount or hang it because all systems with which you hang the work will be visible, becoming part of the work.

Do you think Finnish people have a special sensitivity to light and shadow? When you live in a country with such strong and contrasting seasons, the question of light and darkness is so present and important. I am sure if I lived in a country where it was always summer and always warm and light I would be a very different artist.

At Christmas time, at the end of the year, you feel tired and it's so wonderful with this darkness – because you're allowed to rest in the darkness. Nature itself tells you to rest. It is not just a physical rest, it is a total rest for your thoughts – it gives you the right to rest and sleep in your nest. This is a very long dark period, at least from the beginning of November until March usually about five months.

Many people find the darkness very heavy, but I like it. I think it is very fruitful. I always get back to this fact that in nature everything is always as it should be. Everything is in the right place, nature never fails, the colours are always the right colours, the balance is always right. For me nothing is ugly in nature. ∎

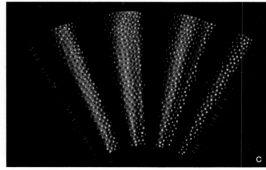

A: GREEN CASCADE. 2002
   5 x 2.2 x 0.5 m
   Stainless steel wire, nylon thread
   Photograph: Rauno Träskelin

B: TRAIL. 2004
   3.6 x 0.5 x 1 m
   Nickel, muscovite (mica)
   Photograph: Rauno Träskelin

C: AT NIGHT. 2001
   0.4 x 0.66 x 0.26 m
   Wood, nails
   Photograph: Rauno Träskelin

■ Edited extracts from interview with
Outi Martikainen, Helsinki, April 2007,
with Lesley Millar

How did you discover the industrial
material you use as your base? I was
invited by an architect's office to propose an
idea for a soft material for a commission of
about 600 square metres. I am not scared
of size, I have seen that it is always possible,
and I have made large-scale many times.
However, for this commission I wanted to
find a way that did not make the work as
expensive as a whole house! I was at a party
and I saw the backrest on someone's chair
and I asked what is this material? I then went
to the factory where the material was made.

Were they interested? I can imagine you
had to persuade them. The contractors
making this work were a little uninterested
at first. However, it was nice to meet
technicians who wanted to test what they
had, to see how far they can go with their
equipment. The size I had in mind was the
biggest the machine can do. We made
some trials and the architects got hooked
because it's technical and factory-made.
And it is the right material for large-scale
architectural work. It is soft and it affects the
environment.

You have taken this very modern industrial
process and then subverted it with
hand work. Yes, and now the guys in the
factory, they know the difference between
weaving and knitting and crochet. And

I am very happy when they identify the
different techniques and say 'I see this is
embroidery'.

Because you come from a textile
background what do you think you bring
to architects? I think I bring architects new
ideas about structures. Perhaps something
soft – I am always textile artist – not artist,
always textile artist. I am trained to work with
patterns, surface design, it does not matter
where it is applied. Patterns are everywhere
and I love the structures. I would like to
design stone streets – I always admire the
beautiful stone streets in Helsinki.

What was the starting point for the work in
the exhibition? I spent a lot of time on the
island near Helsinki, it is called Suomenlinna,
looking at the snow. I lived there when I
was younger and for me it means a place
of silence. There is no traffic, I can walk and
I can think about something from start to
finish without anybody interrupting me.
    Snow is so remarkable with its colours
– and the snow is so different also at
different times, different colours. In one
moment the whole scenery can be blue or
transparent white. Here the seasons are so
strong. I hope they stay like that – otherwise
I'll have to move back north to survive as an
artist. That is something I am really used to.
The seasons are part of me.

I see so many points of contact between
the Finnish approach and Japanese. Yes,
here things always go to the forest. The
Finnish, traditionally have always been very
involved with handicrafts and always in
the forest. It is so strong. We appreciate
the forest. The city is empty for all of June
and July because everyone is going to
the forests. Everybody needs it. It is like
breathing.

METHODS OF MAKING
**Outi Martikainen unites tradition
with new technology and materials,
combining moulded polyester
felt modules with embroidery
and needle felt. Her approach is
informed by her collaborations with
architects.**

NARRATIVE OF MAKING
**Using her various methods of
working, Martikainen references
her extensive visual vocabulary
ranging from folk artefacts through
to landscape. Things seen are
transcribed and become part of
her ongoing commentary on the
embeddedness of cultural continuity.**

SUGGESTED LINKS
**Working with landscape: see Sue
Lawty.**

Lesley Millar

A WINTER'S DAY
3.36 x 3.36 m
Needle-felt, heat moulded polyester
Photograph: Juha Reunanen

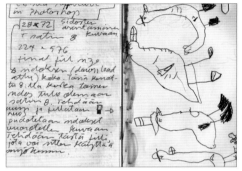

And in the winter you need the dark and the cold. You can also see the air when it is cold – the air smells so good and the light is different and sounds are different. This year the sea was frozen so we went to the east side of Helsinki on the coast and then there you could ski. And it was so great because there was no sound – because it's so far from the big streets. You could only hear the wind where we were skiing. I don't find it scary out there – I found it wonderful standing in the middle of the sea and on the island and listening. I could listen to the sound of this wind – that was so strong I had two jackets and three trousers.

So to get back to the work for the exhibition, which is a new direction for you. I want to give meaning to the natural colour of the felt, and what I can express with the simplicity of Finnish nature, which does not give any excuses. So I made a lot of trials,

and what I found was the beautiful reverse side of the felt that I had needle felted. After I had needle felted synthetic fibres on the felt evenly, I took the fabric to the bigger needle felting machine, which I have just discovered in the middle of Finland. I'm now very happy with the gentle appearance of tiny points on the reverse side, which are forming the image.

Do you like to make the structure apparent? Do you want the person looking to be aware of how it is made? Yes. This issue with structure and making structure visible is, I think, very important. Also to get that feeling that somebody has done this work by hand. The hand is so important to me. My hand touches in the same way a brush touches. My idea was that if you give someone something that is handmade – you feel that the maker is thinking of you. They have touched this and made it for you.

That human sense is transmitted. There is this thing in textiles about it being used and having history. ■

WEBSITE STATEMENT EXTRACT
www.clothandculturenow.com

'I never place myself at a specific point on the designer-artist axis. The ideas on which my works are based can come up at any time, in any situation, from the storehouse of memory and from my emotional-experiential memories.

I am a researcher of materials and am always interested in touching and feeling. That is why surfaces, structures and the feel of fabrics have stayed in my mind ever since my childhood. My grandmother's generation was the last to make almost all the textiles needed in the home.'

OUTI MARTIKAINEN

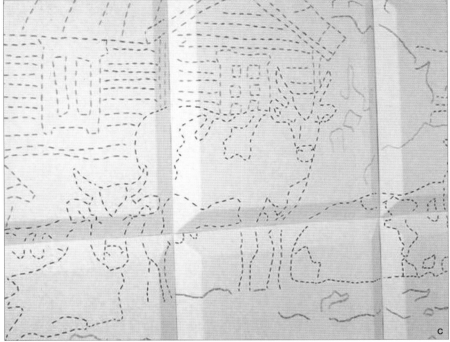

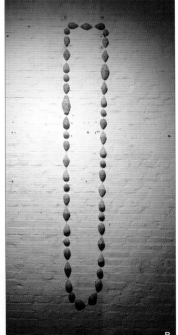

A: MAIN BUILDING FOR THE FACULTY OF
MEDICINE, UNIVERSITY OF OULU. 2004
Heat formed polyester felt
Photograph: Jussi Tiainen

B: DAY IN DAY OUT. 2004
0.3 x 4 m
Laundry tags, sewing
Photograph: Laura Vesa

C: HIETANA (detail). 2005
2.8 x 2.8 m
Embroidery, heat formed polyester felt
Photograph: Julia Weckman

■ Edited extracts from interview with Silja Puranen, Järvenpää, April 2007, with Lesley Millar

You often use your own digitally manipulated image in your work… My work is very autobiographical. I have to start from my own perceptions because I only have my eyes. I do a little drawing, but really I start with photographs. I take photographs of myself by setting up a space and using a timer.

In the work for this exhibition I am dealing with ideas about the belief that new technology can bring control to everything. Just push a button and it is controlled. I have chosen circus as a place where you are very talented, you have skills and must be able to control everything – the moment this control goes, something unexpected happens.

The circus theme is that my husband and myself are performing our own backyard circus – we are performing like a tightrope dancer. But it's not a real tightrope, just an illusion. The tightrope touches the floor because it is so flexible – but you have to be careful because the rope will snap up once you step off.

Of course the circus is a place where a person outside society can be accepted. Yes, that's one way of thinking of it, on the other hand they can only be accepted inside it. They cannot step outside the circus, so they have to be in that world – and they are accepted when the other people look at them from the outside. They are like objects in a way. It is, in one sense, a place to

survive. There is a very strong community in the circus – but it's a community that, when you look at it from the outside, you see very different things than when you look from the inside.

Would you like to talk a little bit about the tightrope and balance? It is between falling and not falling and, of course, the aim is not to fall and the idea is also that you must master it. In this work there is an illusion of total control. I am trying to picture the moment when the tightrope walker understands – uh-ohh, I am going to fall! That special moment when you realise - I can't get myself back into balance.

I'm always trying to picture a moment in time. I try to picture a moment where the figure on the textile looks like they are disappearing. I think about magic and illusion in my work – in a way the whole thing is illusion. First of all, there is this photograph that is not really documentary and then there's this visual illusion of the image emerging from or disappearing into the fabric.

Do you think textiles have a particular ability to communicate? Yes, they are familiar to everybody and they belong to everybody's life. Textiles are popular (not populist, but popular). I use textiles that have already had a use, depending on the theme I have worked with. For instance, when I was thinking about the body, I wanted to use textile materials that are close to the body – so I used the blankets.

For the circus theme I want the picture to feel both exotic and fine. I wanted to use the aesthetic from the circus, but also to employ something foreign from faraway, which is why I used these oriental carpets. Some come from flea markets, some I already had – they are not in a very good condition, but I like the idea of them being worn and that

METHODS OF MAKING
Silja Puranen works on used textiles using an eclectic mixture of digital print and embroidery.

NARRATIVE OF MAKING
Puranen's photographic sources are digitally manipulated images of herself or, on occasion, images of her son. Her approach is that of using autobiographical narrative, communicated through a textile vocabulary, as a metaphor for control/loss of control and illusion.

SUGGESTED LINKS
Mapping the body: see Eglė Ganda Bogdanienė.

Lesley Millar

WITHOUT SAFETY NET (detail)
2 x 2.9 m, 0.5 x 0.5 m
Fabric paint, transfer photograph, soft pastel, stitching on found textile. Needlepoint, wool on canvas (DIY kits – selection of wool, threads, handpainted canvas)
Photograph: Silja Puranen

you can see they are really worn.

It's not so important to me to know who used these materials, but I want them to be used. The digital printing came when I had ideas that needed a narrative and figurative expression that is quite difficult in textile art. Embroidery is like drawing and I like the slowness of it, so it is like a contradiction to these images. It is traditional and commonly mastered and I don't make very complicated stitches – I make very basic stitches.

The narrative in your work is not easy, in a sense you are giving visibility to people who are not normally visible. Yes, well at least in these images with my son. When he came to the opening of the exhibition he was, like – oh, look, here I am, and then here I am again, and he was the real star of the exhibition. There is also the idea that in life everything should be glorious and beautiful – that people should only be young, rich and talented.

However, it is not always like that. There is the dark side, and things that seem to be very beautiful or glorious are not so. I am not forcing a reading of these issues – so in that way I am only a sort of campaigner – the viewers have to see it themselves.

What do you think about the relationship between the person looking at your work and the work? I think they are looking at it as the audience. It is very good for me, when someone tells me they have read a story from my work – that is my aim – but I well understand that it is not the same story that people are reading. A lot of people have

said they have been moved by the work. Many people have been shocked. I have been thinking about how people who are outside of the norm are often laughed at.

Humour is not bad in work, sometimes it is a good way to go through ideas. Lots of women were really amused, and I wondered if they were really amused, or if they were just self-conscious and laughing because of that, because men were not amused – they were a little bit shocked. Very often things that are not so easy are not spoken about. I want to communicate the things I see in society; I am not using a verbal language in my medium, but it is communication. ∎

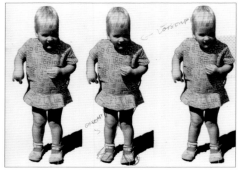

WEBSITE STATEMENT EXTRACT
www.clothandculturenow.com

'In my current works Finnish culture is particularly visible via the attitude to textiles that I had already adopted during my childhood. On the conceptual level, in my works textiles represent protection, refuge, warmth, survival and memory. Conversely, they also represent the human need to decorate the everyday environment and to manifest social identity.

As the starting point for my own works, I am not nowadays really interested in the canonised folk tradition. Instead, the kitschy longing for romantic beauty to the point of banality found in popular taste and in contemporary folk handicraft provides a fertile motivation for my works.'

SILJA PURANEN

A: WORLD'S STRONGEST MAN. 2007
1.98 x 2.85 m
Fabric paint, transfer photograph, soft
pastel and embroidery on found textile
Photograph: Silja Puranen

B: I COULD HAVE DANCED ALL NIGHT
(detail). 2003
1.8 x 1.47 m
Fabric paint, transfer photograph and
soft pastel on found textile
Photograph: Johnny Korkman

C: A MATTER OF CHANCE
(DAISY DUCK). 2005
1.92 x 1.40 m
Fabric paint, transfer photograph
and soft pastel on found textile
Photograph: Silja Puranen

■ Edited extracts from interview with
Kristiina Wiherheimo, Helsinki, April 2007,
with Lesley Millar

What was the starting point for this piece in the exhibition? Mostly I start with the material and then develop the idea. For this work it was the silk and the colour. I had been collecting small pieces of fabric – when I see something I like, I'll just buy it. I choose it if it's a nice colour. With this fabric I really like how it reflects the light.

The warp and the weft are different colours, so when you look at it from two different angles – for instance, here the warp was yellow and the weft red – so it was orange cloth. But when you looked from a certain angle it was red and from another yellow. It was a kind of mystery in this simple weave.

I've also worked with felted wool, I used wool fabric that I felted in the washing machine. I want to see very quick results. For me I think that the backside should always be so good that people can see it. The work I had in the Barbican was double-sided.

You use red a lot... Yes, I do. Red is not my favourite colour and I have been wondering myself why I am using it so much. First I thought it was that when I moved to Helsinki from Lapland where we used to have a lot of fireplaces in the winter – there were suddenly no fireplaces in our house in Helsinki. I was really missing the fires when it was dark in the winter, I think my use of red came from that, from missing fire originally.

24 X RED (detail)
0.6 x 0.6 m (x 24)
Total Area: 5.4 x 2.2 m
Silk on MDF
Photograph: Chikako Harada

Do you do any dyeing? Yes, I do some dyeing. I can really spend many days mixing colours, so that I have a range of different colours around me. I always paint little pieces and cover my space with them. That is something that inspires me. My mother was a weaver and she loved dyeing. She used very strong colours in her work, also black and white. Her textiles were based on the Lap nomad textiles. She started to develop them horizontally. There was a horizon in many of her works.

Is the horizon particularly important to Finnish artists? I was born in Lapland close to the Arctic Circle, in the north the sky is bigger there. In Finnish Lapland the mountains are not so huge, there are soft ones and there is more horizon. Here in Southern Finland the trees are so big you don't really see the horizon. In the winter it is very dark and in the summer it is light.

In February/ March, when the sun rises very slowly, it is so important to see it come, to be sure that from now on it will be bright again – we will have some light. Some people get very depressed in the winter especially in Helsinki when we don't have snow sometimes. In Lapland we always have the snow which makes it not so dark.

Much of your work is made up of units. How did that happen? I don't know. It is not so easy to make big pieces and I cannot just make big pieces for no purpose. Space is really important for me. If I make anything I want to know in which space they will be seen. For me, the work has to have a purpose. To make something that only fills the space would be a bit strange for me. Sometimes it is really only a practical thing, to have something acoustic, that insulates the sound. I am quite a practical thinker. I like a certain purpose.

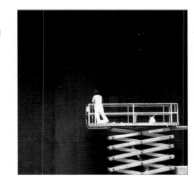

METHODS OF MAKING
**Kristiina Wiherheimo is a designer using a variety of woven and felted fabrics to create architectural installations, often in modular form.**

NARRATIVE OF MAKING
**Wiherheimo explores the ways in which textiles fulfil a specific function: acoustic insulation and the texturing of space. There is a degree of underlying imagery, reflecting her first visual experience as a child growing up in Lapland, most particularly her use of red, referencing the hearth and firelight.**

SUGGESTED LINKS
**Using modules: see Masae Bamba.**

Lesley Millar

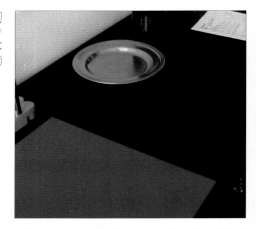

WEBSITE STATEMENT EXTRACT
www.clothandculturenow.com

'The beauty of cloth, the feel of the material and the surface, and the calm quality of a simple weave are basic matters that derive from traditional textiles. They have helped me to find the right material and technique, even though I don't come anywhere near to always using thread or fibre as my material. The warp, weft and weave form a universal structure that is also significant in terms of the expression, when you are seeking to create both concrete and symbolic form.'

KRISTIINA WIHERHEIMO

It is interesting that you speak about the acoustic nature of textile, as I understand you have also collaborated with a musician. Yes, the last exhibition I worked with an Italian composer. I was playing with silk. I asked her to make some sounds for this exhibition – you know music, but not music: sounds – and she wanted to use different materials as inspiration. She had a computer and with metals, for instance, she could translate the thickness of the metal to read into the computer and get some sounds.

But, she said she did not have any sounds related to silk. So we went to the studio, and I was sitting on a chair and wearing a headset and she was behind the glass in another room with her computer. And I had the microphone so I started making sounds with the silks and the composer gave me, every now and then, a sort of signal 'OK that is fine… can you now try such and such'.

She recorded all the sounds I made and she used it in her work. It made me laugh because I don't play any instruments, but I knew there was sound in silk. ∎

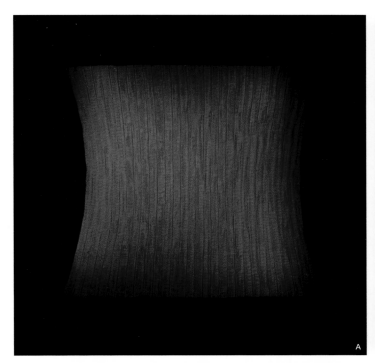

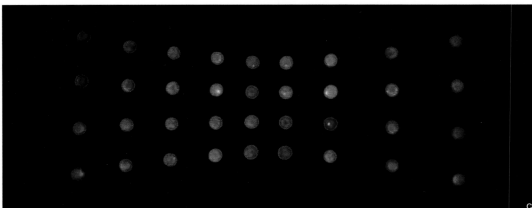

A: BIG FIRES. 1997
2.5 x 2.8 x 0.08 m
Felted wool
Photograph: Jussi Tiainen

B: SOON, THE IRON CURTAIN FOR THE
MAIN STAGE OF THE FINNISH
NATIONAL OPERA. 1993
12 x 20 m
Painted steel
Photograph: Bosse Fagerström

C: SMALL FIRES. 1997
2.4 x 4.3 m
Felted wool, painted MDF
backboard, lights
Photograph: Jussi Tiainen

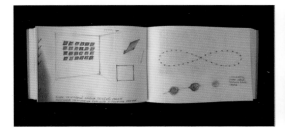

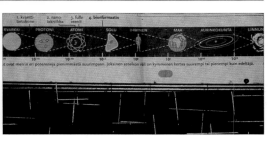

*Your work has a very architectural feel.* All my life, since a baby, I have seen wood being used. I have a strong model in my father who made everything, building all the time with wood. He built his own houses, summerhouse, many houses, also furniture. When I was a child I liked more to build my dolls furniture than to feed them. It is so natural to live and work with wood, wooden constructions – that's the way we discuss in my family, we always discuss the construction, and I want people to be able to see how my work is built; construction is the main thing.

*The technique you use is one that you have developed for yourself.* My technique is my own, I know nobody who is doing this exactly. I originally studied at the University of Industrial Arts in textile art, and weaving was my speciality. When I finished my studies, I worked in Portugal and designed woven clothes – men's shirts, etc. I found it very easy, but it was not for me. When I returned to Finland I started to make woollen 'fur' coats, but then, because of my allergy, I couldn't weave anymore. I had to stop and find myself material, and ways of working that would not irritate my skin.

When I started, I was so poor I used the newspapers that came through my door each morning. However, newsprint turns quickly to dust, it has so many chemicals used in the paper making process. I then found brown paper, which is very durable because the fibres are not broken. It has the natural colour of wood and fibres are long and durable and it doesn't turn to dust.

As I have a tendency to allergic reaction, I must take care what kind of glue I use. Also it should not be too hard, and not smell too strong. I wanted a glue that was easy to use and sinks easily into the paper, making it wet, and then the rolls shrink as they dry. From experience I know how much it shrinks and it is important that it dries hard. The patina on some pieces is accidental. I am using coloured printed papers from flower bouquets, wonderful colours, it gives accidental colouring and it keeps, especially when I shellac the paper.

With my technique it is possible to build almost any form, so I am very strict and use only the most simple forms, ones that have symbolic meaning, like the round form of a sun, for instance, or a star – simple forms that anyone can understand. The pieces are very symmetric, they are just quiet, they don't try and disturb you. They are constructions that express a quiet solemnity

One critic described my works as looking like they could have been made a long time ago, that the works are somehow eternal, and also that the form they take is very modern too.

*There is a strong sense of shadow and light in your work.* I use shadow and light to create a sense of space, and also three-dimensional forms become more alive with shadow and light. When my work is hanging, shadows make it softer. Shadows playing on the floor and on the walls create the atmosphere of being in nature – in the wood or under water. In our language we have many words that cannot be translated, there are tens of words for the 'voice' of snow, and for the light of snow it is the same. These words are the formative words,

METHODS OF MAKING
**Merja Winqvist has developed her own individual technique using paper and shellac to create three-dimensional forms.**

NARRATIVE OF MAKING
**The strong cultural narrative within Winqvist's work is explored through her referencing of archetypal form: e.g. boat shapes as containers. As with other Finnish textile artists, a preoccupation with light and shadow, particularly shadow, influences the final outcome of the work.**

SUGGESTED LINKS
**Light and shadow: see Jun Mitsuhashi. Archetypal forms: see Laura Pavilonyte.**

Lesley Millar

DRY SEASON (detail)
3.6 x 0.52 m
Printed brown paper, yarn
Photograph: Merja Winqvist

MERJA WINQVIST

very necessary for us to survive – this is how our language has developed.

Some people say my work is cold, which surprises me. Maybe people see only the silent forms and don't touch the symbolic level of the work. There are differences, even in Europe, between cultures. Sometimes when my work has been shown in Southern Europe people say the work is very dark, both emotionally and materially. I don't see it that way at all, but maybe it is our way of thinking. For Finnish people silence is fantastic, we enjoy silence. To stay in the forest where there are no noises at all is lovely. In Finland we have such opposite seasons in the year, the light summer and the dark winter. The darkness is a very strong, and long, period in every year, and also mentally there is a very strong area of dark in our minds. The opposition of light and darkness is very interesting. I couldn't live anywhere else where it wasn't so strong.

In the old days, in the winter, people were living inside the houses because it was so cold outside. With no electricity they would sit and talk. Winter was the time people spent inside around the fire. The relationship with fire gives us a feeling of great comfort.

**Many of your works look like they were made to hold something.** The first sculpture I made, I had an idea for making a form that would be floating in the air, hanging and floating, giving the audience the atmosphere of being under water – that's what I thought, but it became a boat, and after that I used the boat form all the time. The shape of the boat is formed by nature, formed by water, the most functional form in our culture, used for fishing, for commerce, for everything.

It is also an internationally recognised form, and it's a form that has not changed. I have been very interested in ancient Egyptian culture since I visited the country eighteen years ago and I made one boat form that had a little house on it, like the Sun Boats of Egypt.

My works may appear to contain 'something' you can't see, and of course a boat is a container. The name of this work was 'Sacred Passenger'. Maybe it was containing someone, maybe it was me. ∎

WEBSITE STATEMENT EXTRACT
www.clothandculturenow.com

'Function has shaped our concept of beauty – what's good is beautiful. This has generally been the starting point for the work of Finnish architects and designers.

I leave the internal structures in my sculptures visible. We often come across the same form language in Finnish traditional log-building, and in contemporary architecture, too – with the bearing structures and joints left visible as part of the overall look of the building, as if to speak of their function and to create tension and rhythm in the space.'

MERJA WINQVIST

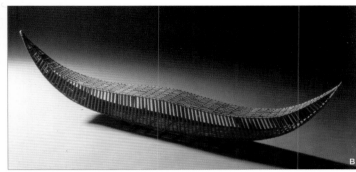

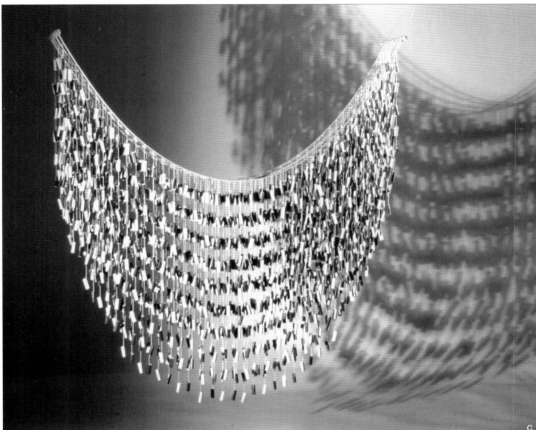

A: BLACK ANGEL. 2006
   1.5 x 1 x 1 m
   Paper
   Photograph: Markku Nurmi

B: SHIP. 1995
   1.8 x 0.5 x 0.3 m
   Paper
   Photograph: Heikki Tuuli

C: WINTER RAIN. 1990
   2 x 1.5 x 0.3 m
   Linen yarn and paper
   Photograph: Heikki Tuuli

**61**

# JAPAN

MASAE BAMBA
HIDEAKI KIZAKI
JUN MITSUHASHI
SHOKO NOMURA
MASAAKI TATE
MITSUO TOYAZAKI

# THE LEGACY OF TWO UNFORGETTABLE DYERS: Tomonosuke Ogo and Toshijiro Inagaki

KEIKO FUJIMOTO
Kyoto Prefecture
Culture and Art Office

One – Appreciation of Japanese dyeing and weaving. Japan has a strong tradition of the appreciation of arts and crafts, none more so than the fabrics used for the tea ceremony, known as kire. Most notable are the many so-called meibutsugire (textiles from the 16th and 17th centuries, associated with either famous tea utensils or famous tea masters) which are so admired by tea ceremony practitioners. Kire may be used for mounting the scrolls that hang in the tokonoma alcove or for making pouches to wrap tea ceremony utensils; even if only a small piece is used, such articles are passed down as treasures. They are delightful, be they kire brought over from China, south-east Asia, India, even west Asia, or dyed or woven textiles capturing the essence of Japan.

Why should they be so highly valued? Not only is the beauty of the design, colours or texture admired, but they are revered because the people who made or used the kire lived such varied lives. In other words, they encapsulate culture itself.

During the Edo period (17th to 18th century), the kosode (literally, small sleeves), a unique Japanese garment which evolved into the modern kimono, underwent a huge development. The shape of the garment itself had not changed much since the Muromachi era of the 15th century, but there was an amazing development in the designs which embellish the outer layer. For example, through the yuzen dyeing techniques, it became possible to express colourful pictorial designs. The wearing of a picture became the fashion of the era, and a plethora of ways of dyeing patterns using novel methods and resources developed.

Japanese people, who have traditionally been surrounded by dyed and woven items, have a close relationship with crafts and have frequently absorbed culture from abroad. Dyeing and weaving have also been closely related to pictures and carvings and have been handed down as 'tools' that make life more enjoyable.

In the Meiji era (latter part of the 19th century), contact with the West and the western idea of separating fine arts (paintings, sculpture) and applied arts (crafts) lead to inevitable change. Japanese dyed and woven products became highly valued in the West and were most popular at international expositions. The 'pictorial' element of these important industrial products increased. Artists set their sights on capturing ever more realistic pictures using dyeing and weaving techniques that combined a high degree of craftsmanship from a number of fields. The result were products that resembled paintings.

This trend continued until the start of the Taisho era (early 20th century) when Japanese dyeing and weaving declined to a position of being considered inferior to paintings. Artistic self-expression was suppressed and creative sensibilities no longer nurtured – and a lot of time was needed before dyed and woven works again became appreciated in their own right.

TWO – The rise of dyeing and weaving artists – participation in the Imperial Art Academy Exhibition.[1] From the Meiji era until the start of the Taisho era (end of 19th century to early 20th century) people engaged in dyeing and weaving were unwillingly restricted because of the perception that dyeing and weaving was inferior to paintings. While hiding their sensibilities as artists, dyers and weavers created designs for kimono or artefacts for interior decoration that placed emphasis on their practical use.

During this time, in the world of crafts, including dyeing and weaving, the sensibilities of artists were being encouraged and in 1927 an important breakthrough occurred that brought individuality to the fore. Craft products were authorised for exhibition alongside paintings and sculptures in the showcase government-sponsored Imperial Art Academy Exhibition (now known as the Japan Arts Exhibition).

The first exhibitors in the field of dyeing and weaving were Seika Yamaga (1885–1981), who used a weaving technique called tuzureori, and Gekka Minakawa (1892–1987), who worked with a type of batik dyeing; in addition, prizes were won by Tomonosuke Ogo (1898–1966) and Toshijiro Inagaki (1902–63). Ogo and Inagaki, aspiring to be artists, were involved in a creative movement at a time when the expression of autonomy and individuality in dyeing and weaving products was being sought. These two individuals had a massive influence on dyers of the period and in particular artists of Kyoto.

### THREE – Excellent instructors – Tomonosuke Ogo and Toshijiro Inagaki.

From 1950, Ogo and Inagaki were engaged at Kyoto City College of Fine Arts (currently Kyoto City University of Arts) and many dyers in Kyoto who are over 60 years old now were trained by them. Thanks to their passionate instruction, the dyeing research laboratories at Kyoto's historic City College of Fine Arts were invigorated, and their greatest achievement was producing the large number of dyers who have continued on that path.

Yet the works and personalities of these two individuals could not have been more different. Ogo was a pre-eminent batik worker. He is quoted as saying: 'Rather than think about the details of technique, you must study outside the creative process' – meaning that first and foremost, artists should consider ideas from a humanistic standpoint, and bring far-reaching concepts into their creations.

Inagaki, on the other hand, was an outstanding stencil dyer, with an analytical personality; through relentless repetition of sketches, he imposed his own reinterpretation on the subject. And as can be perceived from his words – 'When [a piece] is finished, I look at it for ten days, if I am happy with it, I ask the world,' he strove to enhance levels of sensitivity and expression. Because of these differences, they demonstrated to those who followed them good mental balance and the depth of their works.

But they also had much in common. Without getting caught up in learning about materials and techniques which is the fate of crafts, they firmly maintained the intentions and strength of expression of fine artists and strove for satisfaction in both technique and expression. Rather than relying on professional craftsmen for each process and trying to increase the superficial perfection of the creations, by pursuing all processes they improved the expression of the creator's beliefs, and on this point the two of them had an ideal relationship, enhancing each other.

I would like to introduce a few of their works at the same time as explaining a little about their careers.

Tomonosuke Ogo – Ogo was born in 1898 in the centre of Kyoto, the eldest son of a family who made stencils for traditional yuzen dyeing.

Following graduation from Kyoto City College of Arts and Crafts department of design, he was engaged by the long-established Tatsumura Weaving Company working on design. He joined the Shoshoin[2] research group where he made a close study of old dyeing and weaving techniques. He came across an ancient type of design drawn with soft lines called rokechizome, and was struck by the appeal of this long-neglected batik-style dyeing.

He also studied and exhibited both Japanese and western-style paintings. In order to explore creativity, even in the designs that he produced to make a living, he formed a group with some friends from his days at art school, and accordingly tried to express individuality in his works. In 1932, his creative work began in earnest.

In the latter part of the 1940s, when Ogo was in his late 40s, his personal style began to develop as he experimented with batik dyeing,[3] not only by way of technique but by repetition through trial and error with composition and motifs 'catching the subject in a simple shape with bold, carefree lines.' A typical work from that period is 'Rain', the heavy rain expressed with strong colours, the Uji River swollen with water seems to be roaring by.

A work from his later years is 'Tree' (Image 1c), a shift towards rhythmical abstraction, similar to Joan Miró's works, expressing the life-force of the tree. 'Wave' is a kimono design, the huge wave is like an abstract painting, the singular design arrangement of the kimono skilfully brought together in this exquisite work with its perfectly balanced composition.

Toshijiro Inagaki – Inagaki was born in 1902 in the centre of Kyoto, the second son of a Japanese traditional painter. His brother also later became a traditional painter involved in the Association for the Creation of National Paintings.[4]

Initially, he worked in Tokyo Mitsukoshi design department and Kyoto Matsuzakaya design department on kimono as well as other interior decorations. He began to devote himself to creative activities in 1931 at the age of 29. His first exhibited technique was a typical yuzen dyeing technique called norizome in which a starch-based paste is used to form a resist. Rather than subtle sketch-like lines, the distinctive feature of this method is sharp lines formed by the resist.

Then, at the end of the 1940s, inspired by the suien, a highly decorative plate atop the pagoda at Nara's Yakushi temple, Inagaki turned his hand to dyeing with stencils.[5] A creation from his early period is 'Design of Blue Maples' (Image 2c). Created with just five or six 10cm square paper stencils, it expresses perfectly the fresh winds and light of May. The stencils have been turned upside down and back to front to convey a feeling of liveliness in the leaves. The use of only darker or lighter shades of indigo is refreshing. This technique turned stencil dyeing into stencil painting.

In 'Tale of the Heike', Inagaki uses the rationality of paper stencils to create a composition of ordered symmetry as he skilfully depicts the fortunes and failures of the Heike noblemen of the classic medieval story. Another of his works is the kimono 'Grass and Bamboo' with a square hitta design – a traditional kosode (small-sleeved) kimono with stencil designs called surihitta. In this creation he has enabled a rich variety of expression within the design that appears to have no repetition due to the skilful, almost abstract, quality to the autumn grasses and the composition. Rather than clear, simple forms, Inagaki's stencils are known for their elegant style with the quaint beauty typical of the Kyoto style.

FOUR – An introduction to the current project. The current project, organised by Professor Lesley Millar of University College for the Creative Arts, is a gathering together of modern artists who have been influenced by the dyeing and weaving culture in their own country; works by six artists from six countries have been selected to take part in the exhibition. A most interesting concept: not only do works get exhibited, but we are given an opportunity to look into the cultural background of the works.

The culture into which the artist was born and brought up inevitably has a major influence on the act of creation; in addition, the attitudes gained from the influence of other people whom we have met are reflected. In particular, dyed and woven products are intimately related to how the water, earth, plants, etc., which form the core natural features from which raw materials are obtained, are used. It is thought that under these influences, personal awareness of colour and understanding of space is developed.

Ogo and Inagaki, while being aware of the unique qualities of dyeing and weaving works, tried to become universal by traversing the line drawn between dyeing and weaving works, and painting and sculpture; these artists, who uncovered their own personal inner world and reflected their thoughts in their works by using techniques and materials through their own consistent work, attempted to achieve autonomy as artists.

For both of them, the act of creation was an expression of the artist's personality. However, in the current era, divisions and genres are less clear cut as artists attempt to capture the world of art on a new dynamic scale. There is a movement to rethink everything from the point of view of art as affected by the environment, focusing on the qualities possessed by techniques and materials. A method has been developed whereby artists suppress their own will, abandon themselves to the environment they find themselves in, come face-to-face with the very act of the creation process, and apply techniques to materials and quietly watch the process as the materials themselves change.

In conclusion, the era in which Ogo and Inagaki grew up produced polarity with two differing points of view opposing: East versus West, technician versus artist; whereas with the wave of globalisation these days we begin to discover the fundamental points in common on a global scale, affirming the differences between individual regions and environments and seeking the strengths of those environments. In one sense, it is a movement to rethink the starting point of creativity. I feel that it will be perfect if this exhibition enables mutual communication and an interest in the places of origin as participants and viewers alike are stimulated by the uniqueness of the participating countries. ∎

1. Sponsored by the government, the Imperial Art Academy Exhibition was first held in 1907. Now known as the Nitten – Japan Arts Exhibition, it is currently the country's largest general-entry exhibition.
2. A large wooden structure attached to Nara's Todaiji. Holds approximately 9,000 pieces of artwork which are the essence of 7th to 8th century eastern culture.
3. In Japan, the rokechizome style of dyeing using wax to create shapes can be found in the Shoshoin artefacts, but it went out of use. Recently there has been a strong revival of the technique that involves painting the wax on freely with a brush.
4. An arts body established in 1918 by Kyoto's up-and-coming artists. Highlighted new movements in Japanese art.
5. A method whereby starch is placed on paper or material using a template cut in the shape of a pattern. The dyes are then applied by paintbrush or by soaking in liquid dye. This technique was designated an Important Intangible National Treasure in 1956, and thus distinguished from other stencil dyeing methods. It is well known for its high pictorial qualities.

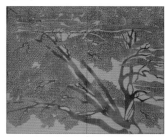

1c. Two-panelled screen, 'Tree', 1960 (National Museum of Modern Art, Kyoto)

2c. Two-panelled screen, 'Design of Blue Maples', 1948 (National Museum of Modern Art, Kyoto)

■ Edited extracts from interview with Masae Bamba, Kobe, November 2006, with Lesley Millar

You have written in your statement about the importance of your discovery of tsujigahana. Can you explain what this technique is? It was a technique popular in the Momayama Period, during the 16th century, and it is a shibori dyeing technique. Many motifs come from flowers, which is why tsujigahana is named this way because hana means flowers. When I saw these patterns I was very moved. Like falling in love. I was 18 and a student when I first saw work from this period. I had just started a textile course.

Before starting university I wanted to study dyeing. At that time I did not recognise shibori, all I knew was I was interested in dyeing. When I was a student in high school I took a design course and at that time I was not dyeing just making paper design. My friends did the kimono dyeing, they used silk fabric, and I wanted to touch the texture. I like the texture of the dye stuff – like paste. I liked the stickiness of the paste. After you put paste on the fabric then the dyer puts on sawdust. I like the way of dyeing and it is strange to me how the sawdust disappears after dyeing. I am interested in using fabric, paste and sawdust and the feeling of the skin touching the dust, paste.

I am interested in the feeling of the materials more than designing on paper. There is a gradation of the dye to the edges of the fabric. The pattern on the fabric looks very different to the paper pattern after it has been dyed. I like the feeling of the bleeding dye – the gentleness and softness of the dye. When I first saw tsujigahana I had a similar feeling. I felt I wanted to continue feelings that were in this work but in a modern way. I did not want to make the same pattern, I wanted to express a new tsujigahana. I wanted to combine tie-dyeing, drawing and painting. I want to make work that brings together different techniques not only shibori.

The forms you use are very organic. Basically, I use only square cloth that I sew and then I tie to make the form, each part of the work is individual. I sew in different directions, diagonals and circles to make the form. In my opinion the shibori technique changes the form from inorganic to organic. I created one installation where the forms look like mushrooms. I think that after everyone returns to the earth, the mushroom also grows in the earth – part of a cycle of life. I want to express that feeling of the earth when I show this work. There are about 6,000 pieces in this installation.

It must take a very long time to make this work. No, not so long, already I have the technique.

Do you always use the same materials? Before I used only cotton cloth, but now I would like to work with other materials, for example plastic bottles. I am interested that plastic is an unnatural, synthetic, material. I use very common fabric – cotton, and plastic is also a very common material. That is why I am using the plastic bottle. But now I am only experimenting, I am undecided whether I will use the materials or not. I don't think about the fact the bottles are recycleable I am only interested that they are made from artificial materials.

FLAME (detail)
Installation
Silk Organza, stones
Photograph: Toshiharu Kawabe

MASAE BAMBA

METHODS OF MAKING
**Masae Bamba is using shibori dyeing technique, influenced by the patterns of tsujigahana. Although shibori is a traditional method of dyeing, she has developed it in such a manner as to create her own style, particularly through installation work.**

NARRATIVE OF MAKING
**Unusually for Japanese textile artists, Bamba acknowledges the importance of content within her work. The cultural and personal narrative within her work is explored through notions of trace elements, originally inspired by her experience of working in Hiroshima.**

SUGGESTED LINKS
**Tradition: see Mare Kelpman.**

Lesley Millar

I think you have strong concepts behind your work. In some of my work I wanted to express traces. I was in Hiroshima making work, and Hiroshima suffered damage from the atom bomb. When the bomb exploded, the shadows of human bodies were cast on the ground or against walls and marked as a trace of the person standing there. People died but left their shadow. When I was in Hiroshima I was very shocked by this. Then I made work to express traces, also traces of animals that have died on the road.

Maybe I have social concept in some of my work. I think Hiroshima was very shocking and influenced me. I live there and teach there. Recently I have become more conceptual in my approach. However, my technique is most important – when I make technical works – I make sure I take time and spend energy to make good technique. But now I would also like to express more of a concept within my work. I know my style is changing. There is structure, but there is freedom. ∎

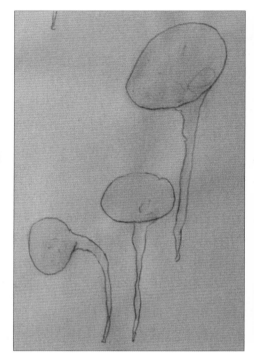

WEBSITE STATEMENT EXTRACT
www.clothandculturenow.com

'Although I remember the feeling that I got from these traditional works, from the start I wanted to create totally new and different works and so my ideas are very different from the traditional styles. With the "solid shiborizome series" my intention was to create something which did not fit any previous category of dyeing.

My desire is to create works that not only look Japanese but are also Japanese-style on a spiritual level.'

MASAE BAMBA

A: TENDER THORNS. 1996
0.3 x 0.15 x 0.15 m.
Cotton cloth
Photograph: Masae Bamba

B: GATHERING. 1995
0.2 x 0.5 x 0.5 m
Cotton cloth
Photograph: Makoto Yano

C: REBORN. 2006
0.05 x 0.02 x 0.02 m (each)
Silk cloth, pin
Photograph: Makoto Yano

**■ Edited extracts from interview with Hideaki Kizaki, Kanazawa, November 2006, with Lesley Millar**

You work in a very traditional medium – dyeing, do you feel that, in Japan, approaches to dyeing have changed very much? I think recent dye work has become concerned only with the surface, with the design – artists are not so concerned with dyeing and materials. For example, the kimono artists today think only about design – a long time ago kimono artist would think about materials, they would take time choosing materials, and then dye. Now kimono artists are much more concerned with surface design, thinking more about product, not the philosophy of making.

In the 1990s, the Japanese economy was strong and designers were very engaged with production and were driven to make more and more – the philosophy of dyeing was not then such an important concern – so I began to feel strongly that this drive for production was not right and I became more interested in the philosophy of dyeing.

I began to work with the Kaga-uzen technique. This is a technique originally developed at the same time as the more famous Kyoto-uzen, at the end of the Edo period. Kyoto-uzen became used for rich people, for the royal family, while Kaga-uzen was used for ordinary people.

Could you describe the dyeing process? First I make persimmon juice – then I make kake-shibu – kake means persimmon, shibu means tanning. If I make a big amount it takes a long time. After I have extracted the juice from the persimmon, I keep it for one year, allowing it to decay and ferment, to increase the strength of the dye. It can take three years for it to become a paste that you can use to paint, but the paste is not good for dyeing. So I keep my juice for only one year. To have enough dye for the piece in the exhibition would take about five litres. Using earth colours is important for me. My feet are firmly on the ground – no socks. I like that feeling on my feet.

Your three-dimensional work has a physicality and strength about it. I am concerned with the construction of the cloth, I want to express the existence of the materials and the form, and this is why I use heavy materials and make large forms. When I was a high school student I made wood carvings – I have continued with the feeling of wood carving in my three-dimensional works.

When people see my work I would like that they cannot recognise that it is cloth. I use jute cloth, which is a heavy material, I feel it has a certain power – the cloth itself has power. I buy a roll of raw jute – it is a beige colour – and then I work it by hand. I do not wear gloves because they just get broken and shredded quickly, and so working with the cloth makes my hands rough. It takes a long time for the material to take the dye.

Jute is not clean – it's not prepared for dyeing when I buy it – it has many bits in it, seeds, etc. The jute is made by hand and I really like that it is produced in this way. Also it is not an expensive material with wealthy connotations. Although jute is made by hand it is still not very expensive – because it's made in poorer countries where weavers are not paid high wages. I feel I am supporting their work by buying the jute.

COCOON (detail)
2.3 x 0.75 x 0.70 m
Jute, Akamegashiwal dye, persimmon juice
Photograph: Toshiharu Kawabe

METHODS OF MAKING
**Hideaki Kizaki is using traditional dyeing methods and natural materials. He has a passionate commitment to both the philosophy and technique of Kaga-uzen and the dyestuff kake-shibu.**

NARRATIVE OF MAKING
**Kizaki is less concerned with immediate visual appeal, preferring a slow revelation of intent through form and construction, weight and solidity. The use of the rough 'common' material of jute contains a narrative linking the traditional use of Kaga-uzen for ordinary people to the working people who weave and use jute today.**

SUGGESTED LINKS
**Form and materials: see Merja Winqvist, Kadri Viires.**

Lesley Millar

Your work is not conventionally beautiful, in the way that much Japanese textile work could be described as beautiful. I don't think I want to make work that is pretty. I think that nature is the most beautiful. The things that I make, or humans make, are not so beautiful. I want to express something more mysterious than beauty, more mysterious feelings than the pleasure of beauty. Maybe I would like viewers to see the work and perhaps the immediate reaction is that it is not beautiful, but then look more closely and slowly understand the beauty of the work.

You have spent much time working in Myanmar, how has this affected your work? I think that Japanese craft's roots are in Asia – so this is why I visited Asian countries to see their craft. In Myanmar I have been teaching textiles using local materials, cotton. Knowledge and skills are then taught by more experienced makers to younger people to make clothes and cloth.

I have learnt a lot about sustainability from this project. I have been particularly impressed by how people in Myanmar make tools when they have limited resources. It made me consider how many tools I have. In Japan we have many things – so it is very easy to throw away. It is better, I think, if people try to keep and reuse their possessions. In Japan we are very quick to throw away something if it is broken, but I observed in Myanmar that people fix and use objects over and over.

I am interested why you choose cloth as your medium? Because the experience was good for me. It was a good fit with me. It was very human feeling for me. ■

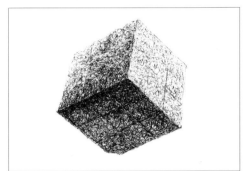

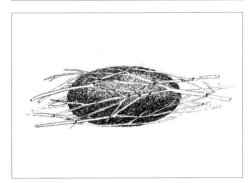

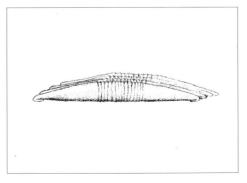

WEBSITE STATEMENT EXTRACT
www.clothandculturenow.com

'The development of Japanese traditional dyeing techniques has a history rarely seen in the world, and the multi-dimensionality of techniques is unique, unseen elsewhere in the world.

Through my involvement in Asia, my own way of thinking changed and this was reflected in my work, which underwent a huge change. I moved away from materials which depend on ever-decreasing fossil resources, and started to use traditional techniques and natural resources that are plentiful in Asia, switching towards a fundamental concept of natural sustainability.'

HIDEAKI KIZAKI

A: EXISTENCE OF CUBIC FORM 2006-1
(GATHER UP SERIES). 2006
0.9 x 1.2 x 0.9 m
Jute, persimmon dye
Photograph: Hideaki Kizaki

B: WALL ORNAMENT. 2005
0.9 x 1.8 x 0.06 m
Cotton, Indigo
Photograph: Hideaki Kizaki

C: FORM OF EXISTENCE
(GATHER UP SERIES). 2003
0.35 x 1.8 x 3.0 m
Jute, persimmon dye
Photograph: Hideaki Kizaki

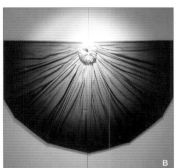

■ Edited extracts from interview with
Jun Mitsuhashi, Kyoto, November 2006,
with Lesley Millar

Very often in your work you include
ordinary objects, but in unusual
juxtapositions. Are you trying to change
the way a viewer might see these objects?
My work can be an entrance into another
world. I try to create a magical world with
ordinary objects – and that is what I want
people to experience. I want people to think
something after they experience the work;
to reconsider everyday objects. I would like
people to notice important things – these
works are a prompt for people to think about
their lives.

I like it when viewers can only see a part
of the installation – a detail – then a viewer
can imagine the rest of the work. This is an
important part of the work, that they don't
see everything all at one time, only a part of
it. In this way people can imagine the feeling
of the work better. I think that under the sun
you do not use your imagination so much,
because everything is visible under the sun.
But under the moonlight, it is a little dark and
there is space for our imagination. There is
not such direct thinking in the moonlight, we
imagine things in the moonlight. I think this is
a very Japanese feeling.

Do you always know beforehand what you
will make – exactly? No. Sometimes the
works that I make are a surprise. Yes, they
are a surprise for me. After I have shown
my works, I find that I see a story. The story
comes after the work. People often ask me

if there is some story with the work – but I
don't talk with viewers about a story. Titles
for my work are very important to me. The
title is a guide for the way people will think
about the work – especially the different kanji
I chose for my titles helps people to imagine
more. For example we have many different
kanji for flower – to use these different kanji
– it is possible to imagine different flowers
– one kanji can be a soft flower image,
another a simple flower image, another a
really gorgeous flower image and so on. So
therefore it is very hard to translate the titles
into English.

It is the same with the kanji for the word
'ma' – which means not only space and
time, but air and silence. It is very difficult
however, to translate these words. The
English words are very direct and straight,
but the Japanese words are not so straight
– they rely on an understanding between the
person who hears the words and the person
who is saying them.

When I look at your work, I have the sense
that some kind of ceremony has been or
is about to be conducted. When we have
a ceremony it is a very special and unusual
time. These times and the experience of
them are very important to me, during
ceremonies I experience a special focus in
my mind, I think this is true for many people.
When I make works I feel a similar focus. My
works are not so special, they use ordinary
things and by including these objects in
the work I give them a special value. When
people see the work, they have to use their
imagination. The work can remind a viewer
of the water or the sky. Viewers can feel the
world in their minds.

How did you start to make these kinds of
Mitsuhashi worlds? I started dyeing works
and using batik to make two-dimensional
work when I was a student at university.

MURMUR OF THE RAIN (detail)
1.39 x 0.91 x 1.61 m
Cotton, bamboo, thread, brass,
aluminium, mineral, feather, wood
Photograph: Toshiharu Kawabe

METHODS OF MAKING
**Although Jun Mitsuhashi trained
as a dyer, the starting points for his
works are images and drawings,
rather than the expression of
sensation through materials and
techniques. Materials are chosen
and used for their appropriateness
in the development of the idea.**

NARRATIVE OF MAKING
**Mitsuhashi's drawings and final
outcomes are a part of a continuous
interior narrative, from which he
extracts tableaux that become
self-referential worlds revealing the
secret life of everyday objects.**

SUGGESTED LINKS
**Hidden narratives: see Silja Puranen,
Lija Rage.**

Lesley Millar

At that time, I drew demons – for two-dimensional works. These were creatures – crawling and dancing. My ideas still come first from images, not the materials. The idea comes first. I have a picture in my mind. I make drawings of the installation at the start in preparation.

I have equal feelings for all my materials – wood or silk or metal or paper, and equal feelings about using them. I make aesthetic choices and decisions about materials on a day-to-day basis. Sometimes I want the tactile feeling of using textiles – so I use cloth and dye it – but I can also control the way the cloth can look through dyeing. Sometimes I use wood and metal. Cloth is for the sight experience – I like the feeling that dyeing evokes – and what it looks like. But if I need a texture, I will use wood or metal.

Do you want to make people smile when they look at your work? Yes, I do. ∎

WEBSITE STATEMENT EXTRACT
www.clothandculturenow.com

'I am fascinated by Japanese culture; the pleasure of subtlety and exaggeration, harmony and contrast, light and shade, can be discovered in so many places.

My works are not brightly coloured, they do not release an overwhelming sense of being, but quietly and inconspicuously, the installations move you, showing that there is a world among the small and trivial; it is like peeping through a window.

I believe my works reflect my own perception of Japanese culture.'

JUN MITSUHASHI

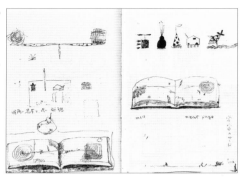
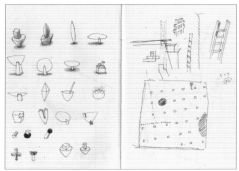
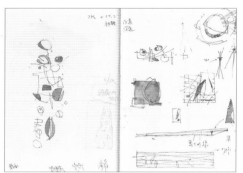
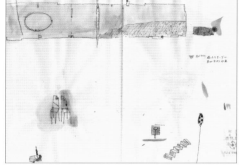

A: RAIN CIRCLE. 2000
   Installation
   Seaweed paper,
   brass wire, wood, acrylic colour
   Photograph: Jun Mitsuhashi

B: FLOATING GARDEN. 1998
   Installation
   Silk organdy, brass wire,
   stone, feather
   Photograph: Koichi Nishimura

C: WATER SCENE. 2003
   Installation
   Silk cloth by batik, wood,
   brass wire, feather, mineral, glass,
   coral, thread, stone, shell, bamboo,
   acrylic colour
   Photograph: Koichi Hayakawa

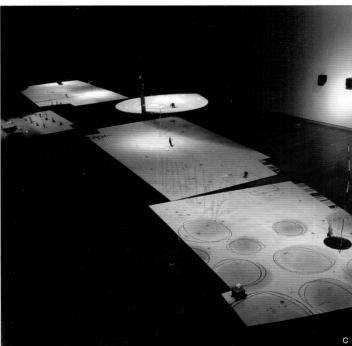

■ Edited extracts from interview with Shoko Nomura, Kyoto, November 2006, with Lesley Millar

Could we discuss a little history? How did you start working with paper? When I was a student at university, I studied weaving and went to a scroll-mounting shop and wanted to touch the paper. I became very interested in paper work. The master from the mount shop taught me how to make the scroll mounts. He used a special glue, dempun nori – it is starch. After I had studied how to make the mounts, I began to make paper works.

There is a long history of paper-making in Japan. Do you connect with this history in your work? I am interested in the material of washi paper more than the history of washi. I am interested in how you can see light through washi, it is a soft light. I like this feeling. In my early work, I cut my paper to get a very sharp edge. This sharp edge is most important to me because washi is very soft and the cut edge is very hard which makes interesting contrast.

How do you make the work? Paper on acrylic board then dempun nori. Five or six layers of paper, almost 20 layers, I think, at the thickest point. In the earlier works, it was very important for me to make a pattern. I was most interested in natural patterns – for instance the natural patterns you see in a leaf, and I trapped the leaves between the layers. Now I am not thinking so much about pattern.

When I make my work I layer the paper in such a way that, finally, it is not possible to recognise which part is the start and which the end. I would like to express this no start/no finish in my work. In the same way I cannot understand which is Japanese culture and which an outside cultural influence. Trying to find the dividing line is difficult, I feel many cultures in the heart – culture is not only an object.

I think that Japanese culture is a movement not an object and I think the more important things about Japanese culture are internal. For instance, an example – tea ceremony is an aspect of traditional culture – I feel it is only the form of tea ceremony that is passed on. Now we only understand the surface value of it, we do not understand the spirit of it, which I think is more important. It used to be that tea ceremony was important for your soul/spirit, but now I think that is no longer the case.

How would you like people to respond to the work? I feel that traditional culture includes action and gesture. This is why I make work out of paper. The action of laying the paper is as important as the work itself. When I have an exhibition – I want people to feel something deep down – a resonance in their hearts. I think an emptiness is what they will access, this is what I want. This emptiness is difficult to translate. It is a feeling. I want the viewer to feel ku and ma – this is the blank space. It is a spiritual feeling. Then there are also margins around the blank spaces.

When I make the work I feel the reverberation around the work, the energy around the work. When the work is in a gallery, I want viewers to feel an energy coming out of the work into the space of the gallery. At that time when looking at the work the viewer also recognises the action involved in making it.

METHODS OF MAKING
**Rather than exploiting the softness of washi, Shoko Nomura uses the traditional technique for scroll mounts, which produces a hard structure. Nomura interleaves and layers tiny strips of washi and glue, retaining one of the essential qualities of washi – that of the softness of permeated light.**

NARRATIVE OF MAKING
**As with many Japanese textile artists, Nomura is using the concept of ma, which is notoriously difficult for non-Japanese to understand. Ambiguity is at the heart of her work, the non-visibility of the beginning and ending of the process, the space at the centre of the work, and its relationship to surrounding space. The cultural narrative is carried through process, through the action and gesture of making.**

SUGGESTED LINKS
**Space: see Agneta Hobin, Helena Hietanen.**

Lesley Millar

LANDSCOPE (detail)
4.8 x 4.4 x 2.4 m
Washi, wood
Photograph: Toshiharu Kawabe

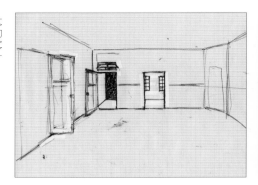

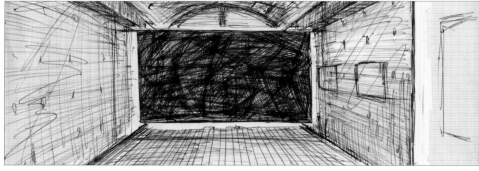

WEBSITE STATEMENT EXTRACT
www.clothandculturenow.com

'As you layer washi it appears thicker and the pieces get out of alignment. The more you layer it the more the outlines become blurred and you cannot see what is inside. In fact, the act of layering is also an act of subtracting or taking away. These pieces become blank spaces with no centre.

For me the blank space created inside and on the back of the layered papers reflects an essential aspect of Japanese culture.'

SHOKO NOMURA

Your work could now be described as installation, how did you move into this area of practice? I was thinking about cycles and I made a work based on the pattern of a whirlpool – like a ripple spreading out. The work was suspended above the floor so that you get reflections, and fitted wall to wall so that a concave effect was formed and visitors could not enter the room. After that I made a screen, a kind of wall, it is called 'LandscOpe'. I have mixed two words landscape and microscope, thinking about the microcosm and macrocosm. The light is coming through only from the back, you can't see through. I would like people to see both sides and then people can see a different view.

I have also made work that creates a white cube. I wanted to cut the space and used the piece to break up the space. This work is both paper and acrylic and so the work can stand by itself. The exhibition was about the border between one world and another and in the work I have made an entrance that is like Nigiri-guchi – this is a small entrance that we have in tea-houses. People have to bend down to enter through Nigiri-guchi, this bending action is very important because it makes people aware that they are entering the tea ceremony. I made my Nigiri-guchi and people had to lift the paper to enter.

Usually artists put an object in the space – and so people see only the object. I want viewers to see not only the object, but the whole space. ■

A: LANDSCOPE LANDESCAPE. 2007
2.5 x 4 x 2 m
Washi (Japanese paper)
Photograh: taniQ

B: HI-LINE 49SENTIMENTAL. 2006
Hi-line: 0.8 x 0.8 m
49setimental: 0.49 x 0.49 m
Washi (Japanese paper)
Photograph: taniQ

C: SYNCHRONIZE X CROSSING. 2005
2.4 x 4 m
Washi (Japanese paper)
Photograph: Shoko Nomura

■ Edited extracts from interview with Masaaki Tate, Osaka, November 2006, with Lesley Millar

Your work is very spare in terms of decoration. When I am making my work, I want to show the characteristics of the cloth and the dyeing materials. I don't want excess decoration. Traditionally such work would have been very decorative, whereas I am concerned with describing the essence of the material and the idea in the simplest way. In my work I would like to bring together material, technique and intuition. I feel that using intuition is the artist and using skill is the craftsman and it is important for me that both coexist in my work. I have found that I achieve the best results when I have allowed my intuition to guide my technical skills.

I always use cotton, this gives me the opportunity to be independent, to control the whole process in my studio, rather than having to depend on others. The cotton fabric is about 114 cm wide and it is very difficult for one person to stretch and get the tension right. It is a slow process, tensioning along one side then the other, adjusting all the time. I first put the wax onto the cloth under tension, then remove it from tension to iron it so that the wax melts through the surface. The cloth is then re-tensioned and I brush the dye onto the cloth. Doing it this way makes the colour more intense and also gives a graduation of colour, particularly where the wax has not penetrated.

I got the idea for this wax technique when I saw someone use a hairdryer, not an iron,

to melt wax, but the wax was only melted partially and I thought it was an idea worth developing further. I use many different weights and textures of cotton, and also different waxes.

You also use a very restrained palette. My early work was much more colourful than my recent work. I began this current body of work in 2005, using very subtle, dark colours so that the pulled threads, which create the white lines in my work, are more visible. The white line represents, and communicates, the structure of the cloth. Using the idea of pulled threads began when I accidentally did just that and I discovered the effect of revealing the undyed threads, and that this not only served as a pattern, but also made the structure of the cloth clear.

How do you plan your work, do you make lots of drawings? I plan the work very carefully, often using computer drawings, this is now very useful as I am now interested in not only making vertical and horizontal lines, but also diagonal and circular lines. This is a very delicate operation, requiring the threads to be cut as well as pulled.

What drew you to work with textiles? My father has a kimono shop, and so I always saw and touched kimono as a child, it is a very familiar fabric to me. Recently kimono has become more expensive and children don't have the opportunity to touch kimono cloth, but as a child my life was surrounded by kimono. When I went to University it seemed natural for me to go into the textile department and I assumed that

MASAAKI TATE

METHODS OF MAKING
Masaaki Tate is using traditional dye techniques, which he has developed into his own style through the pulling of threads, very subtle use of wax resist and the use of computerised drawing to visualise the work.

NARRATIVE OF MAKING
Tate brings his finely tuned aesthetic judgment to traditional craft processes, contrasting the density of dyed surface with the structure of the cloth revealed through the pulled thread.

SUGGESTED LINKS
Surface: see Diana Harrison.

Lesley Millar

I would work in my father's shop. However it is very difficult now to make a living from kimono, so my father suggested I look outside kimono for my career, although I have still made kimono on a few occasions and sometimes, under my father's name, I organise fabric to be sold through my father's shop. ■

HYPOTHESIS AND VERIFICATION AND RESULT (DROPS SERIES) V75 H75
0.90 x 0.90 (x 12)
Rozome dyed cotton
Photograph: Toshiharu Kawabe

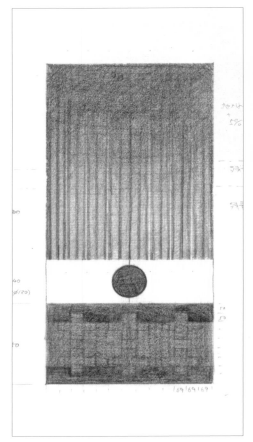

WEBSITE STATEMENT EXTRACT
www.clothandculturenow.com

'In their desire to make the best possible artefacts, craftsmen adapt and improve materials, techniques and tools in many ways. This also comes across in my own works and it has been a source of influence for me.

I create my works by exploiting the special qualities of the materials. This is because I have considered how the weaving and dyeing ought to be. I believe that the essential ingredients for success are the creator, the materials and the technique.'

MASAAKI TATE

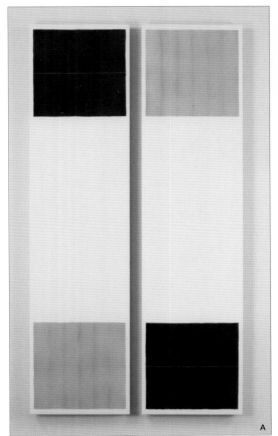

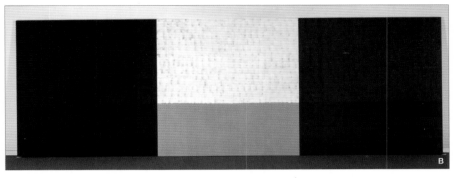

A: TRINITY 05-10. 2005
   Two pieces, each 1.62 x 0.40 m
   Rozome, cotton
   Photograph: Yuji Doi

B: UNSETTLED – THE BEGINNING. 2004
   1.8 x 5.4 m
   Rozome, cotton
   Photograph: Masaaki Tate
   Collection of Some-Seiryukai

C: TRINITY 06-2. 2006
   1.6 x 3.2 m
   Rozome, cotton
   Photograph: Masaaki Tate

Your work is very concerned with pattern.
Someone said that Japan has two patterns
– Jōmon pattern and Yayoi pattern. The
Jōmon period was before Roman times, and
the patterning is very powerful, not simple,
with many decorations. This pattern comes
from water. Before research was made
into Jōmon culture, it was believed that
Japanese culture came from Yayoi culture –
being quiet and simple – this is what people
thought was the Japanese aesthetic. But
research into Jōmon culture showed there
are now different opinions about Japanese
aesthetic. My roots come from Jōmon – in
my work I would like to have no space within
my pattern.

When I was a textile student at university, I
became interested in stencils (they are called
katagami) and I made traditional stencil
work. However, I wanted to make freer work,
more influenced by the accidental patterns
of nature. In the end I made work with shirts.
There was no draft, no stencil – I did it by
eye, and the pattern was created by burning
tiny holes. I used incense to burn the shirt,
just freely making marks straight on to the
cloth.

Your button works are often huge
installations – do you make a plan for
these works? I think about the space and
then draw it out, and I think about colour
combinations, some of the works have up

to 8,000 buttons. These button pieces are
very important. When I make something
using buttons, I use them as a material, the
buttons are just a circular shape so I can
make works using the button. The buttons
give me inspiration.

In one case I collected the buttons from
shirts and made a button tower. One of my
button works is called 'Tama-tama, Mizu-
tama'. Tama-tama means 'by accident'.
Mizu-tama means 'water circle' or it can also
mean 'dots'. The fact that it is made out of
circles refers to the total shape and also the
individual shape. It references the cosmos
– from small tama comes everything … like
an atom. Button-tama.

Your collection of buttons is delightful,
colour coded and stored in candy jars.
However, you also have collections
of other objects. When did you start
collecting objects? After the earthquake
in Kobe. I live in Kobe but my house was
not damaged – though everyone around
me suffered, their houses were damaged
and people threw away everything. At that
time I had a very simple life – no tools,
no collections. But after the earthquake I
decided to collect good things, good tools
for my house– as a kind of recovery. I don't
know when I will die so I collect good things
for the time being. If an earthquake comes
again and my collection is damaged, it
is OK because I have already been given
something by my collection. I continue to
collect things, I have a good eye for my
favourite things, and I want many, many
things, so I continue to collect small objects.
I have no space for collections, so objects
are getting smaller.

How do you decide what to collect? I like
an object to have a function; I like this more
than sculpture or painting. That is why I
collected craft objects – knives, etc. I like

**METHODS OF MAKING**
**Mitsuo Toyazaki trained in dyeing
and katagami – traditional stencil
technique and his work is concerned
with colour and pattern, expressed
through a variety of materials and
methods. His specific affiliations
are with Jōmon culture, a very
different aesthetic from that normally
associated with Japan.**

**NARRATIVE OF MAKING**
**Toyazaki's concepts of pattern
move from traditional forms to
ways of working that are wholly
contemporary, carrying a cultural
narrative through that relationship to
tradition, the seriousness of intent
purposely disrupted by the use of
unexpected materials.**

SUGGESTED LINKS
**Pattern and making: see Michael
Brennand-Wood.**

Lesley Millar

PASSAGE OF TIME (detail)
6 x 2 m
Buttons
Photograph: Toshiharu Kawabe

MITSUO TOYAZAKI

not only old objects but also new objects. Sometimes the function and way to use some of the objects is a mystery, I like that there are no instructions for these objects. I have a limit on my collections – I have a limit on height – the object must be no more than one finger high and fit in the hand. That's the limit. I would like to collect things that we recognise but we are not quite sure what the object is. I am particularly interested in who made this object, and when they made it, but I have so many collections now I have no time to research. It is not the purpose to research the object. I record how much it cost, where I bought it – not for all the objects, but for most of them (I don't make a record for the cheap objects).

You have a very wide range of references and interests. I like to think of new things and many things. The Japanese word zome is translated into English as 'dyeing', which has only one meaning. I am not comfortable with the translation because zome has many more meanings than simply dyeing. In Western Europe textile is weaving. In Japan weaving and dyeing are very different, and textile is not only weaving. The emotion comes through the dyeing. There is a famous Basho haiku using the word Shimi-iru, which means to 'infiltrate' or to 'saturate' or to 'penetrate', this can apply to dyeing but also to inside the rock. The sound of the cicadas penetrates the rock. Of course, the cicadas sounds do not actually go into the rock, but it feels like they do. ■

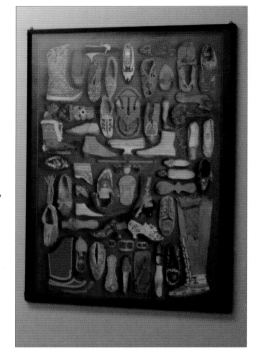

WEBSITE STATEMENT EXTRACT
www.clothandculturenow.com

'When I first started working, I wasn't aware of it, but I have discovered an aspect of "Japanese-ness" in my own work. Recently, I have been working to understand "Japanese culture" better and have been leaning towards historical Japanese forms in my own work.

My way of approaching my work is to entrust the shape to the materials, then experiment with the method and techniques and finally work in tune with nature – self-expression is not my primary objective. I generally work by focusing on the method and materials.'

MITSUO TOYAZAKI

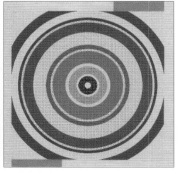

A: A SHELL. 2005
   Installation (in church)
   Used shell buttons
   Photograph: Mitsuo Toyazaki

B: KARA. 1994
   0.74 × 0.54m
   Used shirt (burning incense
   sticks), used hanger
   Photograph: Tadasu Yamamoto

C: OVER THE RAINBOW. 1987
   Installation (in park)
   Dyed sneakers
   Photograph: Michiaki Suzuki

# LATVIA

ZANE BERZINA
IEVA KRUMINA
UNA LAUKMANE
LIJA RAGE
PETERIS SIDARS
DZINTRA VILKS

# LATVIAN TEXTILES: from historical to contemporary

ASTRIDA BERZINA

Cloth & Culture Now is a celebration of cross-cultural encounters, in which we gain an unprecedented opportunity to travel through the history of numerous cultural identities, searching for both the unifying and the surprising, as well as answers to questions about textile art from historical and contemporary perspectives. Latvia is one of six cultures being examined more closely during this project through the work of selected artists of various generations.

The long and complicated development of Latvian identity has been influenced by much contact with other peoples, their cultures and attitudes. Research by the Indian linguist SK Chatterji[1] indicates that the Latvian and Lithuanian languages have their roots in the tribes that travelled from India and settled by the Baltic Sea 4000 years ago. Like Celtic, modern Latvian and Lithuanian have preserved a close relationship to Sanskrit. It is possible that this was when the first real crossing of cultures occurred, which over time has been reflected in the unique mentality and cultural identity of the Baltic peoples.

Due to its geographical position and the ice-free ports, making it the 'gateway to Western Europe', the territory inhabited by Latvians has always been attractive to foreign traders and invaders. Until the 20th century, this territory, a meeting point for the clash of forces and power, passed from hand to hand – invaded at various times by Germany, Lithuania, Poland, Sweden and Russia. Having come with good or evil intentions, all these forces left their differing material and spiritual imprints on the people living by the Baltic Sea. Ethnic culture, assimilating the rich experience of other influences, has proved to possess a notable capacity for survival considering the political and cultural pressure from outside.

In the post-war period, Socialist Realism ruled all genres of art in Latvia and demanded the glorification of Soviet ideology. At this time, Latvian art was totally cut off from creative processes in Europe or the world: it developed in an isolated space. The only spiritual nourishment for the creative intelligentsia was their ethnic heritage and the cultural experiences of the short period of pre-war independent Latvia (1918–40), when art had been naturally included within the European context.

In the early 1960s, suppressed creative energy searched for pathways of free expression and manifested itself in textile art. Soviet censorship defined textiles as a decorative-applied genre, with a purely decorative function, within which it was not possible to express anti-Soviet ideology. This is why textile art was not subjected to censorship as was painting and literature. Artists quickly grasped the priorities of creative freedom and the dynamic development of textile and fibre art began.

The founder of Latvian modern professional textile art was professor Rudolfs Heimrats, who in 1960 exhibited the tapestry 'To the Song Festival', which, in an unusual way for the time, synthesised ethnographic tradition with classical principles of tapestry and figurative painting. One year later, he founded the department of textile art at the Latvian Art Academy.

The first students to graduate, for example Edite Vignere, blazed a bright trail for the new textile art, which was notable for its unrestricted creative daring. Despite the political isolation of Latvia, these processes coincided with the renaissance in the whole European textile scene, as exemplified by the Lausanne Textile Biennale, founded in 1962. Since then four Latvian artists have taken part in this exhibition in various years: Ruta Bogustova, Inese and Ivars Mailitis, and Peteris Sidars.

Soon there was talk of the Latvian national textile school. Latvian artists received state commissions not just from their own country, but also from Moscow. They were invited to represent the USSR in international exhibitions. A paradoxical situation was created, where national art was stimulated and also financed by the central occupying power, although it did not always express a message friendly to this ideology.

Between the 1960s and 90s, a coded system based on the Latvian mentality was consolidated in all artistic genres, a type of 'Aesop's language' using special, often amusing metaphors to express unpleasant truths, which could not be understood by outsiders. Artists learned to express their message in ways that escaped through the net of Soviet censorship, and audiences learned to 'read between the lines'.

Imaginative narrative was a general

characteristic of professional Latvian textiles since their beginnings in the early 1920s, when the first wall decoration woven in the tapestry technique interpreted mythological themes. Figurative compositions are still popular today, while those based on social, political or literary sources reached a peak in the 1970s and 80s. Interestingly, at that time this approach contextually corresponded with European textile trends.

In Latvia this concept also corresponded with the time when the air vibrated with the premonition of the 'Singing Revolution', which in 1991 led us to the second proclamation of an independent Latvian state. Artists in all genres, and particularly textile artists, returned with heightened enthusiasm to their ethnographic heritage and its symbolism. This resonated with a rapidly growing need for a confirmation of suppressed identity.

On the eve of the Singing Revolution, during the second half of 80s, a huge internal tension – a combination of strength and desperation – manifested itself in large, almost iconographic compositions, which in their contemporary form referenced the idealistic life assumptions of the pre-war period (Aija Baumane, Viesturs Berzins, Arvids Priedite, Egils Rozenbergs) or searched for philosophical references to humanity's collective subconscious system of images and global cultural contexts (Georgs Barkans, Astrida Berzina, Lija Rage).

Some fibre and textile artists turned to the possibilities of incorporating three-dimensional objects within public spaces (Inese Jakobi, Edite-Pauls Vignere). Subsequently, textile art was 'on a wave' and exhibitions were filled with visitors. Textiles had been transformed from decorative compositions concerned with design or style, taking on a deeper significance or even a political statement, representing the story of nation's self-preservation.

In independent Latvia today, cross-cultural exchange initiates a stimulating dialogue, enhancing the development of creativity. Nevertheless, we are also confused by the defencelessness of human nature and its fragility during the course of rapid transformation. We are concerned about how this will influence the spiritual, delicate substance, which cannot be grasped, and which, irrespective of technologies or materials used, allows the Japanese to maintain identifiable signs of cultural belonging, and Latvians and Finns – their own signs.

We worry about the mentality and spirituality which long ago was carefully guarded and maintained by all peoples, passed from generation to generation in the form of the wisdom of the heart, experience and craft skills. Does there exist – and if yes, then where – a line of moral duty which one should not cross in the contemporary process of globalisation, for us not completely to lose the uniqueness which makes us interesting in the global colourful diversity? These are questions which live quietly in each of us, being particularly important for the cultural identity of small nations.

Contemporary Latvian textile practice, like that of most other countries, is based on ethnic heritage. Through the mediation of design, texture and colour combinations, textiles reflect the spiritual characteristic of a people or ethnic groups, giving also intimate information about the individual, their feeling of belonging and status. These characteristics of ethnographic textiles are most prominently demonstrated in Latvia by the folk costumes, which are still worn with pride and nostalgia at times of national celebration, such as during song or dance festivals. It could be said that ethnic costume is still a source of inspiration for contemporary Latvian textile art and design.

The practice of Latvian ethnography

is characterised by the culture of skilled craftsmanship. Many centuries ago, Latvian peasant women would weave by firelight elaborate overshot 'Drell' patterns using up to 32 shafts. From early childhood, girls prepared their dowry under the supervision of their mothers, comprising everything needed for future family life. The making of the dowry was a sort of meditative initiation in the transformation of a girl into a woman (Image 2d).

In Latvia's north and midlands, colours were more restrained, viewed through fine nuances of grey, while on the western coast in Kurzeme, where boats from Germany, the Netherlands and Spain often docked, after the appearance of chemical dyes in sailors' baggage, fabrics flared up in shades of orange, red, blue and purple. Wealthy women from Kurzeme treated themselves by buying the joy of colour.

In his early works artist Peteris Sidars manifested his feel for his roots by weaving tapestries in which he improvised the richly saturated, bright colours and motifs of western Kurzeme (Image 1d). It is interesting to observe that, after the artist's later creative experiments with various materials including hot glue, fibre optics and snake skins, in his most recent work 'Gloves from Southern Kurzeme', Sidars directly reflects on the ethnographic legacy of his own region. The knitting of an anonymous female inhabitant of Kurzeme is transformed into an object of art, through an extended transformation process and an interaction with the wearer – the artist himself.

In the Latvian mentality aesthetics have always been organically linked to everyday life. This is manifested in the universal principle: beauty is practical, while the practical is beautiful and natural. Deep understanding of the natural and nature resonated with Latvian traditional practices.

These basic cultural values are organically

integrated in Dzintra Vilks' subtle, light structures created in sisal fibres, which have associations with visions of an ancient historical style or the cultural signs from a half-forgotten age. By contrast, the textile objects by Lija Rage have an architecturally clean form referencing the harsh beauty of Northern nature. Through the touch of a loving hand, rich with a many-layered associative cultural experience and spiritual intensity, the works of the artist offer a journey through the world of archetypal cultural signs.

For centuries Latvian tradition undoubtedly resonated the positive and spiritual: vital joy about the world and existence as a united whole with clearly defined categories of good and evil, the beautiful and the ugly. This harmonious world view, deeply experienced in the form of metaphors and symbols of nature, is manifest in the Latvian folk songs called dainas – quatrains. These are similar to the Indian rigveda, and speak through polysemantic encoded metaphors about the rhythm of human life and basic values, from cradle to grave, always in the presence of the divine.

In the 1920s in Latvia a contentious theory was introduced, which suggested that the Latvian dainas could be interpreted as a type of 'backup' for the information encoded into Latvian ornamentation. Latvians have a set range of basic archetypal patterns, which are based on an unusual principle of coding (Image 2d). This principle allows countless variations through the interpretation of various weavers, although in their essence, they always retain the encoded message. This explains the large diversity in textile practice in individual regions and even villages.

The Lielvarde belt (Image 3d) can be considered the most striking example of encoded information, in which, over generations, weavers have woven the story of the people from their beginnings to the future. Each motif holds a symbolic meaning, which, in the process of weaving the belt, evolves into a visually completed story, etched into the collective memory. Therefore in the Latvian ethnographic context we can speak about the interrelationship between text and textiles, which is currently being studied in this and other contexts in Latvia and around the world.

In Riga the interaction between text and textiles manifests itself in the concept of the e-text+textile project. One of the co-authors of this project is the London-based artist and designer Zane Berzina, who investigates the influence of technology and science on text and textile-based practices and our cultural environment in general. Born and raised in Latvia, educated in various Western European countries, Berzina's intensely creative life is focused on her desire to reach out, connect and then assimilate new experiences and value systems into her artworks.

The historically determined principles that have formed Latvian history and spirituality, in the context of their contribution and losses, themselves are a metaphor for various models of cultural interaction. What the future for the development of Latvia and its culture will be, after a short period of renewed independence and after re-integrating with Europe, will become apparent over time.

As Latvia opens the door to contemporary cultural discourses and concepts, interdisciplinary and cross-cultural dialogues are taking place more often, new technologies and materials are becoming more accessible – this all providing the opportunity for fantastic discoveries and synthesis in the space where craft, art, design, technologies and theories overlap. But as participating artist Ieva Krumina comments: 'It is not a question about textile art or some other art. Any creative motivation resides in the artists themselves, in their creativity and joy of ideas.'[2]

Latvian textiles are at the crossroads of crucial changes. The selection of artists for this exhibition is an attempt to demonstrate a few directions in Latvian textile art now – both by more established practitioners and those just emerging. These artists are already shaping the future, each from their individual perspectives. ■

2d. Mittens from Akniste (late 18th century – early 19th century)

3d. A Lielvarde belt (early 19th century)

1d. A married woman's costume (Rucava, mid-19th century)

1. Chatterji, S.K. (1968) Balts and Aryans – In Their Indo-European Background. Calcutta. Indian Institute of Advance Study
2. Krumina, Ieva. (January 2007). Author's interview.

All objects courtesy of the National History Museum of Latvia. Photographs: L Balodis

■ Edited extracts from interview with Zane Berzina, London, April 2007, with Lesley Millar

You are a Latvian artist, living in London and dividing your working time between London, Latvia and Germany. How is this reflected in your work? I am not working with identity, it never has been one of my concerns, but then, of course, we all start from a very specific place – for me: Latvia, which has a specific cultural and political environment. It has formed a lot of my work and I cannot escape that. Nevertheless, I think that Soviet times were a very difficult period for a young girl – but I did not know anything better. Now there are actually a lot of things I am missing from Soviet times – a more ecological approach to life and way of living, without branding.

There was not this terrible sense of consumerism. There were only two types of bread – black and white. Competitiveness wasn't a driving force in the arts community, which I think was healthier. There were pluses and minuses. Now I read books about that time and I realise I had forgotten most of it, and then I remember everything – I remember those queues, for instance. But with a bit of perspective I think I am a little proud – perhaps this is not the right word. But I am proud to have had that experience.

Could you talk about your proposal for the exhibition? Well, that will be part of my 'Skin Stories', in which I have been looking at merging two different practices

MEMBRANES IV (detail)
0.14 x 0.19 x 0.08 m (x 40)
Manipulated fabrics, pins, wooden boxes
with glass covers
Photograph: Zane Berzina

between an artist and a scientist. I was really interested in biological mechanisms and I have been looking into how skin mirrors our psychological or mental health.

I'm creating those very little textile pieces, hybrid fabrics, in a very time-consuming way, working not only with nice silks, but a lot of technical fabrics, and modifying them. I'm treating them as small specimens, referencing the human skin surfaces and presenting them in specimen boxes, like the boxes you buy for preserved butterflies – systematising the butterflies, organising them into families . But when you go into the shop the butterflies in their cases become a kind of decoration.

How did you start to work with scientists? I started to work with scientists during my PhD when I began to investigate new materials. I visited research institutes and I realised that the scientists were interested in what I was doing and I felt really free in this unknown zone. I was allowed to ask silly questions because I was an outsider and was very free in communicating with them and in many cases I got really interesting responses.

Was it difficult to collaborate? No, that's the thing, I think it is very difficult sometimes to collaborate both for artists and scientists, but I was made to feel very welcome and I started to learn how to be understood and how to address my questions. It made me more and more methodical in my process of exploring the skin or the fabric by looking at it through the microscope, and I made amazing discoveries by looking in that way. Then I felt I had to make that process visible, to organise that information in specific ways using a more clinical approach. In this way the work becomes more abstract.

METHODS OF MAKING
**Zane Berzina's approach is primarily investigatory. Using combinations of natural and new materials, she draws on both textile knowledge and scientific methodology to create her installations.**

NARRATIVE OF MAKING
**Berzina occupies a middle ground between art and science. Applying the sensibilities of the artist to a scientific procedure, she uses the close relationship between cloth and skin to carry the narrative of this investigation.**

SUGGESTED LINKS
**For methodology: see Maxine Bristow.**

Lesley Millar

WEBSITE STATEMENT EXTRACT
www.clothandculturenow.com

'The choices of yarns, colours and patterns reflected not only on the specific region and its landscape, but also expressed the weaver's individual sense of taste, her values and her dreams in a beautifully crafted non-linear textiles narrative.

In order to create new readings and meanings I combine traditional textile processes and materials with technically highly advanced new materials and methods.'

ZANE BERZINA

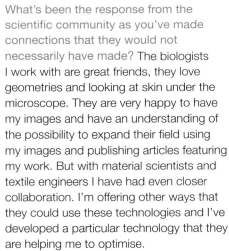

**What's been the response from the scientific community as you've made connections that they would not necessarily have made?** The biologists I work with are great friends, they love geometries and looking at skin under the microscope. They are very happy to have my images and have an understanding of the possibility to expand their field using my images and publishing articles featuring my work. But with material scientists and textile engineers I have had even closer collaboration. I'm offering other ways that they could use these technologies and I've developed a particular technology that they are helping me to optimise.

I'm not a typical designer – in that I am looking for a fabric to be industrialised or manufactured. I'm interested in that in-between space, how to suggest something through working with scientists and bring it out in textile design that other people can develop into a product. I have a problem calling myself an artist or designer because I'm interested in all these unfinished things, most of which are, I think, in between art and science. This can be a very uncomfortable position sometimes. Not too many people work this way so I cannot find exactly where to locate myself.

**Do you have a concept before you begin?** Yes, always. I can't just do something led by intuition, it always comes from research and I work for many years on one thing. I never have a precise image. I may have a rough shape, but the image comes out of the material as I work with it. I think in shapes as an end product. I think I have a good sense of space. It is a kind of shape and then everything else comes out of that, but I'm not drawing or sketching too much. I might do some technical drawing. For me it is not enough just to be aesthetically pleasing. I find the measurements beautiful.

**What would you like people to understand from your work?** I would like people to see something wondrous – that it makes them inquisitive. There is so much beauty around. I would like them to see that through the microscope. I want to take them into another world for a while.

**Do you think there would come a time when you didn't translate your research into an artistic outcome?** That would be a sad moment in my life. I hope I will always be able to make the work. ∎

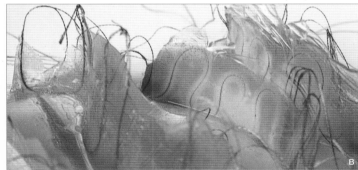

A: TOUCH ME WALLPAPER. 2005
   3 x 1.5 m
   Thremochromic inks, fire retardant
   non-wovens
   Photograph: Zane Berzina

C: MEMBRANES III. 2006
   Size variable
   Manipulated textiles,
   glass slides, magnifying glasses
   Photograph: Raimo Lielbriedis

B: SKIN ARCHITECTURE. 2004
   Approx. 0.25 x 0.15 x 0.06 m
   Silicone, conductive threads,
   thermochromic inks, encapsulated
   aromas, power supply
   Photograph: Zane Berzina

■ Edited extracts from interview with
Ieva Krumina, October 2006, with Lesley Millar

Much of your work has been in woven tapestry. Why have you chosen this medium? Tapestry is fascinating. It is so labour consuming to make and it is so, so rich, this technique. It is possible to fill the work with different thoughts and different and very beautiful inner values. When I look at old tapestries, they are very rich, not with material value, but rather like a container of the artist's ideas and time. I am fascinated with this very deep inner value, this time-value that is held within the work.

Also when I see a lot of tapestries in old museums, I experience something like the smell of sweat in the air when I start to think how much work it has taken to weave these tapestries. Now I feel that only specialists, professional artists can value – can see how – what is done in tapestry – and how serious was this work. For people whose life is quite far from textile, for them it is not important, they are somehow indifferent.

Traditionally tapestries have been used to carry a narrative, to tell a story. Story is very important for me. My colleagues sometimes criticise me because they feel that there is too much influence from literature in my work. My mother was teacher of literature, I have such a background, I can't escape from it and I don't want to. For me the work should contain some message or some reason to think of something deeper. Even in very abstract work I need to know something more. I want to know what I am looking at.

In Latvian fairy tales a butterfly is a beautiful creature, but very light minded, and only lives for one day. However, in Eastern mythology the butterfly is something like a soul, a symbol of eternity. One day a very ordinary Latvian butterfly sat near to me on the bench. I looked at the design on the wings and suddenly saw that it was a little like a map of the world.

This inspired me to begin working with the idea of maps, and I had the idea that there are two butterflies, like two worlds maybe, and finally made the tapestry titled 'We and They'. We like to divide society into We and They: We the Christians, They the Muslims or Buddhists, or We the White or They the Black – people divide. Sometimes it's very sad that we have such strict borders between us when, really, we all are the same.

The work for this exhibition is about as different in technique from tapestry as possible. My current work is with silkscreen print, heat and garbage bags, and it's quite fragile. I melt the images together at certain points, using an iron, just for a few seconds, and the effect is very reminiscent of lace. However, the material shrinks all the time and it's never the same, the process is quite capricious. It tears easily, but it's also possible to melt it back together with

METHODS OF MAKING
**Ieva Krumina is a tapestry weaver and printer. She is also an illustrator and drawing plays a central role in visualising and developing her ideas.**

NARRATIVE OF MAKING
**Krumina is using the traditional narrative role of tapestry, and the inherent narrative of cloth; the choice of technique has thematic meaning. Her selection of images has strong symbolic significance within the narrative.**

SUGGESTED LINKS
**Tapestry: see Shelly Goldsmith.**

Lesley Millar

NOBODY (detail above)
1.5 x 1.5 m
Polyethylene (garbage bags), screen print,
artist's own technique
Photograph: Ojars Grikis

a warm needle. Not all garbage bags are equally suitable for this technique. Some are thicker and some are thinner, so, there are different nuances, and sometimes I use two layers of the finest garbage bag – I'm becoming quite an expert on garbage bags.

You have been using images of butterflies and there are both links and dissonances between the garbage bags and the fragile, transient nature of the butterfly. I have silkscreen printed butterflies on garbage bags, on polyethylene. Garbage bags are not biodegradable, they are made to be used for just a few minutes and thrown away, but they'll take maybe a hundred years to degrade. And this one-day-being butterfly is printed on one-day material. I've been experimenting with other kinds of images of fragility – moths, disintegrating fabrics, corroded surfaces – the intention being to find correspondences for the transience and fragility of life, things that had meaning once, but over time the meaning has changed or disappeared.

Also I am thinking about a new series of silkscreen images to make a larger size work in this technique. I've been thinking about a lost, forgotten army, that has also forgotten the reason they began to fight. A devastated army, full of holes, but still very organised, still standing, doing its duty – to be against somebody, just to be against. Through the work I would like to show that there are two sides, by revealing the aesthetic beauty of the shapes made from a material that has absolutely no value.

Sometimes I try to think about the implications of what we do. For example, the silkworm, the mulberry butterfly. For us the value of this insect lies in the silk. The kilometre of silk each silkworm produces represents the value of its life, and, depending on how thick the fibre is, **100** that kilometre will make approximately 10

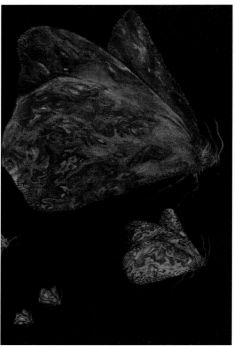

WEBSITE STATEMENT EXTRACT
www.clothandculturenow.com

'Since I was born, have been living and working in Latvia, my works are Latvian, too, in some respect. It is like the colour of the sky – seemingly the same everywhere, and, yet, different at home.

The features of other cultures certainly come into my works; I remember what I have seen in books, movies or museums elsewhere in the world, but I know that it is not African, American or Asian art as such that has affected me, but the images, colours and shapes that "carry" an idea which is of importance to me in a certain period of life.'

IEVA KRUMINA

centimetres of cloth, and the harvest of this tiny amount of silk causes the death of the silkworm. So if I use silk in my work, I can't play with that knowledge, that the silk somehow contains that death, the work must be a serious work. ■

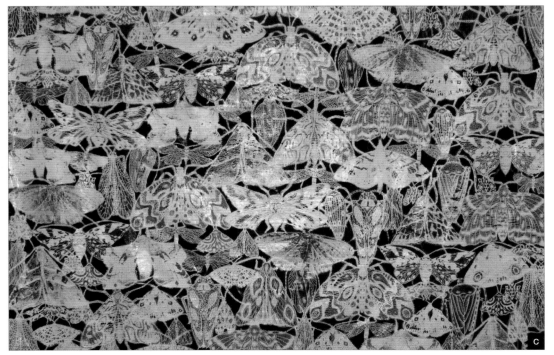

A: WE. THEY. 2006
1.27 x 2.11 m
Wool, cotton, linen, silk,
tapestry (basse-lisse)
Photograph: Ojars Grikis

B: FRAGMENT FROM UNFINISHED
WORK – THE ALLOY. 2007
Polyethylene (garbage bags),
screen print, author's technique
Photograph: Ojars Grikis

C: SILENCE. 2007
1.1 x 1.5 m
Polyethylene (garbage bags),
screen print, author's technique
Photograph: Ojars Grikis

■ Edited extracts from interview with
Una Laukmane, via email, September/October
2007 with Lesley Millar

In the past you have worked in theatre, has this influenced your work with textiles? The interplay of emotions and movement are definitely present in my textile work. It is important for me – both in theatrical design and textile – to transmit certain visual images, and in fact my textile work has had an influence on my work in the theatre. For the theatre I work with material, costumes, cloth, colours. This gives extra texture to whatever happens on the stage.

I had worked with textile already before I worked in theatre, so in a sense I returned to textile again after having studied stage direction, with the idea to introduce movement into material – textile. When I speak about 'movement' for me this describes the possibility to work outside strict limitations, with no precise trajectory, but it affects my textile work giving it extra depth. I don't think about 'movement' like moving, I am speaking about textile, or different materials, which can move the emotional senses. Maybe it is too difficult to explain.

Why have you chosen the techniques you are using? Because these are the techniques that provide maximum freedom for me. And sometimes certain materials take on new meaning and begin to create stories of their own. For example, when I work with plastic granule, I have ideas about

images, what I want to make, what I want to see after work and perform with this material, but when I start to work with that material, I realize that granule can do more than I imagined when I started to make the work.

Is it important that your work tells a story? It certainly is for me, it is my way of communication. For me, every work begins with a story, and as I work further it acquires particular colours and shapes, and the story might develop in new and unexpected ways.

I am not a writer, I'm not a musical either, textile is my medium of telling. When I work with books I illustrate somebody else's stories, when I work for theatre I also create visual images for the purpose of a story, which strictly speaking is not my own. My textile work brings out my own story. It is not my intention that the viewer understands my story, but it is important for me that my story resonates with the individual stories of the viewers. It is delight if the viewer is on the same wave (thread) length.

First of all it's a connection of materials. It is connection with all the different materials, and of course connection with and between the viewer and the work. Best of all if the materials supplement the story of images, or assist each other to tell the story. Sometimes the materials themselves create the story, then I can only help to make the images after materials tell me their story.

Is your work autobiographical? It is not strictly autobiographical, and yet concrete events, experiences, doubts and passions have influenced each particular work. For example, I have researched and been influenced by my grandmother's life 86 years ago, however her story is changed by my emotional and technical interference in the story. I give to her story something from the present, something from me. The dates

METHODS OF MAKING
**Una Laukmane has developed a technique combining digital print and embroidery, working with images that have autobiographical reference.**

NARRATIVE OF MAKING
**Laukmane builds complex layers of narrative, forming timelines between the past and present, connections between personal biography and universal experience. Materials, technique and narrative are combined in a manner contrived to deliver the sensation of balance.**

SUGGESTED LINKS
**Importance of sense of time: see Sue Lawty.**

Lesley Millar

DIARY. SEASONS (detail)
2.2 x 2.6 m (x 4)
Digital print, fabrics, embroidery
Photograph: Normunds Braslins

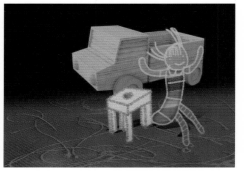

and months are concrete days from my grandmother's life. Of course I change that time in my works, because I was not alive in 1921, and I when I show this time in present time, I show it as I see today, at this time with my vision about time.

In the work for the exhibition you are using text – could you explain why? There are a number of reasons – firstly, the texts come from the diary of my grandmother who kept this diary through the year 1921 – in

that sense it is very personal. On the other hand I was very attracted by the ornamental pattern of the handwriting, and in that sense the factual content, the story itself was not so important. Anyone from anywhere could relate to the story, the image in their own way.

Do you see your work linking to Latvian textile tradition? Yes, I think it is like the connection with different materials, but with common generation roots. ■

WEBSITE STATEMENT EXTRACT
www.clothandculturenow.com

'My first encounter with textile took place in childhood, in a very traditional sense – those were the loom, flax yarn, bits of wool and reed, the scent, colour and texture of which lured me into a mystical world where I wanted to stay as long as I could.

I suppose that in the process of creating something entirely new, in absorbing unexplored currents and traditions it is essential for me not to lose this connection with history.'

UNA LAUKMANE

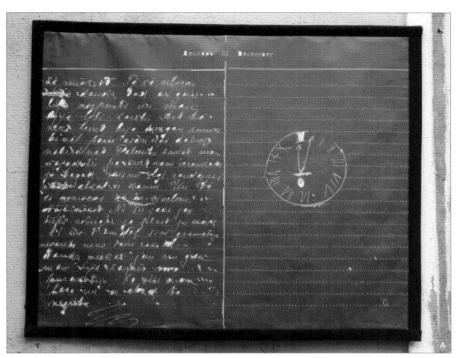

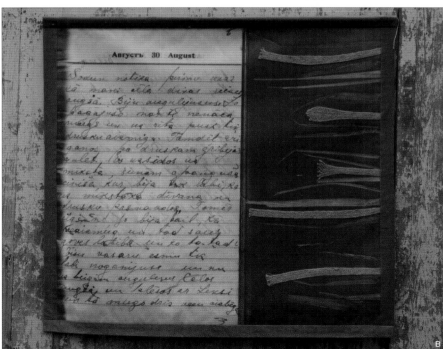

A:  DIARY. DECEMBER. 2006
0.11 x 0.13 m
Digital print, fabrics and embroidery
Photograph: Janis Nigals

B:  DIARY. AUGUST. 2006
0.11 x 0.12 m
Digital print, fabrics and embroidery
Photograph: Janis Nigals

C:  BALANCE (detail). 2000
0.15 x 0.12 m
Plastic, embroidery
Photograph: Janis Deinats

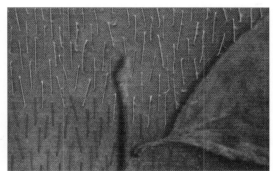

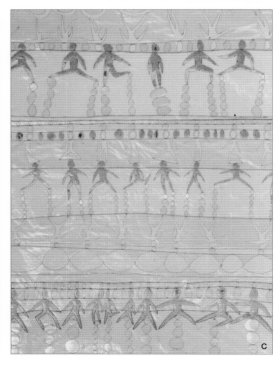

■ Edited extracts from interview with Lija Rage, Riga, October 2006, with Lesley Millar

*We are surrounded by red, here in your studio.* Red, this is my colour – all colours from orange to coral and brown. It's from the old city with its eroded surfaces, and I have used it my whole life. One day I was travelling to middle Asia (Uzbekistan). The colour was amazing and the monuments were not renovated. Many women had coral jewellery, a little bit red. I liked this and I think at that time my work changed.

*You mention coral – how about amber? There is amber everywhere here in the Baltic region.* No, only coral. Amber is different, because in Soviet times artists made old-fashioned work from amber. The amber is associated with a degree of nationalism, it has associations as a Latvian material. Latvian colours are yellow and brown now – heavy colours.

*You trained in traditional Gobelin tapestry?* Yes, I was educated at art college and the Latvian Academy, but I don't think it was – but I don't think it was very serious. I learnt from other artists. Magdalena Abakanowicz was our tapestry influence at that time. My beginning was not traditional. I was departing from the traditional style, it was modern work I was making, with textures. Now I've been working for 25 years everyday and I've developed my technique through my hands. I've developed my own style and I'm trying to change all the time.

*What are the starting points for your work?* I start from a small drawing to make the tapestry – I don't have a cartoon behind – I just come each day with my particular feelings to make the tapestry. This is my method and in the evening, at the end of each day, I'm always very tired.

*Your tapestries are full of stories with strange visual clues for the viewer.* I make tapestries as cultural symbols, but the cultures I think about are in my head so that people are free to make their own stories. I think always the work we make, all tapestries are self-portraits. Tapestry is interesting for me, and each year it grows more and more interesting. I'm not a painter or a graphic artist – tapestry is my way to communicate my ideas. These tapestries can take a long time to make. I certainly feel that tapestry is a physical presence of time.

There are many layers – cultural layers and centuries. Yes, like archaeology. I am interested in rhythm and vibrations. It's a feeling or understanding, rather than a visual image – maybe a kind of a philosophy. I read often about language, culture, architecture – not very sophisticated books, more like children's books, but I read them, none the less. I'm interested in history – art history, people's history, where we come from, and I like thinking about this. Japanese culture particularly interests me, and Zen Buddhism, all this is very close. We are all small countries and there is sameness.

*You have two very distinct ways of working – flat tapestry and three-dimensional forms. How did you start with the three-dimensional works?* I started a long time ago, about five years ago, maybe more. It's interesting for me to make modern sculpture in textile materials. Working with copper is like working with light. The copper is also

**METHODS OF MAKING**
Lija Rage works in woven tapestry and with her own personal technique for developing three-dimensional forms using meat skewers, bamboo and copper wire.

**NARRATIVE OF MAKING**
Rage uses tapestry and sculptural form to create a self-referential personal and cultural narrative, which emerges through the making process.

**SUGGESTED LINKS**
Tapestry: see Sue Lawty.

Lesley Millar

BEFORE EUROREPAIR
1.7 x 0.9 m, 1.9 x 0.2 m, 1.9 x 0.2 m
Silk, metal, wooden sticks
Photograph: Ojars Grikis

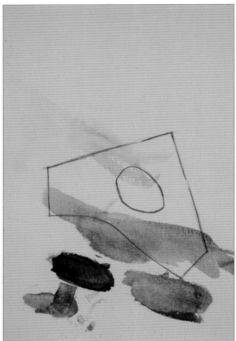

valuable to me because of its colour, which is sometimes a little bit green or yellow.

Do you see them as separate bodies of work or together, what is their relationship? I get very tired from weaving, I weave in silence and after about five hours I'm ready to stop and do something different. I make the three-dimensional work as a break from weaving, but I make these works at the same time, working with the same emotions. I show the tapestries and the three-dimensional works together, making whole installations, which I think is more interesting. I like having different things in exhibitions. I asked my daughter about this – I like some secrets, some story in an exhibition. I need this emotion.

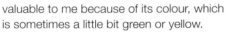

Do you want your work to make people smile? Oh, yes, of course. I'm very happy after weaving time and I look forward to the next day's weaving. Every day my feelings change, but the feelings are really not too serious. I think in this technological age, people need something more tactile. ∎

WEBSITE STATEMENT EXTRACT
www.clothandculturenow.com

'I believe that modern world culture cannot be closed. Each of us grows up from the culture we live in, through centuries, which further on is subjected to other impacts and becomes interwoven with the world culture influences.

Long-term theatre work has contributed to my sense of space around the textile object. Just as the theatre stage comes to life by light; my works also come to life by light – copper, silk and wood, and a play of shades of light helps to create an image.'

LIJA RAGE

A: ON THE RIVER. 2005
   1 x 1.8 m,
   Silk, metal, acrylic, linen
   Photograph: Lija Rage

B: BLACK SQUARE. 2005
   0.45 x 0.45m
   Wooden sticks, silk
   Photograph: Lija Rage

C: WOODEN LACE (detail). 1998
   2.5 x 1 m
   Wooden sticks, glue, fabric
   Photograph: Lija Rage

■ Edited extracts from interview with Peteris Sidars, Riga, October 2006, with Lesley Millar

**Did you train as a tapestry weaver?**
No, I started in ceramics, working in the place I was born, in the South-West part of Kurzeme. Three years later I joined the Red Army – the Soviet Army – and after that, I moved into working in interior design, at an applied art school. Then I worked in textiles because a friend of mine, a teacher said – Peteris, try textiles. He recommended textiles because he thought I would suit the colours – he said textile is nice for your colours.

I thought this was a good idea, I had shared ideas already with textiles and I felt that if you worked in textiles you were freer to express yourself. Not like in painting, which was always under control, not just the teaching but also the outcomes were controlled. Abstract painting was forbidden completely, so it was not only political content that they were looking for – to censure and ban – but also abstract qualities in painting. That was forbidden.

Despite being strong in realistic representation, drawing and painting – I understood after three years in the Latvian Academy of Art that I could express myself more clearly and freely in abstract ways, and that in the decorative arts – ceramics, textiles, interior design – much more was permitted. There was not the same kind of control.

PETERIS IN COURLAND
0.3 x 0.2 x 0.2 m (x 2)
Wool, plexiglass podium
Photograph: Peteris Sidars

During the Soviet times – to be a textile artist was to be a radical… Although I was not allowed to travel for international symposiums or exhibitions, as other artists were, I was free at that time. For instance, textile artists could draw for themselves, materials were cheap – you just needed ideas. During one national movement (not the open national movement), an important thing was happening, textile and applied artists wanted to use national patterns and ornaments.

I used some patterns form the western coast where I was born. I used these patterns enlarged as if you were looking at them under a microscope. I think that both Lithuanians and Latvians share something that comes from the earth – a feeling. A special feeling or sense in art – it is quite heavy – visually and mentally. The use of colours link to sadness.

**If Latvia had not been occupied by the Soviets, would you have been a painter?**
Yes – but people are different and have different tastes. Someone will choose paintings, someone else will prefer stone to textiles. The differences in taste are written in us already. A journalist once asked me, would I like to use stone at some point in my creative work, and I said, no, never. It's not something that I can feel.

Here is what I think. If one is trained in textiles, one is dealing with construction, the surface is created from the way the fabric is constructed, from the inside, and the textile artist would approach making sculpture in the same way – from the inside to the outside. This is a sophisticated question about the outside going inside and outside. I felt this when I first worked in wool. I think I got the ability to work from my father – I had my father's work ethic – and I liked weaving. I thought there is something

METHODS OF MAKING
**Peteris Sidars works largely with found objects, often manipulating through the use of heat and glue gun. Much of his work is in the form of installation, with elements of performance.**

NARRATIVE OF MAKING
**The narrative of Sidars' work is given impetus by his transformation of found objects, which through his intervention take on a theatrical/performative role within the gallery context.**

SUGGESTED LINKS
**Performativity: see Eglė Ganda Bogdanienė.**

Lesley Millar

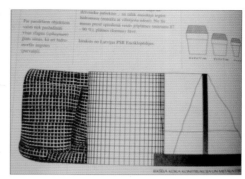

more here to develop. I was making experiments with different materials and felt I had a special feeling in my brain and in my fingers. I thought there was something to develop here.

Have you found it? Yes. I made one of my pieces in Norway – for a symposium. I made the piece using glue – normal glue – you know, with water, sticking pieces together – but it was a long and slow process because you had to wait for the glue to dry. So I started to use hot glue and once I got some mess on the table – and I thought, oh my god, I must clean up my mess when I saw, oh, it's art!

This is when I discovered hot glue as a material for me to work with. Now I collect everything I can find – plastic things. Things people have thrown away. I don't have a special purpose in mind. I just build a composition without thinking what it will be. I have this urge all the time to work with my eyes closed – to make signs on the walls at home or on paper. I think it is like playing like a child – serious playing.

What is the link between all these materials? Apart from Peteris. I often think about that question. What links all these materials? Actually, no link exists – if I see a material and an emotion or thought comes and I feel I can express myself then I do. I use the material. ■

WEBSITE STATEMENT EXTRACT
www.clothandculturenow.com

'In my early work I used motifs from the region of Southern Kurzeme (Courland). Ethnography, improvisations combining dense colours, experiments with novel materials and glorious colours.

I have always been interested in a synthesis of seemingly disparate things, a skill to notice new dimensions in various mundane materials, be it textile, textile fibre, children's building blocks, copper, wire, glass fibre, pots of clay or peat, hot glue.'

PETERIS SIDARS

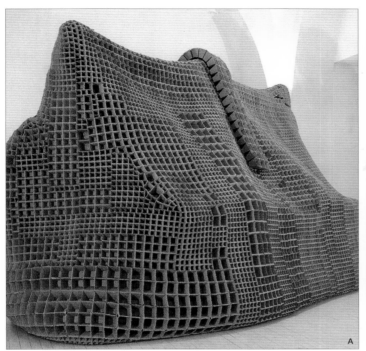

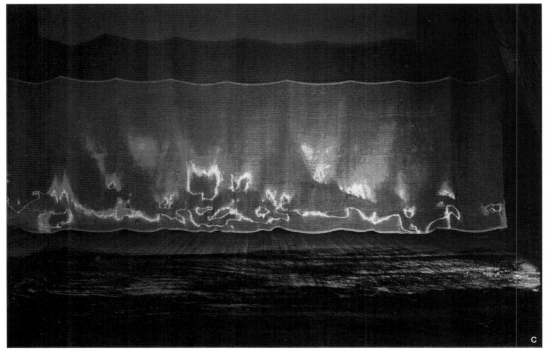

A: MY HOUSE. 1996
   3 x 6 x 2.3 m
   Peat moss pots, PVA glue, wooden
   construction, author's technique
   Photograph: Peteris Sidars

B: PASSIONS. 2003
   Dimensions variable
   Hot glue, synthetic threads, author's
   technique
   Photograph: Peteris Sidars

C: MIRAGE. 1986
   2 x 7 m
   Copper wire, flax, author's technique
   Photograph: Peteris Sidars

■ Edited extracts from interview with Dzintra Vilks, Piebalga, October 2006, with Lesley Millar

Your drawings are really very accomplished. Did you always see yourself working in textiles? No, first I studied in the art school in Riga, I always liked to draw, not painting so much. My dream was to be an artist, I didn't know what kind of artist, but I always knew that I would be an artist. When I wanted to start at the Latvian Academy of Art, the textile department was new and encouraged a free style. Painting was not so free because of the Soviet system, so I learnt hand sewing – not weaving.

Everything you can make by hand – sewing, knitting, all different craft techniques. And still I always make my work by hand – with a needle and thread. I don't use glue and it is not felted fabric. I am like a small insect working, very slowly. I have only one thread in the needle and in my mind I think that this is drawing with a thread.

This is a very distinctive technique. How did you start to develop it? We had art days in Old Riga in an open area and we made a big project with ropes and different materials. The government had no money to pay for this project for us, so we got sisal ropes from a fishermen's cooperative. I couldn't throw anything out, so afterwards I put all these sisal ropes in a small house where I kept firewood, and two years went by with the ropes in the small house.

Then I saw a work by Edite Pauls-Vignere in which she used just green grass and small flowers – I had no idea that you could use materials in this way, so simple and I thought it was the best idea I had seen in my whole life. Seeing this, sparked my memory and I remembered I had the sisal in my woodshed, and I was so excited.

I'm very interested in your three-dimensional work. What was the starting point for these works? We had a mini-Gobelin exhibition and I had no idea what to make for this exhibition. I was standing drinking coffee when I noticed that one of the napkins was torn, not perfect. So I made something like these napkins, but very small. I cut them and twisted them and then glued them together in one place. It is a large piece of work made from many small pieces. Since then it opened me, suddenly bigger work was not an issue. I think this is such a simple idea, cutting and sticking and making the work. I have practised with this technique and it makes very interesting shapes.

There are recurring symbols in your work – lizards, birds – do they carry specific meaning or are they a decorative? My work contains stories, but it's also very decorative. All my ideas come from nature. One day I was invited to take part in an exhibition in Germany on the idea of Freedom. The work I made for this exhibition changed my life. The title was 'Spring'. It reflected my opinion about people who were in Siberia and then returned to Latvia. I used small mirrors, some had numbers because people in Siberia had numbers – they had no name just numbers. Now when they came back to Latvia from Siberia – they had freedom. It's Spring. It is hope.

METHODS OF MAKING
**Dzintra Vilks has developed her own techniques, working with needle and thread and using sisal, wood and cotton. Her observational drawings form the starting points for much of her work.**

NARRATIVE OF MAKING
**Wilks invests the forms she constructs with a strong personal and cultural narrative.**

SUGGESTED LINKS
**Development of personal technique: see Merja Winqvist.**

Lesley Millar

MEETING OF THE WORLD TORN WINDS
1 x 1.1 m
Bamboo, cotton
Photograph: Didzis Grodzs

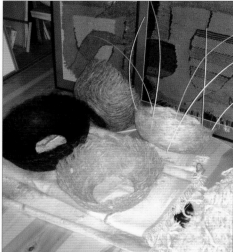

You made this work after the fall of communism? Yes. However, when I realised that the other artists in the exhibition were showing nice tapestries, which were easy to sell, I was not so happy. I too needed to sell work and this work was very conceptual, and not commercial – but this was the piece that the selectors wanted from me. And as I expected, some artists sold their work but not me.

Then one day an old man, Herr von Seydlitz, came to the exhibition and asked me what the piece meant. I explained about my project – it is not only spring – it is people. He came back and said that he wanted to make a special exhibition of my work, he offered to support me financially and all I had to do was make the work.

This was fantastic as at that time my children were small and we had a very bad situation with money and lifestyle. Then, when I made this first exhibition in Hamburg, they sold three or four pieces and I got 10,000 or more Deutschmarks, I felt like a

millionaire. This was the beginning of a long relationship with the von Seydlitz family.

So making something that came from your heart, changed your life. My father's brother died in Siberia – he was an architect. I made another work, titled 'Altogether'. The work contains fifteen birds because we had fifteen republics in the Soviet, which stood together. The eyes of the birds were different, some had red eyes some had no eyes, some black eyes and three of them were hanging from ropes. I love birds. They represent many things from my soul, they talk about freedom and our dreams.

I would like to know how important the tradition of textile is in your work? Very important, because in the north textile is absolutely necessary. In my heart I have a warm and light feeling when I make something with thread. It is necessary to warm up your heart, this is my philosophy. ■

WEBSITE STATEMENT EXTRACT
www.clothandculturenow.com

'All my life and work is closely related to the culture of my country, nature and people. I think, because of this reason, my Latvian identity is appreciable in my works: both wittingly and unawares. It could be tonality of the colours.

I hope that in the age of developed technologies a person will still long for… an artist's work inspired by nature, cherished by ancestors, created by hand.'

DZINTRA VILKS

A:  WHITE FIELD (detail). 2002
    0.7 x 2 x 3 m
    Bamboo, cotton
    Photograph: Gvido Kajons

B:  AFTER THE WIND. 2005
    1.5 x 2 m
    Bamboo, cotton
    Photograph: Gvido Kajons

C:  FLOWERBED. 1999
    3 x 2 x 2 m
    Sizal, wood
    Photograph: Gvido Kajons

# LITHUANIA

EGLĖ GANDA BOGDANIENĖ
SEVERIJA INČIRAUSKAITĖ-
 KRIAUNEVIČIENĖ
LINA JONIKĖ
AUSTĖ JURGELIONYTE
LAIMA ORŽEKAUSKIENĖ
LAURA PAVILONYTE

# ART AS A MANIFESTATION OF BEING

VIRGINIJA VITKIENĖ

A general return to national heritage has become an inseparable part of culture today and this is also reflected in the arts. As trends and the inherent references in art have become increasingly similar, artists are turning towards the search for identity, in-depth introspection and a common social voice. The area of textiles, with its central role in human existence, becomes a solace in this search for identity, by presenting an inter-textual relationship between text and viewer.

During my years studying the importance of materials in contemporary art, I have returned to textiles repeatedly, as it has offered me archetypal and referential layers for many other art forms and techniques, crossing the boundaries between the fine and applied arts, and emerging at the periphery of the existential and marginal. Today, art embraces any material for expression, even the most unexpected, however, textiles represent the most expressive.

In this article, and by means of examples, I will try to reveal the intertextual force that textiles enjoy (as described by the post-structuralists), the relationship between Lithuanian contemporary art and textile heritage as an expression of national identity, and discover the differences of expression between textile artists and artists from other disciplines that use textile materials.

Etymologically, the word textile is related to the word text, which itself went through something of a transformation during the post-modern era, no longer being limited to the notion of written text, it began to function as an axis for cultural discourse. Roland Barthes in his explanation of the theory of text calls any work of art, expression and even human being a text of that particular context and culture. In his work, text emerges as a 'net' or 'fabric' of meanings, lacking both purpose and axis (main idea, common formula). The text (in this case, the work of art) is peculiar in its plurality and incompleteness of meaning and its principal openness.

Post-structuralists see reality in art as a textualised world (based on intertextual relationships); that is, one meaning opens the door to another, and the latter invites opportunities for understanding and interpreting still more meanings emerging from different experiences. The application of fabric and other textile materials in the practice of contemporary art is assuming a more prominent place than ever, since the physical and referential potential provided by such materials most certainly establishes them as fundamental categories in the post-modern worldview: transience, impermanence, metamorphoses of forms, the impossibility of representation, the removal of boundaries between the real and simulacrum, destruction, fragmentation and most importantly, the offer of an assertive, almost conspiratorial opportunity to establish contact with the viewer – the illusion of tactility.

It is not surprising that many conceptual artists have employed textile materials (e.g., Claes Oldenburg, Robert Rauschenberg, Joseph Beuys, Louise Bourgeois, Annette Messager, Yayoi Kusama, Christo). I would like to define some of the approaches to communicating meaning in works of art by means of:
• the characteristics of fabric (surface, structure, surface processing techniques, transparency);
• archetypal references (interpretations related to national identity and heritage);
• 'feminised' material and textile techniques which, by the way, are inseparable from a critique of the customary patriarchal culture.

I will explore the last two notional levels and support my view with reference to several works by Lithuanian artists.

Before discussing the crossroads between contemporary Lithuanian art and textiles, I would like to turn back to the 20th century, which historically marks a period when Lithuanian national identity and the struggle for its preservation is verbally defined. Almost throughout the 20th century, professional textiles developed alongside painting and sculpture, while constantly referring to the heritage of folk art. From the mid-60's, the subject matter in tapestry reflected folklore, folk songs (Ramutė Jasudytė), customs, and domestic and farm work (Juozas Balčikonis, Vladas Daujotas). However, the old technologies for weaving, felting or embroidering involved craftspeople (non-artistic), hence, only small groups of enthusiasts continued this tradition at home.

Only in the 1990s did the separation of art into applied and performing arts gradually subside. The need to redefine national identity emerged during this period, and during the early post-Soviet era textiles served as a metaphor for the existence of national identity, which was employed in various interdisciplinary art projects: performances, installations, objects and assemblage. Artists used direct references to textile techniques and frequently employed archetypal interpretations **119** of clothing and uniforms as a polemic – from existential concepts about puppets or fringe existence to artistic interpretations of existence for women.

Motifs from wedding gowns, pioneer or military uniforms, hats of beggars, tattered clothes, and, ultimately, hand-woven towels or bandages in the works of contemporary art have emerged as a chain of intertextual references. These suggest different meanings depending on the experience of the viewer, going beyond the simple search for national identity and entering an awareness of cultural identity dominated by a painful history. Such artists as Robertas Antinis, Česlovas Lukenskas, Marija Teresė Rožanskaitė, Eglė Rakauskaitė and Valentinas Antanavičius have employed the expressive potential of fabric in order to expose the wounds of a traumatised society while at the same time healing them.

Valentinas Antanavičius, a classic Lithuanian Modernist, constructs characters known as 'human-things' or 'human-animals' using old household tools and handmade fabric, deconstructing and destroying the model of 'rural' nationality/identity overly idealised until the end of the Soviet era. Antanavičius verges on nihilism in the questioning of the myth of the Lithuanian 'lyrical' and 'noble' descent. In his assemblage 'One-eyed in White' from 2001, a one-eyed figure is created through the skilful pleating of white towels decorated with lace. The woman's white garments and veil resemble a bride's wedding gown, as if referring to Lithuanian family values and stability, ensuring outward neatness and orderliness (an allusion to the romanticised stability and values of a patriarchal Lithuanian society). The perverse and disfigured face of the woman, who not only has one eye, but also only one arm pressed to her chest, and decorations about her neck resembling the burial decorations and 'whitened coffins', all offer comparison between femininity and decorated burial ceremonies, alluding to the destruction of idealism and a painful confrontation with

reality in disguise. The gaze of this 'One-eyed' one evokes inner disharmony, ripping off the 'laced' cover and exposing the inner pain, self-consciousness, spite, powerlessness and spiritual death, ungracefully hidden in the starched lace.

Eglė Rakauskaitė in her installation 'Time: 4 Days' 1997, includes a handloom containing a work in progress – a white woven rag rug almost half a metre long. White garments, ripped into long strips waiting to be woven, lay beside the loom on the floor, and a white wedding gown and linen undergarments hang on the framework of the loom waiting their turn. As the wedding gown goes through this metamorphosis, Rakauskaitė subtly portrays the change in the status of women in society: a beautiful, 'ritual' garment is turned into a ragged piece of cloth that is then doggedly woven into a rug to wipe ones feet on, or perhaps, a tablecloth for the family dinner table. The fabric in the loom, woven from the skirt of the wedding gown evokes strong associations of a 'trade-off' in the work, drawing parallels between a woman and a practical object. Where Antanavičius employs certain archetypal characteristics in the image of the woman in 'One-eyed' to speak of the disabled spirit of the nation and universal experience, Rakauskaitė uses elements of folklore to touch upon the feminist discourse emerging in Lithuanian art only in the last decade of the 20th century.

Although textile artists have chosen to use the language of contemporary art: installation, performance, photography, sculpture and video art – they have also preserved the expressive value inherent in textiles to contribute to meaning in their work through the use of archetypal elements and technical skill in the use of textiles technology. In my opinion, the ability to interpret tradition by employing contemporary art language is one of the strongest characteristics of contemporary Lithuanian textiles, facilitating individuality and originality as well as a national and cultural introspection.

Traditional sewing and embroidery techniques offer considerable potential, becoming a subtle means of expression for Lithuanian contemporary textile artists. Works of art by Lithuanian artists in this exhibition and others, for example Vita Gelūnienė, Inga Likšaitė, Jolanta Šmidtienė, Žydrutė Ridulytė, Feliksas Jakubauskas, Jūratė Petruškevičienė, Loreta Švaikauskienė and Monika Žaltauskaitė-Grašienė are prominent in their original creative solutions. I will describe some artists from this exhibition – those who portray their experience of cultural heritage most prominently.

Lina Jonikė uses embroidery – one of the oldest techniques of textile decoration – to apply a lyrical, secretive and intriguing pattern to large format photography, and, thus, 'silently' offers the viewer clues to a number of potential stories and interpretations. By choosing to portray (or dress up in embroidery) a naked body, the artist compares it to a blank canvas, on which, through the application of stitching, rather than painting, she creates a destiny for an imaginary human being. The textile technique and the textile itself semantically form a parallel expression of individuality.

A thread in Jonikė's hands is more than a tool for creation. It serves as a century-old opportunity to reveal both national and cultural identity (determined by family relationships and social-political processes). Jonikė often employs subconscious codes from the Lithuanian mindset that are inseparable from religion, intermingled with a mythical heritage and mysticism (interpretations of the motives of the Pensive Christ, Virgin Mary and little mermaids). She is also not afraid to transform metaphors and attribute to them new meaning. For example, in her work using three colours (a reference to the Lithuanian flag), named 'LIE-TU-VA' (LIT-HUA-NIA), she does exactly that by portraying the country's idyll through the concept of a family.

Jonikė portrays the topic of motherland, a reflection of oneself as a part of the nation, in

**120**

a number of her works. By choosing feminine topics and perspectives, as well as an ancient technique (embroidering), the artist is able to speak about the archetypal experience of contemporary women, and focuses not on feminist or cultural frustration or audacity (as, for example, is the case in the embroidered works by Ahmer), but on the search for an inner peace that is only possible through realising ones identity.

When speaking about innovative solutions in the ancient technique of embroidery, it is impossible not to mention the work 'Life Is Beautiful' (2005) by Severija Inčirauskaitė-Kriaunevičienė. The metal pot lids are decorated with traditional cross stitch pattern and the flower motifs popular in Lithuania, even glorified in folk songs. The objects portrayed by Inčirauskaitė-Kriaunevičienė could be said to follow a purity of aesthetics and concept.

Kriaunevičienė applies textile techniques in order to reveal the inner world of women. Her works invite the viewer to take an 'inside out' view instead of the drastic alternative of seeing things as objects. The artist offers a new and more valuable relationship with oneself and the surroundings by removing the practical and user-friendly aspects from utilitarian objects. Contrary to examples of radical feminism, which have incorporated textiles in an expressive manner, she manifests an accurate display of woman's inner contradictions in her works by employing aesthetic, rather than objective means.

Until recently, Lithuanian artists had no opportunities to use computerised looms, yet, over the last decades, their refined use of hand looms highlighting the expressive use of weave, has been acknowledged at international exhibitions. Most prominent as an example of conceptualised weaving is Laima Oržekauskienė, who chooses weaving and ancient Baltic patterns as a structural element to portray the ritual, during which both the creator and the creation itself fulfil each other. In order to reflect Lithuanian

Baltic heritage, Oržekauskienė presents the anonymous (faceless) image of a woman's torso in her tapestry, at the same time manifesting a matriarchal worldview – of woman as deity.

Another example can be seen in the cycle, 'Women – Arhats: Danutė, Lina, Violeta, Kristina' (2003–05) . This work is impressive in its monumentality and psychology: each torso (without face) communicates a different emotion and character. The conceptual and material elements bring out a sense of 'liveliness' and ritual (an impression that is hard to describe) – Oržekauskienė manages to portray the outline and form of the figures by weaving women's hair of different colours into the surface of a fabric woven from light gold-coloured thread. In doing so she breaks several taboos – attributing the female sex to the male deity (Arhat) from Buddhist philosophy, and as if enchanting the viewer, she uses hair (according to Lithuanian custom, cut hair had to be safeguarded or even burnt so it could not be used by enchanters), thereby ignoring local custom and creating new myths about women's identity.

In conclusion, I would like to note that these artists are reflecting on the absence of identity in today's culture by glancing back at their own cultural heritage. The broad scope of references and significance inherent in textiles is particularly useful in contemporary art, manifesting itself in the multifarious search for identity. The creators of installations, performances or objects incorporate textile materials as a means of emphasising their ideas that very often are radical, destructive or socially and politically biased. Textile artists conceptualise the very process of creation and textile techniques, which in Lithuanian tradition were attributed solely to the woman's sphere of activity.

The most important rituals in a woman's life were related to weaving and embroidery: birth, preparation for marriage, weddings, childbirth and death. Having crossed the boundaries of ancient technique, from which certain codes of

meaning are intuitively expected, Lithuanian textile artists still preserve a relationship with their heritage, stressing its importance in the creative process and even a dependence on it.

The difference remains not in the results achieved (both are convincing), but in their creativity and thought processes. Rather than searching for identity in their artwork, textile artists experience the creative process as the establishment of identity. Quoting Arthur Danto, we could call the artwork of these latter artists 'the art after the end of the art,' free from aesthetics and any imposed canons or goals. Art is the manifestation of being, an inner necessity and depth. ■

1.  Roland Barthes, 1991. The Pleasure of the Text (Vaga, Vilnius), p 313.

2.  Lithuania entered the 20th century under the oppression of Tsarist Russia: work-shops and dry-goods shops were closed, the Lithuanian press was banned (1864–1904), many parents refused to let their children attend public schools. 'Maternity Schools' became an alternative, teaching children how to read and write from books smuggled in from Lithuania Minor (which belonged to Prussia), passing on oral traditions and cultural customs along with textile skills. After World War I, during the formation of the independent state of Lithuania, professional textiles were brought back to life, and artists openly expressed their views on the necessity to search for folk ornamentation in modern designs. All art conveyed the idea of 'folk style' regarded as the highest form of expression, important for Lithuanians and capable of attracting the world's attention. Distinguished Lithuanian thinkers of the interwar period stressed the importance of lyricism, closeness to nature, and dignity, as Lithuanian national traits, crystallised over many centuries. The preservation of references to Lithuanian cultural heritage (folklore, trades, including weaving and sewing), as a survival technique for the na-tion, assumed a certain form of resistance/metaphor in Lithuanian art (1940–90).

3.  The cycle won the highest award in an international biennial textile event in Kau-nas, 2003 and at Shanghai international biennial (awarded 'outstanding') 2004. In 2005 she received the Lithuanian National Prize for this and other works.

■ Edited extracts from interview with Eglė Ganda Bogdanienė, Vilnius, May 2007, with Lesley Millar

You have an amazingly wide range of work, not just felt or weave or print or installation. What is your favourite way of working? I want to make things that are beautiful, foremost in my work is the sense of aesthetic, I hate ugly things in my work. I can understand that someone can do that, but I can't. My way of working depends on the idea, after that the possibilities of execution come. I never know how I can execute my idea beforehand. I can't say very strictly what is my favourite, sometimes I like to weave Gobelin, it is really like praying.

It is hard for me to weave at the moment, with all my other commitments of teaching and family – because you have to forget everything to just sit and weave. I absolutely miss weaving. I dream to have a holiday, to have a year and to weave every day. It doesn't matter what I weave, I could weave a plain white cloth – but just to sit and weave and think and sit. Felting is very good, I like to sit and felt with needles because I can do it everywhere, on the bus, anywhere – when I have just a few minutes I can take it out from my bag.

Much of your work is about performance… Maybe because of my parents, who were in the theatre, I'm not afraid to show myself, to use my body, my form. It's not embarrassing for me. However, I could also use your body, it doesn't matter which body

ŽEMNYA (detail) (Lithuanian Goddess of harvest and fecundity of earth)
2.7 x 1.5 m
Wool
Photograph: Auste Jurgelionyte

I use. What is important to understand is that when I'm working in this way I'm not Eglė, I am everybody – I can be you. I try to work with problems and situations that are understandable to everyone.

I am a woman and sometimes I try to be a man also, but most of all I am a woman – but not Eglė, no! It's strange, people try to find the history of my own life in my work. For example the work I made about Judith and Holofernes, with the male heads on the pillars, people tried to find physical similarities with my husband.

I found this strange because I never think about depicting particular people – I made one of the heads, for example, during a symposium attended by eight men. During the evening I would talk to one or other of the men and as we spoke I would be needle felting the head, basing the nose on one man, the eyes on another, so that head is the mix of different people, but it doesn't matter to me – they are just men.

Could you describe the starting points for the work in the exhibition? It is a further development of a collaborative work made last year based on ideas of fruit and the human body. In Lithuania the goddess of harvest is the second most powerful god after the god of thunder. She is very important because, for Lithuanians, the most important relationship is with the earth. We are not a mystical people, we stay in one place, growing the harvest, depending on the earth. This goddess was very important for our grandparents, our ancestors.

The idea is to put the work on a table in the same way that a body is laid out before a funeral. The body is laid out on a white cloth on the table, not wrapped up, just the body. My idea is to put the work on the table with the white border of the textile hanging over the edge. My idea at the moment is that in the exhibition the

METHODS OF MAKING
Eglė Ganda Bogdanienė's process is much concerned with the performativity of the final outcome. She works primarily with weave, both tapestry and cloth, and with felt, but will use whatever technique she feels appropriate to the final outcome.

NARRATIVE OF MAKING
Bogdanienė is a storyteller and performer, much of her work directly referencing the body. Traditional culture and traditional textile are central elements in her visual vocabulary, with the method of making and final outcome each informing the other.

SUGGESTED LINKS
Narrative and the body: see Silja Puranen.

Lesley Millar

'body' will be covered initially with a white cloth, so that the textile relief appears like a real body underneath the cloth. I am not sure how, but after some time the cloth is removed and reveals not a real body, but fruit and vegetables. The fruits I have chosen are those that you can find everywhere in Lithuania. You could not find them 100 years ago, but now these fruits and vegetables you can find here. The fruits and vegetables that I use to depict the body are like a local harvest.

The border of the work is very different to the centrepiece, with a very subtle design. The ornament around the edge of the work is taken from the old sashes of Lithuania. The ornament is very simple; we call it a 'rake' sign, like a comb and you can see it in the border of my work. The sash is the most important thing for Lithuanian woman, worn round the neck and round the head like a crown, around 6 or 7 cm wide. Before marriage the sash is worn like a crown, but after marriage women use a big scarf, so the hair is hidden. You can recognise married women in this way.

Traditionally, when women get married they have to make sashes for everyone who takes part in the wedding party. Special sash for the husband's mother, special sash for the husband's sister, for brothers' wives, for kitchen women who are preparing the food, for everybody. Sashes were also made for the well, for the oven. These sashes were woven by the bride, and every young woman who wanted to get married began these sashes from five or six years old, plus all the trousseau, the bed linen, the 'bottom drawer'.

All your works are very narrative, I feel that you are a story-teller. Absolutely. For me the stories are much more interesting than the art. It's interesting for people to know the stories behind the work. But perhaps not everything or everyone, Let's leave space for each to bring their own story. ∎

WEBSITE STATEMENT EXTRACT
www.clothandculturenow.com

'I spent my childhood in Soviet Lithuania, in the city of Vilnius. Despite the occupation, Lithuanian traditions could not be erased from our cultural life. I was also interested in the culture of the old town, which is like a mix of the aesthetic sensibilities of the ordinary local urban culture and that of the nobility.

At present, I believe that our textile school is rather interesting and unique – we do not have the latest equipment, nor expensive materials – we have to follow our enthusiasm, be inventive and creative.'

EGLÉ GANDA BOGDANIENÉ

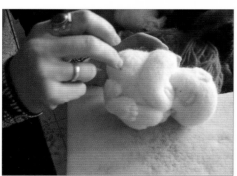

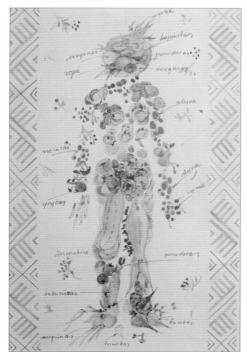

A: WAKING (8 WORK CYCLE). 2004
   0.08 x 2 x 1 m
   Silk, viscose; painting on silk,
   photo print
   Photograph: Vaiva Abromaityte,
   Eglė Ganda Bogdanienė

B: HAPPINESS / LESS. 2006
   1.2 x 1.5 m
   Wool, felting
   Photograph: Auste Jurgelionyte

C: GOOD NIGHT, JUDITH. 2003
   Carpet: 4 x 3 m
   Figure: 2 x 0.80 x 0.3 m
   3 pillows: 0.5 x 0.5 x 0.2 m
   3 heads: 0.35 x 0.35 x 0.35 m
   Wool, felting, embroidery
   Photograph: Eglė Gande Bogdanienė

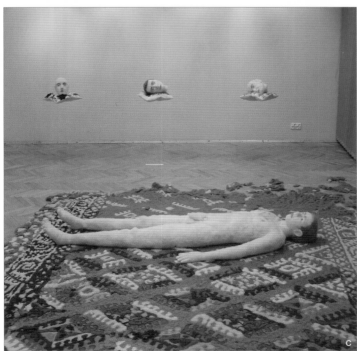

■ Edited extracts from interview with
Severija Inčirauskaitė-Kriaunevičienė, Vilnius,
May 2007, with Lesley Millar

Would you like to talk a little bit about your
embroidery? Are the patterns you use
traditional? These patterns come from my
head – of course you can see that I have
embroidered flowers and these are typical
Lithuanian flowers. You can find these
flowers everywhere. I am interested in what
could be described as ethnic kitsch. I like to
use images from kitsch art, and flowers are
often employed in kitsch work. My position
is a little bit ironic. When I was studying to
write my thesis, I was also doing practical
work that was close to questions about
identity – looking for connections between
modernity and ethnic culture.

After Independence we were thinking
about how we can represent our country.
Thinking about how we were different from
other neighbouring countries, or on a wider
scale from the rest of the world. But now
fifteen years on we are thinking more about
our similarities, but at Independence we
looked for difference in our identity. We
had one identity in Soviet times, and that
is important, but now we have a different
identity. Then also, of course, we have
another identity from before Soviet times
when were an Independent republic.

Another issue was the European Union
– it's important in this union to represent
our country's identity. This interests me
– for example, you see a lot of restaurants
in Lithuania that serve food that are the
'national dishes'. This is one way, to
represent our country – this is not only
true in Lithuania. So I made plates with
Lithuanian national dishes embroidered
on them. Fried egg, for example. I'm not
sure if this a real Lithuanian national dish
– I am not sure if there is really such a thing
as a Lithuanian national dish – but it is a
comment on what is happening to us as a
country as we try to define our identity.

These traditional restaurants are often
decorated in similar fashions – they go to the
countryside and dig up 'old things' for an
authentic Lithuanian experience. They hang
all these old things in the restaurant. We
have many restaurants like this. I'm trying to
be humorous and ironic in this work. I think
there are more interesting ways to represent
our country than through some mythical folk
past.

Is it important that the objects you work
with have already been used? It is really
important to use real things from daily life.
Often people value special days – wedding
days, birthdays, but for me the everyday is
most important, just daily life. Therefore I try
to use everyday objects. In the work for the
exhibition I used objects that I found in a
village, they are real objects – watering can,
buckets. I just found them – the objects had
been discarded and I wanted to transform
the objects.

I wanted what other people had
thrown away. I embroidered flowers on
to them because I think they are beautiful
symbols and transform the objects. It's
really important in my practice that I use
real objects. This work is called 'Autumn
Collection' – because it's brown, because
these objects are rusted – a process that
comes about when it is raining – in autumn
there is a lot of rain. Also the colour of the
metal is from autumn.

METHODS OF MAKING
**Severija Inčirauskaitė-Kriaunevičienė
is essentially an embroiderer,
working with found objects and the
built environment.**

NARRATIVE OF MAKING
**She employs traditional embroidery
techniques as a method of
subversion of, and commentary on,
popular understanding of Lithuanian
cultural identity.**

SUGGESTED LINKS
**Cultural identity: see Freddie Robins.**

Lesley Millar

AUTUMN COLLECTION (detail)
Installation
Old rusted metal things, cotton,
embroidery
Photograph: Severija Inčirauskaitė-
Kriaunevičienė

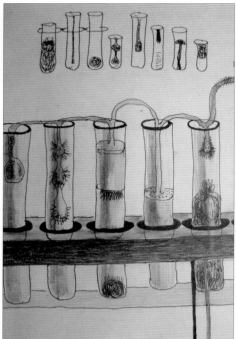

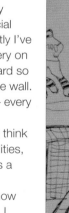

**How do you make the holes?** First my father helped me, but now I have special tools to make the holes myself. Recently I've been working to make larger embroidery on walls – I am drilling holes in plaster board so that it looks like embroidery through the wall. It is very difficult to make these holes – every time I need to be careful when drilling because the boards can break easily. I think this work has real architectural possibilities, I imagine you could create this work as a design idea for real flats – real spaces.

It took me a long time to figure out how to make these large wall embroideries. I have to prepare quite carefully, but actually making the embroidery takes a relatively short time. With the wall embroidery, I had difficulty with materials. I use a very large needle because the stitches are so large – the embroidery isn't like a meditation, it's very hard work!

**128** My next step is to embroider a car… ∎

WEBSITE STATEMENT EXTRACT
www.clothandculturenow.com

'The market of global production initiates the creation of "Lithuanity" which is often referred to as "the image of Lithuania" – a face that should be attractive both to foreign investors and the tourism industry.

I think ethnic culture is not only what marks people out as different, but also forms the basis for communicating with other cultures. There are many things that are common to ethnic cultures and sometimes these things are obvious. Moreover, a lot of textile techniques, considering their archaic origin, can become references to ethnic themes as well as relationships to a universal form of intercommunication.'

SEVERIJA INČIRAUSKAITĖ-KRIAUNEVIČIENĖ

A: LIFE IS BEAUTIFUL (detail). 2005
   Installation
   Metal covers, cotton, embroidery
   Photograph: Severija Inčirauskaitė-
   Kriaunevičienė

B: TRADITIONAL DINNER. 2005
   Installation
   Cotton, cotton threads,
   printing, crochet
   Photograph: Severija Inčirauskaitė-
   Kriaunevičienė

C: SNOWDROPS. 2006
   2.1 x 1.15 m (x3)
   Wool, synthetics, cotton, felt
   Photograph: Severija Inčirauskaitė-
   Kriaunevičienė

*This is a very mysterious image you have
used for the work in the exhibition.* During
my summer holidays I saw a little hut with
a government sign marking it as a special
place, a memorial. It was very dilapidated
and it got more dilapidated year on year. I
liked this place because when I was a child,
I used to go with my teacher and draw old
houses and this house reminded me of that
experience. And I liked this place because it
was not very clean but very real.

*What was the building used for?* It was an
ice-house, for keeping fish. The hut was built
near the river and in the winter ice was dug
out and kept in the hut, then fish or other
food would be kept in, in preparation for the
summer. But now people who live in the area
have refrigerators, so there's no need for the
ice-house. I think it's a very special building
and I find it interesting that I had never
encountered this type of building before – I
never used a building like this.

I don't know when these buildings went
out of use. I think it was a long time ago –
because it was such difficult and heavy work
to prepare and keep these houses. I think
that in England this would not be considered
a very old building – only 100 years old – but
here, in Lithuania, that's very old. I don't
know exactly how old the ice-house is. I
wanted to ask but nobody knew the answer.
That information has passed out of memory.
I decided that I wanted to take pictures and

record this moment, this place.

I have a photograph of the house and an
old woman who lived nearby. I really like this
woman and I am interested and impressed
with the house. When I asked to take her
photo – the woman said wait a minute, I
prepare for the photo – and she went off to
get flowers. She didn't go and touch up her
make-up – her eyes, her lips – she went to
get flowers. I don't know if this woman is still
alive, I last saw her a year ago. But I called
her son and he said she is in hospital. The
title of this work is 'Memory of Architecture',
but I speak about the old woman, and I have
embroidered only forget-me-not flowers on
to the images.

*The idea of memory is important in your
work?* Yes, of course – I use forget-me-nots!

*How did you come to embroidery?* As
a student, at first, I wanted to weave – I
thought it looked more like textiles – but my
teacher (Laima Oržekauskienė) encouraged
me to find my own technique, and this for
me was embroidery. Now, I cannot live
without embroidery. When I finish a piece
of embroidery work I say – that is enough
– but after about a month I start preparing
new work. I work from photographs. For
example, if I am working with images of
flowers, I will draw flowers to prepare the
images that I will embroider.

In earlier work I would take a small photo
and then make simple composition with a
cartoon. I sometimes still make a cartoon
– but often I make the embroidery by eye. I
am interested in using a variety of materials
and techniques for embroidery. Plastics are
very difficult – when I work in plastic my
nails become very blunt and I get strong
arms for working with plastic. I think now
I'm finished with plastic. Recently, I've been
experimenting with digital printing on cotton

**METHODS OF MAKING**
Lina Jonikė is an embroiderer
working on a variety of materials
(cloth, plastic, photographs),
that create the feeling of three-
dimensional form. Photography is
also important as a starting point for
the work.

**NARRATIVE OF MAKING**
Jonike uses embroidery to create
a textural narrative working in
apposition to the base image, which
is frequently photographic. That
narrative is a complex mix reflecting
cultural tradition and personal
experience.

**SUGGESTED LINKS**
Mapping of place: see Una
Laukmane.

Lesley Millar

ARCHITECTURAL MONUMENT (detail)
0.97 x 1.32 m
Digital print on canvas, hand embroidery
Photograph: Lina Jonikė

LINA JONIKĖ

and embroidering on top or 'drawing' with burning. At first I tried embroidering on paper and then burning it.

Why burning? I was thinking about maps and also historical examples of burning houses. The burning I'm doing refers to the destruction of things. I used a little stitch that I took out after the burning. I think it makes a very beautiful surface. The beauty of the surface is of most importance to me – the aesthetic quality of the surface.

You often use your embroidery to 'clothe' the subjects. I like it that textile is the material of clothes and I often embroider elements of clothing onto the images of naked people. In one work I asked for nude pictures of people, not just women, however I had difficulty getting naked images of men.

I asked twelve men, but they said they could not do it. In this work I used three colours – yellow, red and green – these are the colours of the Lithuanian flag, which is very important to me. I especially used these colours for the man, woman and child. And I was thinking that the flag and the family was the future of our Lithuanian nationality. It is a simple philosophy.

How do you want people to respond to your work? I like it when people smile at my work and I also like it when people cannot understand how it's made. From a distance it looks very different from when you are up close. There's a Lithuanian saying that when you look close at work that is very labour intensive, it smells because of the sweat and labour that has gone into it – there is too much work in it! ∎

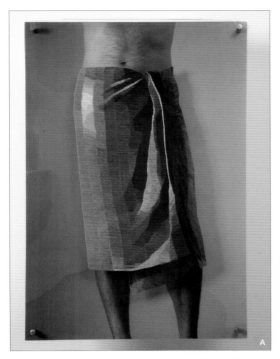

WEBSITE STATEMENT EXTRACT
www.clothandculturenow.com

'One of my grandmother's was a weaver, the other did patchworks, and my mother worked in a textiles factory. A lot of textile things surrounded me throughout my early childhood.

The majority of the ideas for my work are taken from Lithuanian folk art… In some of my works I use the ornaments from Lithuanian folk costumes.'

LINA JONIKĖ

A: TU. 2005
0.90 x 0.60 m
Photograph, plastic, embroidery
Photograph: Arunas Baltenas

B: VA. 2006
0.90 x 0.60 m
Photograph, plastic, embroidery
Photograph: Arunas Baltenas

C: TRIANGLE. 2006
1 x 1.4 m
Digital printing on cotton, embroidery
Photograph: Lina Jonikė

■ Edited extracts from interview with Auste Jurgelionyte, Vilnius, May 2007, with Lesley Millar

On the one hand your work seems very simple, and yet it is full with so many different narratives, and the animation is also such a complex process. In my creative life I have really wanted to show two sides. On one side, I wanted to show a history of life and feelings – the other side is more technical. I like showing new techniques, how you can use them. I like thinking about life and funny stories. And I remember my life as a student. I also like the work of children – my life is like a child's world. I want what you see to make you feel very good, I don't want you to feel bad or sad, I want you just to think life is beautiful. I see a lot of contemporary movies for children – that are not so positive. I feel bad after I see these movies.

So often life just passes you by – so if you make an image of it, or an animation, you fix it. I fix the stories of my life and my friends' lives. In the city I watch people and make sketches of interactions and people's facial expressions. I like telling stories. When I'm at parties or with friends you hear a lot of stories. I like this. Sometimes I have commercial work – taking photographs of weddings. I find these events very interesting. I look at the people who are getting married, I watch the families – I'm interested to see what's going on within families and the stories of relationships.

What is delightful about your animation is that you're making something very simple with modern technology out of ancient materials. I like it when I make a felt picture and then let it rest for some time. After that time I like to come back to it and add in to it things that have changed. For instance, add in new ideas or experiences. Felt is good for this. I think it's very nice to constantly add more into work over time. You know, add in fun stories from my life.

Felt is an interesting material. I think it moves a little bit. The loose fibres have inspired me. I noticed that some animals crawled into the wool and made it move and seeing this inspired me to make animation using the felt. Before making this animation I didn't especially use felt. When I was here in Vilnius studying at the Academy of Art I used a variety of materials.

In 1998 I studied in Paris and was exposed to a lot of video and photographic work. That was when I started thinking about using film and photography in my work. It was a big point in my life. When I was in Paris I made lots of photographs of my life – how I felt in my new flat, in this new place, new rooms. My work then was about dreams, because my dreams are sometimes like a film. When I returned to Vilnius, I worked at night and made work about dreams using photo emulsion paper.

I've made one work that's like a book of my life, for example there's an image of the bus – when I was about twenty I was travelling, hitchhiking, and I was working in Paris – and I dreamed about owning a bus, so I could travel anywhere and sleep anywhere.

You don't need any equipment to make felt. You can make felt anywhere, you can travel with felt. Yes, felt is in my life. It's lovely to be able to travel and make felt. No problem. You can teach felt-making

METHODS OF MAKING
**Auste Jurgelionyte is a felt maker and animator, exploring the evolution of an image, which moves freely between the static and fluid.**

NARRATIVE OF MAKING
**Jurgelionyte works against the qualities of felt normally exploited through traditional felt making – those of substance and solidity. Her felt is constantly moving – telling stories about life that are funny, beautiful and unpredictable in ways that give the viewer a sense of well-being.**

SUGGESTED LINKS
**Personal narrative: see Jun Mitsuhashi.**

Lesley Millar

1. 'PLANE' (detail)
2.5 x 2 m
Non-woven felt, wool
Photograph: Auste Jurgelionyte

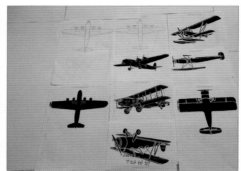

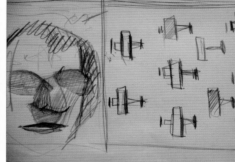

anywhere and felt is born when people are travelling. Maybe you want to build a house quickly – you can do that by making felt. Felt houses help you feel connected to nature. I think it's very important for artists to be connected to nature, because now with technology many people have lost a connection and relationship to nature. They don't know so intimately what a tree or the grass is.

I was born in the city, but now half the year I spend in the city and half in the countryside. I work in the countryside – I find it a good place to work – I made the animation there. It's very inspiring in the countryside. I pick strawberries, make jam, listen to the birds. I look forward to not wearing shoes and seeing the dew and the mist. It's so beautiful.

The work for the exhibition combines animation and an actual felt work. It is a diptych to be shown on the wall. The animation is one part and the other will be a still image made of industrial felt. The animation will be a moving extension of the still image. The idea is that it's like a game. The pilot is smiling. Then he opens his eyes and says goodbye. In the animation you see him take his glasses off, then smile, then he is a little bit serious – but then his mood changes and everything goes crazy. Like life.

Do you start with ideas and then find materials, or with materials and then have ideas? First I have ideas, and then I just look for what material can help me to do it. Felt is very comfortable with me. First I thought I just wanted to make a film about life, but then I thought, ahh!… felt is very good. ■

WEBSITE STATEMENT EXTRACT
www.clothandculturenow.com

'I am especially keen on Lithuanian folk traditions as well as modern Lithuanian culture and the new tendencies in art.

I was very interested in the fairy tales my grandmother told me – her stories and her songs. It is impossible to remove oneself from the impact of childhood – its memories.'

AUSTE JURGELIONYTE

A: ILLUMINATED SIGN. 2006
   1.3 m, lamp's height 0.26
   Felt technique, wool
   Photograph: Auste Jurgelionyte

B: AUSTE'S SIGNS. 2006
   1.58 x 2.25 m
   Felt technique, wool
   Photograph: Auste Jurgelionyte

C: CARS. 2006
   1.3 x 1.8 m
   Felt technique
   Photograph: Auste Jurgelionyte

**137**

In some of your work you have used
human hair. I use only women's hair, and in
the work you can see the lines where some
hair is darker and some lighter, showing
where one woman's hair ends and the next
begins. A colleague presented her hair to
me, but of course this was not enough for
the project. So I wrote in the newspaper for
help, that I need women's hair not longer
than 20 cm – and it was wonderful. I met
so many women, from grandmothers who
brought me hair from their children, mothers
from their daughters.

What do you think about people's reaction
to human hair in the work? I think there's
something taboo about hair, something
magical. From Gothic time, from the Middle
Ages or even further back, hair has been
symbolic of the universe and of woman's life.
Of course so many tales begin with the witch
and her hair. In my work I use gold threads
which are a symbol of God, so by using
the gold thread to depict the woman, I am
changing the perception of God. The hair
represents the everyday, the common life, so
I mix only two threads, gold and hair.

In the particular work we are speaking
about, 'Women – Arhats: Danutė, Lina,
Violeta, Kristina', there are four parts, each
named after the woman who posed for
the image. I invited these women to my
studio and photographed them, then put

the photos in the computer and cropped
the images so that only the torso is visible.
It was important for me that the women
are ordinary women, from daily life. We
recognise that they are just like us.

The position of the women in the work is
very important. I took the photographs from
one point so that the body appears to be
standing in a line. I wanted to give the feeling
that this line of women goes on and on, to
infinity – so many women standing without
finishing.

You are still very involved with these works
as you describe them. No, when I speak
about work, it is from a distance. But when
I'm making the work I never talk about it. I
have to go inside the work, discover what's
inside me and inside the work – and then
you're at one with the work. Later, after the
work is finished, and I am distanced from
it. I can speak about it and wonder what I
was doing. Often I do something that I don't
'see' – then later I understand how much I
went inside the work.

Can you talk about the work for Cloth
& Culture Now? I want the work to be
exhibited on the floor. The work shows
a man and a woman, and the title of the
work is 'The Best Position'. In my young
days there were not enough beds for all
the children and they were put to bed after
dinner for a couple of hours and then they
would sleep in the same bed head to toe.

Then when I was young I saw many
people travelling by train and they would
buy just one ticket for two persons and lie
head to toe on the seat, and now, in this
work, I'm showing when we are old, this is
the optimum position. We're going to death
– man and woman – in this position.

In this work I put a digital print on the
warp, then when weaving, I 'dressed' them.
I'm 'dressing' through my weaving. The

THE OPTIMAL POSITION I, II
I: 0.54 x 1.52 m, II: 0.54 x 1.52 m
Tapestry: digital print, double weaving
Pure wool, gold, transparent threads
Photograph: Vl. Oržekauskas

METHODS OF MAKING
Laima Oržekauskienė has developed
her own personal double weave
technique, which incorporates
digital printed warps, enabling her
to create images within the woven
construction.

NARRATIVE OF MAKING
Much of Oržekauskienė's work is
concerned with the mapping of the
body, and the mythological status
of women. Her narrative is further
developed through the use of
women's hair and gold thread within
the weft.

SUGGESTED LINKS
Use of human hair: see Helena
Hietanen.

Lesley Millar

LAIMA ORŽEKAUSKIENĖ

WEBSITE STATEMENT EXTRACT
www.clothandculturenow.com

'Technically and visually, my works are based on traditional techniques and old Lithuanian stripe motifs (traditional Lithuanian stripes are accessories to our national costumes).

I bring my ideas to life by integrating the narrative of our historical heritage into modern digital technologies. The method I use is weaving, which I see as a traditional ritual.'

LAIMA ORŽEKAUSKIENĖ

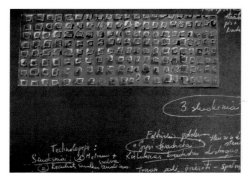

man has blue thread and, of course, the woman pink. And the rest of the weft is gold. And because they are lying head to toe, the body of one fits to the torso of the other and becomes like one. As usual, I'm using double weave, and the symbol of the swastika, which is a creative symbol of the universe, of nature, of everything – of birth, of death, of good and bad. All things.

Because I made the photo from one side and put it on to the warp, the lines go vertical, and when I weave the horizontal it becomes a typical plaid, a blanket. I didn't imagine this would happen, but by the weaving it happened. For me the association with the blanket is really important, because

you wrap it around the body. My ideas are based in daily life, common people and the beauty of every moment of life.

And always it is weave? Yes. In my young days I made so many things from different techniques – paper, three-dimensional, etc – and after all I returned to weaving. I weave because the vertical is the warp and the horizontal is life. Also it is so important for me to be able to make the work alone, by myself, without anyone having to help me. It's so important for me to have my silence, my peace and my dialogue with what it is I want to do. After I have finished the work, it's over, it's not important. It's on to the next one.

Weaving for me is like the man sweeping the street, his peaceful daily life job. I remember in India I was working in my studio and I heard this noise – swoosh, swoosh – and I recognised that noise. I am doing, like him, a simple daily job and the sound of my weaving, throwing the shuttle was swoosh, swoosh, the same sound. No words, just sound and daily life job. Life for man in nature is just to do a job, just do a job. The rhythm is the ritual, rhythm of textile, rhythm of sweeping. I am the sweeper. ■

**140**

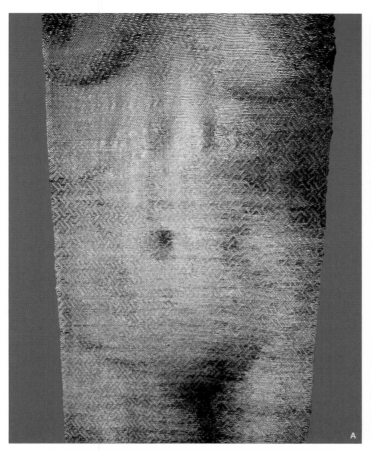

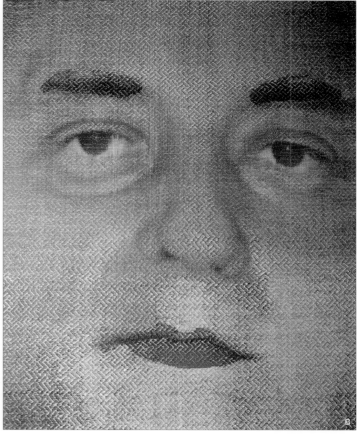

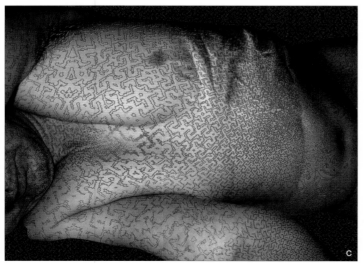

A: WOMEN DANUTĖ. 2002–2004
2.2 x 0.9 m
Women's hair, gold thread,
double weaving
Photograph: Vl. Oržekauskas

B: HER NAME WAS EGLĖ. 2005
1.9 x 1.5 m
Synthetic and gold thread,
digital print, double weaving
Photograph: VL. Oržekauskas

C: CLOTHES. 2005
0.97 x 1.4 m
Cotton, digital print
Photograph: Vl. Oržekauskas

**141**

■ Edited extracts from interview with Laura Pavilonyte, Vilnius, May 2007, with Lesley Millar

Your work is installation but it's also performance. I don't want to sit in the studio, hang up my pictures and not communicate with the people who are looking at them. Perhaps this is why I go directly to people, to communicate the making of art and ask them to make art with me. My projects are a form of exchange, sometimes I exchange my work for other things from people, and then make an exhibition of these things. I am very happy since I have such a good collection of objects – such as things from handbags.

This approach has been very popular with the public, because people want to discuss art, the value of art, and sometimes they want to buy art but can't afford it. The possibility of making an exchange for the art was really important, because sometimes, rich people know good brands, but don't understand art – whereas people who love culture don't have money and cannot buy.

When you are making a performance, do you become someone else, take on a different character, like an actor? When I'm performing I don't become a different person/character – I only forget that I am a mother, a woman, a Lithuanian, I am just part of my idea. I'm interested in working in different spaces, different architecture, and now in nature. I think about communication and prepare myself for that. Sometimes I worry that I may encounter

difficult situations, for example at the bus station where I encounter people from very different social backgrounds. But I haven't had contact with any aggressive people – perhaps I'm lucky.

Bus stations are a place of transition, of movement from one place to another. The centre of that installation is rather like a huge felt carpet, and I was thinking about Islamic carpets. I sometimes think carpets are very wonderful things, because in the folk tales we have carpets that fly. I made this performance near the bus map in the station, and I felt that the installation somehow hints at travel, simply by its nearness to the map. People were sitting watching me like in the cinema, with the question: 'You are doing all this for us?'

Your latest work doesn't have that same sense of personal interaction with people. When I was making my performance at the bus station, it was really important that I communicated with people. The work was about 'community', about giving and taking. Now the spirit of the work is about man and nature. I want to ask the questions – How to be happy? What are the spiritual values in society?

I'm the first in my family to grow up in the town. My father and mother are from the countryside, and I wanted to make a new relationship with the countryside. I have bought my own earth, one hectare, my own piece of land. I decided I didn't want to build a house or grow food, but I will make it like a gallery – for me to fill the land with my work. Perhaps in future I'll live there, but at the moment I want to fill it with my art.

I am interested in cycles and have been thinking about the relationship in ancient times between those people and nature. Then people lived together with nature, with the seasons – and everywhere you

METHODS OF MAKING
**Laura Pavilonyte's methods of making are governed by the performance outcomes, in particular the potential of the methodology to communicate the idea. Felt has been the material most closely integrated into her performance.**

NARRATIVE OF MAKING
**The colours that Pavilonyte uses – red and white – carry the narrative of her cultural identity, a theme further developed through her research into the ancient ornamentation of Baltic sculpture.**

SUGGESTED LINKS
**Cultural narrative and ornamentation: see Kadri Viires.**

Lesley Millar

HOW TO BECOME HAPPY
Installation
Wool, wood
Photograph: Auste Jurgelionyte

**143**

can find the idea of a spiral. For this reason I have chosen to work with the idea of the labyrinth, an ornament that relates to the spiral.

My idea is to make a big, flat labyrinth, lay fabric on the ground, on the grass and watch what will happen. As I've chosen linen felt that will decompose in nature over time. I'll print some design on it and see what happens to the different areas of the fabric, where it is printed and not printed. In some places the grass will grow through, maybe where I leave holes in the fabric.

You have also used thread to create a labyrinth. I am now working with more geometric forms. In fact it's quite difficult to achieve the correct geometry for the labyrinth, quite mathematical. I've been researching ancient ornamentation, particularly that found in Baltic sculpture. This contains so much information – but we no longer know how to access it, how to 'read' it. Through this research I discovered more about spirals, became interested in notions of time, and wanted to reflect this through my labyrinth.

I want to lay the thread down, and then someone else can re-wind it back into a ball. The thread will be white or red. These are contrasting colours that do not represent opposites, or good or bad, as black and white might be seen as good and bad – opposite poles. This use of the two colours also goes back to my grandmother. In Lithuania we have pillows decorated with these two colours. My grandmother gave me such a pillow when I was a little girl and I slept on it, for me it has beautiful and safe resonance.

How important is it for you that your practice has meaning other than referencing textile? My work may not appear to be autobiographical, but I feel these things very deeply inside. I start from myself, and then reflect what is outside – sometimes I joke that I feel responsible for the world problems.

I need to understand how people lived in ancient times. I think that they had their own high culture. I've done research on the Baltic people in pagan times, and even more ancient times, and for me it's very

important to go inside my roots. I think we can remember this knowledge, we can find our way back to this knowledge – maybe through the labyrinth. ■

WEBSITE STATEMENT EXTRACT
www.clothandculturenow.com

'First of all, I think that Lithuanian folk traditions had an impact on my perception of aesthetic beauty. In my childhood I slept on pillows that were traditionally made by my grandmother. During festive seasons I used to spread hand-woven tablecloths on the table. This embedded an appreciation and love for rhythmic compositions [and] combinations of red and white.'

LAURA PAVILONYTE

A: AMERICAN CHEESE. 2002
   Performance
   Colour woodcut, Vilnius
   Photograph: Laura Pavilonyte

B: HOW TO BECOME HAPPY. 2007
   7 x 7 m
   Felted yarn, installation
   Photograph: Laura Pavilonyte

C: WOMAN AND EGGS. 1999
   1.5 x 9 m
   Object, paper, textile, author's
   technique
   Photograph: Laura Pavilonyte

# UNITED KINGDOM

MICHAEL BRENNAND-WOOD
MAXINE BRISTOW
SHELLY GOLDSMITH
DIANA HARRISON
SUE LAWTY
FREDDIE ROBINS

# OURSPACE: tradition and innovation in contemporary british textile art

JENNIFER HARRIS

'The past not merely is not fugitive, it remains present.'

Marcel Proust, Remembrance of Things Past: The Guermantes Way (1913-27)

In her influential essay, 'The Originality of the Avant-Garde,' the American art historian Rosalind Krauss interrogates the idea of originality as the one fairly constant theme in vanguardist discourse.[1]

One of the 'myths' of Modernism, she argues, is that artistic originality involves far more than a revolt against tradition and a rejection of the past; it is conceived as being literally without antecedents. The avant-garde artist is him/herself the origin of their work. Acknowledgement or appropriation of what has gone before is discredited. Where then, in the discourse of contemporary visual arts practice, does this leave textile art since, as a category, it may be said to be characterised by the creative interplay between tradition and innovation?

Textile art thrives on the freedom found in the interstices between the two ideas of tradition and innovation. Work by artists in what is increasingly a global community of textiles practice is nourished by and creatively re-invents the forms, techniques and symbols associated with both vernacular and indigenous craft traditions, but is often conceptually closer to the concerns of contemporary fine art. The acquisition and implementation of skills associated with traditional craft media like textiles also requires the investment of time, another commodity not easily assimilated into the rhetoric of the avant-garde, with its insistence on a fast turnaround of ideas and their visual articulation.

Let us proceed, perhaps, by examining a little more closely the idea of tradition and its role in contemporary culture. Sue Rowley, the Australian writer and critic, has suggested that the idea of tradition does not arise in those communities where its presence is deeply naturalised, arguing that it is a construct of modernity itself – the latter's 'inescapable dialectical other'.[2]

This is analogous to Eric Hobsbawm's thesis in The Invention of Tradition, where he makes a distinction between tradition and convention or custom.[3] Customs can change and evolve but he posits 'invariance' and 'repetition' as the defining characteristics of tradition. He further distinguishes between tradition in industrialised societies and custom in 'traditional' ones. Traditions are most commonly invented within societies where rapid industrialisation or some other transformation has weakened or disrupted social patterns and relationships.[4]

The rapid and early industrialisation of the textile industry in Britain is well documented. Spinning and weaving, closely followed by textile printing, were the first industries in the UK to become fully mechanised and this had a huge impact socially, economically and culturally. The development of mills involved the mass movement of workers from the home to the factory and from the country to the city, with textile workers often living in appalling conditions. It is, therefore, interesting and paradoxical that textiles as a practice in the UK is still quite firmly rooted in the popular imagination as an artisanal activity, associated particularly with the vernacular textile traditions of quilting, embroidery and knitting. Equally hard to shake is the notion that textiles are irrevocably linked with women and with the domestic economy, a romanticised and highly inaccurate view of an industry that has been mechanised since the end of the 18th century. The global trade in textiles has also been an important influence and a degree of cultural fusion has defined the 'britishness' of British textiles for centuries.

Michael Brennand-Wood, Maxine Bristow and Sue Lawty all have their roots in the textile heart of the north of England. The cotton and woollen mills may have long since closed but family ties and the industrial landscape itself have both played a part in forming and shaping their attitudes to the medium in which they work. 'Textile history is writ large on this land,' writes Sue Lawty; and Brennand-Wood remembers a grandmother who worked in one of Lancashire's cotton mills and, before that, ancestors who fashioned the wood and metal printing blocks that left traces of memory in the carved and inlaid wood surfaces of his lace-related works in the 1990s. In his study of 'invented' traditions, Hobsbawm argues that post-industrial societies have been obliged to invent or develop new conventions more frequently than earlier societies.[5] As objects or practices become no longer constrained by everyday use they acquire ritual and symbolic functions. Thus, artists deploy domestic and artisanal craft skills that are no longer required in the textile industries of the West, and which can therefore be liberated for symbolic and ritual use, for the 'making of meaning'.

Hand knitting epitomises the homely, functional view of craft. It has flourished in the West as both a middle-class pastime, aimed at keeping idle hands busily occupied, and, until its place was taken by mass-produced machine-knitted goods in the post-war period, as a means of keeping families cheaply and warmly clothed. Its association with an idealised view of a simpler, more wholesome past also placed hand knitting at the centre of the craft revivals that took place in the 1960s and 1980s. Freddie Robins' work plays with the cosy, domestic connotations of hand knitting to draw the viewer in, but her 'mutant knitwear' flouts any suggestion of functionality.[6] There is a deliberate disjuncture between the homespun technique and the vaguely unsettling subject matter that disrupts the continuity with the past and with craft traditions.

The tradition of plain, functional sewing – patching and darning, the turning of seams and the binding of buttonholes – also expresses the dedicated labour of pre-industrial, domestic textile making and exists like a folk memory in the social and psychological make-up of many contemporary textile artists. It has informed the work of Diana Harrison through the use that she makes of the techniques of British North Country quilting. Like the Amish who traditionally produced quilts in plain fabrics pieced in bold geometric patterns, quilts made in Wales and Northumberland were characterised by wide striped or single colour tops, wadded, backed and then quilted together with complex patterns in a plain running stitch that, at their best, demonstrate the ingenuity and imagination of their makers in working within the constraints of tradition. In Harrison's work the techniques are combined with new and inventive approaches to the dyeing and printing of cloth.

In post-modernity quilting, like knitting, can function as a sign of an alternative community-based creativity that is at odds with the modernist ideal of individual self-expression and the notion of the artist as a lone genius. In the past quilt groups in the UK and quilting 'bees' in the US met a whole gamut of social, psychological and creative needs for women who were often isolated within the home, but contemporary artists often invoke this and other alternative attributes of craft to reflect critically on questions of social formation and human relationships.

For over a decade now Maxine Bristow's stitched and painted serial works have self-consciously invoked the 'meanings' and associations of craft while drawing much of their power and impact from an equal acknowledgement of their debt to the visual language of Minimalism and to contemporary critical debates in the visual arts. They articulate the labour of pre-industrial domestic textile making – the precise and repetitive work involved in the execution of hand-stitched textiles, the quiet dignity of plain sewing, the time invested in the processes of hand crafting ('it takes an hour to stitch one square inch of needlepoint'), and the sense of community that is invoked when the artist works with groups of other makers, on the needlepoint projects, for example. Bristow's work thus frames itself in opposition to the idea of modernity through its use of craft sensibilities and traditions, but sets up a deliberate dichotomy by confronting these with the serial repetition, repetitive language and modular configurations of form that acknowledge the artist's interest in Minimalism, in some ways the apotheosis of modernist idealism. Her stated intention is to subvert or transcend these conventional definitions of meaning through the process of exchange embodied in her work.[7] Michael Brennand-Wood's mixed media constructions offer another challenge to one of modernism's core tenets. In its quest for an artistic tabula rasa early 20th-century modernism pushed ornament to the very margins of Western taste and aesthetics. Along with notions of craft and an acknowledgement of tradition as an element of innovation, ornament was devalued and, until recently, with the stranglehold of modernism loosening, systematically excluded from the mainstream of Western art making. In the contemporary context, however, of increasing global connectivity and cultural influence and integration, pattern can have a unifying role.

Floral imagery, for example, is found in many indigenous textile traditions all over the world, widely in Europe, Asia and in the Americas. Brennand-Wood's most recent work has taken floral ornament as its subject matter, translating flat two-dimensional motifs into almost holographic three-dimensional constructions, 'crafting' the works with the aid of a computerised embroidery machine. Floral imagery is just the latest in a series of contested areas of textile practice that Brennand-Wood has chosen to work in, lace and embroidery being earlier examples. Like Maxine Bristow, the defining characteristic of his work is the attempt to produce a conceptual synthesis of contemporary and historical source material. Both deliberately undermine any perceived dichotomy of tradition and innovation, drawing on the former to realise the latter. Modernism has shaped our way of seeing over the last hundred years, but has not easily been able to embrace those working

in traditional craft media such as textiles. Its ideological imperatives – the emphasis on artistic originality and unadorned form – pushed notions of craftsmanship to the margins and set up false dichotomies of art and craft, tradition and innovation. As a dominant aesthetic discourse it is now in retreat, along with the power of the West to determine where cultural value lies. In art and artefacts from other parts of the world, much of Asia, for example, where there have been long histories of building aesthetics around craftwork, artistic practice frequently invokes tradition, especially in relation to creative and symbolic practices such as narrative, popular culture and craft, and these have been better integrated into society generally.

In a multicultural society the art/craft divide in recent Western culture seems increasingly irrelevant, and the pluralism, interdisciplinarity and hybridity of contemporary visual culture are better able to embrace craft skills, practices and objects as a means of delineating indigenous, local or other identity. Homi Bhabha's essay in The Location of Culture, 'How newness enters the world,' argues that cultural difference is the prime mover in the production of creativity. Post-colonial theory and ideas like Bhabha's on the 'in-between' spaces – 'the interstitial passages and processes of cultural difference' [8] – have allowed artists the freedom to work outside the mainstream. Contemporary art textiles thrive on the freedom found in these alternative spaces. ■

1. Krauss, Rosalind E. (1985). 'The Originality of the Avant-Garde' in The Originality of the Avant-Garde and Other Modernist Myths. Cambridge, MA, and London. MIT Press. p 157.

2. Rowley, Sue. (1999). 'Craft, Creativity and Critical Practice' in Sue Rowley (ed), Reinventing Textiles, Vol 1: Tradition and Innovation. Winchester. Telos Art Publishing. p 11.

3. Hobsbawm, Eric. (1983). 'Introduction: Inventing Traditions' in Eric Hobsbawm and Terence Ranger (eds), The Invention of Tradition. Cambridge, England. Cambridge University Press. p 2.

4. Ibid, p 4.

5. Ibid, p 3.

6. Robins, Freddie (2002). 'Freddie Robins in conversation with Linda Theophilus' in Freddie Robins, Cosy. Colchester. firstsite.

7. www.clothandculturenow.com/Maxine_Bristow.html

8. Bhabha, Homi K. (1994). The Location of Culture. London. Routledge.

I feel your work is very much about synthesising ideas and processes, how important is the actual making for you? I really like making, I am totally unapologetic about it, this is what I do, and I make things. To me it is very important that I personally make an artwork. I like my handwriting and I am probably at my happiest when I am listening to music and making something. I have always looked at textiles with the view that you can be inspired by the technique or the materials, but once you understand the context of the work, how it has been used, you can also access those ideas as well. I think that materials have a spirit – that is, there is sensitivity, an understanding. For example, for me an evocative description of lace would be the encirclement of space. I work with something to the stage that I understand what it wants to do and try and go with that. I would choose that material to develop a certain idea, knowing that it will enhance that idea rather than make it feel visually uncomfortable. I am responsive to contested areas of practice and I deliberately use terms like embroidery, patterning or lace.

In recent work you have been much concerned with floral imagery… I am very interested in historical textiles, where you can't avoid the predominance of floral imagery and in 2001 I worked on a collaborative project called 'Stars Underfoot'.

STARS UNDERFOOT – RANDOM
PRECISION (detail)
1.13 x 1.66 x 0.10 m
Embroidered flowers, acrylic, wire, glass,
fabric, thread, mosaic on wood panel
Photograph: Stephen Brayne

This was based on a book I had read on Indian Mughal Era carpets called Flowers Underfoot. I thought it would be interesting to do an inversion: textiles have always been influenced by floral imagery, and I wondered what would happen if you use real flowers to reconstruct a memory of a historical textile. I took thousands of fresh flowers and I worked in the studio with a photographer, and we ended up with a series of 1.20 m sq. photographs, which were the exact size of the flower installation pieces.

Did you ever think about making an installation of the flowers within a gallery space? I did do some private installations. However, as the photographs worked really well, and I was excited to continue the other side of the circle and go back into the textile again, I decided to take that exploration back into cloth, into stitch. It sounds perverse, but in many ways I am not that interested in flowers. I am interested in the geometrical sub-structures that are underneath a lot of historical textiles. In a sense I was mapping those geometries and the flowers became a marking point of geometrical intersection.

The flowers were purposely symbolic, because I didn't want to try to recreate a rose. And that is where the 'Field of Centres' exhibition came from. I use titles quite deliberately, as additional referencing; to me titles are colours, enhancing meaning and hinting at subliminal connections. 'Field of Centres' as a title is derived from a critique: people say that a good carpet has a 'field of centres' and by that they mean it has a geometrical multiplicity. Within the visual field there is a sense of illusionary space, an implied arena within which something might happen.

**METHODS OF MAKING**
Michael Brennand-Wood's critical awareness of the continuum of textile practice underpins his approach, one that is firmly rooted in his research, technical understanding and material knowledge, accompanied by meditative contemplation of historical artefacts.

**NARRATIVE OF MAKING**
Brennand-Wood's approach is one of mapping space and cultural narrative. The field of centres in a carpet, or minute observation of structure: the structure of flowers – these elements become entry points for his making process. The interaction between Brennand-Wood and both his study of structure and the structure of his work could be seen as one of the closest symbiosis.

**SUGGESTED LINKS**
Historical artefacts and making: see Mitsuo Toyazaki.

Lesley Millar

That sense of something happening, not knowing what to expect, is very present for the viewer in the works where you use found objects to create the pattern... Recently, whole series of mnemonic shapes have gradually superseded the flower shapes. I do small drawings, keep notebooks of line drawings, which are references to things that I have thought of, or seen and I do that, on a relatively daily basis. I have always been interested in scripts, particularly early forms of communication, ideograms, pictograms, visual writing. The 'Field of Centres' exhibition had more than one line of enquiry. In particular there was a group of work that became quite military, a use of skull shapes and mine shapes. This came from somebody who said to me that the work was 'pretty' – and that really irritated me because I thought they couldn't get past that. Then I thought, I could use that aspect to make something that was superficially quite attractive but when you get closer you realise the shapes you are looking at have a much more sinister dimension. For instance a skull flower that at distance looks like four petals but when you get closer you realise it is four or five heads.

The geometry of pattern has a strong musical base in the way shapes interlock together. One very noticeable aspect is the use of rhythmic repetitive devices. When you mix a musical composition you draw from a multitude of pre-recorded tracks, bringing sounds backwards and forwards in the mix to create the final piece. I think I do that, visually, in exactly the same way creating an orchestration of colour, image and collage. In that sense the 'Flower Works' are a true synthesis of many references, which – hopefully – harmoniously gel into a coherent statement.

Your work has always been three-dimensional, but the work you are creating for the exhibition engages much more overtly with the surrounding space... What had persistently fascinated me has been the relationship between the art object and the wall, that tradition of illusionary pictorial space that you see from the Renaissance onwards. The early flower pieces were, for want of a better word, quite holographic in construction. They were reliefs, enabling the flowers and the collage material to be constructed at different levels. The idea was that the viewer, walking past the piece, physically interacted with it.

I started to work with piano wire with single shapes attached at the end of each length that protruded out of the surface of the work. This enhanced the dimension of the work as the shapes literally moved, giving an ambient, sense of optical movement. The piece that I want to make for this exhibition is developing that idea and extending it to a much larger arena, working with many more component parts. This offers me so many more interesting possibilities, working at different levels on the wall surface, creating shadows so that the work physically has an additional dimension, extending literally into space.

This connects with a lot of things I enjoy, you can look at an historical carpet and you can see it has a visual reverberation. I always think that the magic carpet has nothing to do with the idea that you get on a carpet and fly somewhere, if you look at a carpet you are transported somewhere visually; it is a meditative surface, hallucinogenic in its synthesis of shape and colouration. I am drawn to complex, to use the vernacular 'trippy', images, that particular fusion of colour and pattern, you move backwards and forwards within the picture frame depending on what your focus is and where you are standing. ■

WEBSITE STATEMENT EXTRACT
www.clothandculturenow.com

'The two primal materials in my work, textile and wood, relate directly to my maternal Grandparents. My Grandmother worked in an industrial mill in Lancashire, as a young woman, weaving cloth for the cotton industry. As a child I literally played with cloth, learning to sew and knit before the age of 10.

I believe the most interesting artists locate themselves within unfamiliar territory. Habitat, studio, material choices and imagery have all been influenced via travel, the beauty of which is the unfamiliar.'

MICHAEL BRENNAND-WOOD

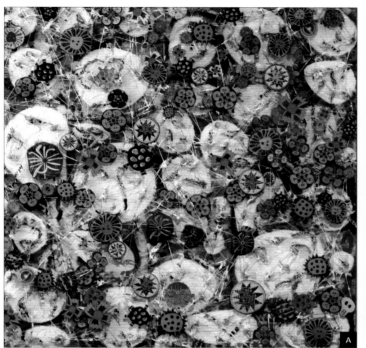

A. TIME LOVES A HERO. 2006
0.9 x 0.9 x 0.04 m
Embroidered imagery, acrylic,
thread, fabric, toy soldiers, resin
on wood panel
Photograph: Joe Low

B. A FIELD OF CENTRES (detail). 1996
2 x 5.8 x 0.04 m
Inlaid fabric into painted wood base
Photograph: James Austin

C. STILL LIVES – THIS FINAL TWIST. 2007
0.68 x 0.68 x 0.55 m
Embroidered imagery, wooden
figures, wire, medals, and red wax
Photograph: Joe Low

■ Edited extracts from interview with Maxine Bristow, Manchester, June 2007, with Lesley Millar

**Can you talk about the work you have proposed for the exhibition?** It is a development of past work where I have been thinking about our bodily relationship with spaces and the built environment – and in particular points of physical contact, points of touch. Previous work was very much focused on finger touch and hand touch. A few years ago when I used to go the gym I started looking at those gym pads that you adjust to the body. I was also thinking about the notion of 'padded paintings'.

I was thinking about the positioning of ourselves in relation to those gym pads – how if it was a padded painting at body height, instead of eye height, there would be a kind of ambiguity. This got me thinking about other anonymous pads. You know the kind you get on the tube – where you pull a seat down, or the kind that you lean against. I like that idea of it being hinged so that on the one hand we read it as a kind of framed painting, and then in your imagination you pull it down – the work playing between furniture and painting.

**There are three of these pads. Do all three have to be the same?** Yes – no individuality. I don't know why three, really – back to past serial work – and the strangeness that they would all be close together. And going back to the bags, the multiples, gives you a larger surface area. You would read the stitching as

a horizontal band across the three.

I am not thinking about furniture in any ergonomic sense. It is just an upholstered pad – which takes me back to the anonymity that is within most of my work. In recent work I have been employing strategies that purposely conceal; strategies of restraint or reduction in order to make things all the more articulate. Exploring if, in paring back, reducing things to their essence, you pick up on the nuance of things, and the cloth itself is allowed to speak.

What interests me with textiles are the stories, the kind of real or imaginary narratives which we associate with cloth. I think this partly stems from the work I did for the light switch pieces and the handrail pieces (for 'Through the Surface' exhibition) where I kept a record of when I was stitching and where I was stitching. There was a mass of documentation that lay behind these quite blank neutral works. I am interested in the generic signifying potential of textiles. It does not matter that we know the particular history behind them – we kind of invent the stories in our imagination.

The strategy of keeping the works blank and neutral is that they become more resonant; they become more universal – paradoxically both tangible and immaterial at the same time.

**That takes me back to something you wrote about, when you referred to Clement Greenberg. Greenberg was about a non-referential surface, no narrative and yet you are talking about the fact that the narrative is very important to you...** It's that Greenberg idea of autonomy, the thing about cloth is that, no matter how much I adopt those strategies, no matter how much I kind of silence it, the potency of cloth is so strong it speaks volumes, and it is that which is really key. Going back to the pads and tubes and buses: I was also thinking

METHODS OF MAKING
**Maxine Bristow uses the traditional techniques of plain sewing as an expression of modernity: the grid, the abstraction, the repetition and the essentially autonomous surface. The method she employs also connects to the domestic resonance's of needlepoint, a universality of constructing cloth, which has a commonality and potential for communication across cultures.**

NARRATIVE OF MAKING
**Bristow employs an autonomous modernist aesthetic to map the relationship of the body to space and the built environment. She is using methods of textile production that essentially lack subjective potential. Instead cloth is seen as a silent witness, Bristow's pads could contain a forensic pattern of stories of everyday life.**

SUGGESTED LINKS
**Mapping space: see Helena Hietanen. Mapping the body: see Zane Berzina.**

Lesley Millar

BACKRESTS REF. 762/398 (detail)
1.19 x 1.71 x 0.12 m
Cotton cloth, embroidery cotton, wadding, timber, powdercoated steel fabrication
Photograph: Maxine Bristow and Damian Chapman

forensically about what stories they could tell – all those narratives that are imbued within the pile of the fabric – the idea of cloth as a silent witness to the routines of our daily lives. What interested me with the recent canvas work was the contrast between the very detailed record that I kept of the work's production and the finished work which remained resolutely silent.

Would you like people to know that? Maybe, I am wondering how this documentation could be developed as a kind of parallel aspect of the work.
I am making a connection between the repetitive routines that the pads bear witness to and the repetitive processes that I use in the work – how through the process of stitching the work is literally imbued with my own DNA. Using darning or canvas work or other methodical processes I am echoing all those narratives and repetitive routines –

both time and space become concentrated and collapsed in the work.
The invisibility of these imaginary narratives goes back to the whole idea of plain sewing. It is those hidden aspects of textile production that interest me – the quiet anonymity and unassuming modesty of everyday utility. Ironically, it is the very universality and ubiquity of these utilitarian processes which accounts for their invisibility.

With your light switch pieces people brought their own narratives... That's the thing of it being quite neutral – it does invite a multiplicity of meanings. Yes, it is still operating under that cloak of an autonomous modernist aesthetic, but subverting that at the same time. While the work clearly draws on the subjective potential of cloth I want at all costs to avoid sentiment and nostalgia. I think a

lot of textile art draws on what I call 'the bit of antique lace and a sepia photograph of granny aesthetic' in an attempt to confer meaning and significance. I want the work to have resonance, however, all the time I am trying to counteract those resonances.

And the textile itself as the medium of communication... I was thinking about universal characteristics, simple methods of construction and issues of touch. What has always attracted me to Textiles is the tactility of good quality cloth, something that communicates across all cultures.
I suppose in relation to this project again it is the idea of the plain sewing being a universal language. You may see different stylistic conventions within textiles from different cultures, but techniques of seaming, darning and quilting are basic methods of constructing, strengthening and repairing cloth that are common to all cultures. ■

WEBSITE STATEMENT EXTRACT
www.clothandculturenow.com

**'It has been a silent inheritance; knowledge and skills transferred through tacit acquisition – an unspoken language communicated, as with much craft practice itself, through the continuity of touch.**

**I recognise a family, and indeed, wider cultural inheritance, in among other things, the appreciation of skills and traditions; the care and respect for tools and the quiet dignity of utilitarian objects.'**

MAXINE BRISTOW

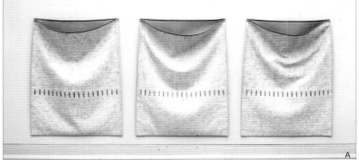

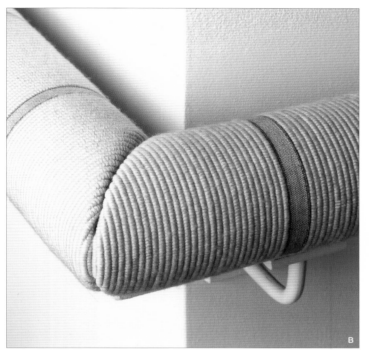

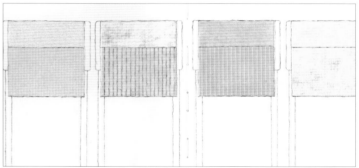

A. 3x19: INTERSECTING A SEAM. 1999
   1.63 x 4.18 m
   Linen, cotton, gesso
   Photograph: Dewi Tannatt Lloyd

B. NEEDLEPOINT: ref.7510, 3x63cm
   SURROUND. 2001
   1 x 0.63 x 0.43 m
   Tapestry canvas, denim,
   tapestry wool, metal fixings
   Photograph: Brian Slater

C. LIGHT-SWITCH: ref. 203/18. 2003
   2.6 m x variable
   White concrete, plaster, granite
   chippings, carborundum powder,
   tapestry wool, tapestry canvas,
   electric fittings
   Photograph: Peter Huggins

What were your starting points for the work in the exhibition? I carry my ideas around for a very, very long time. The first set of dresses from the children's home was an idea I had for a long time. And this globe piece, I kept drawing it and drawing it in my sketchbooks and then, two years later, I am making it. My ideas mutate as they travel through time, thought processes and references. Then again through the making, that is when I understand what the work is about. This is how I work. I feel passionate about something, I can't let it go, it keeps coming to the front of my mind.

For people looking at my work it may be the same, often people don't get it straight away. My work is not a quick fix – as in the way that it is made, or the way an audience receives it. I don't think it hits you between the eyes, it is a slow burn sort of thing.

This work links back to earlier work through the use of dresses, and the reference to water... I keep going back to the same things and thinking I really must move on. But then I look at other artists' work and realise that they too are grappling with issues for years, so it's OK for me to re-explore the same themes. I have a passionate dialogue with particular issues that I keep on struggling with, and I am trying to find new forms and ways to explore them. I suppose there are so many questions and no true answers.

ROBBING PETER (detail)
Installation
Mercerised cotton
Photograph: Damian Chapman
and Ian Forsyth

In this piece I am very interested in the idea of transference, the ways that we transfer matter, the relationship between the body and the earth, linked and mirrored cycles. We only have one body of water on the earth and it just keeps going round and round again, transferred and reused and although I talk directly about this cycle, it also presents itself, in the work, as a metaphor for other issues.

I was looking at satellite images of the globe while thinking about humankind, the globe and ideas surrounding clothing, especially the dress as a contained whole garment. I have pared my ideas down to a very simple white woven garment, with thoughts of a ghost version, a 'ghost dress' – though utterly recognisable. I will use a tapestry technique, not for symbolic or historical reference points, but for technical ease. Most people will not know it is tapestry. The reason to work in this way is because I need to build in copious amounts of extra thread and a series of holes. I may use the idea of darning, or retain the 'bundle' of thread used in the weaving technique as a metaphor for building up areas of excess and other areas that are very lacking. The piece will ultimately change through the process of making. Again I am referencing drought and flooding, but also starvation and food mountains, global warming and ice ages starting. Of course it gets blown out of proportion in my mind and quite fictional, it reaffirms my understanding of what might happen and what has always happened on the globe.

So the narrative is as much in the process as the outcome? This weaving is almost about the weaving of our globe and the reweaving of it. The relationship of woven to unwoven cloth, the relationship of differing quantities of thread to holes and the options for darning is really critical to this work. My

METHODS OF MAKING
**Shelly Goldsmith has been exploring ways that tapestry can be liberated from its traditional place on the wall. Her creative journey has been one of maintaining craft skills within her developing personal visual and technical vocabulary.**

NARRATIVE OF MAKING
**Goldsmith's process is one of a long gestation period from original concept to realisation, allowing each stage to influence and change the final outcome. The body, represented by body parts and clothing, is the essential element in the narrative of her work. She is concerned with the cyclical nature of water as a metaphor for the cycle of life, the interconnected and interrelated nature of all things.**

SUGGESTED LINKS
**Mapping the body: see Laima Oržekauskienė.**

Lesley Millar

SHELLY GOLDSMITH

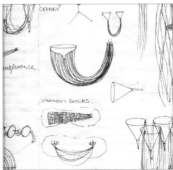

Dad used to do all the darning when I was little. He learnt it in the Navy, and he does it really well. He taught me how to do it. He sometimes found a bit of yarn from the garment to darn with. I just love that – it's sustaining itself. In the proposed dress piece I want to draw upon that notion of using a part of the whole to repair, mend or heal itself. I am hoping that there will be areas where there are layers and layers of thread borrowed from other parts of the garment.

As you describe it, there are so many references in your works – your research is also part of that narrative process. Textile has a wonderful substance in itself, but there are also other levels of research. Weaving itself draws on such a lot of the historical references of cloth and clothing. There is such a lot of research that goes into each piece of work. Gaston Bachelard in Water and Dreams, talks about different types of water – violent water, turbulent water, dark water, as well as about Edgar Allan Poe, water and death. Much of my work seems to be about loss, grief and a feeling that something difficult is about to happen.

The word I want to use about your work is immanence... Yes! It's the way I have always seen the world.

What is the relationship between your woven work and your printed work? I feel there is no relationship between my digitally or heat transfer printed work and the woven pieces. I very rarely ever put them together. I see them as very different voices, almost like two parts of a persona, two parts of this thing water. The woven is the deep darkness, the depth of the water, and the printed images refer to being on the surface – like the reflection. In this globe/dress work there is nothing to be said in the surface of the cloth. It is all about the form and the

movement of the substance. The thread I am using is as plain and simple yarn as possible, an un-dyed mercerised natural cotton, very beautiful in itself. Because I am using this nice clean yarn, it will get quite dirty as I am handling it, hand weaving it, and will undoubtedly show the engagement of time and evidence of the making, and I am happy for that. ■

WEBSITE STATEMENT EXTRACT
www.clothandculturenow.com

'My engagement with dressmaking, construction and deconstruction, is long standing. My childhood activity of making clothing for my dolls naturally extended into garments for myself and has assisted and underpinned my understanding of working with textiles as an effective and accessible vehicle for the expression of ideas.

Ultimately, these garments are very strongly rooted in a domestic, familial, English and Christian context, which is my experience, the cultural, ceremonial and historic references. My intention is that this would become apparent to others who have grown up within wider cultural parameters.'

SHELLY GOLDSMITH

A.  FORMING VAPOUR. 2005
    0.42 x 0.6 m
    Limited edition (50) Giclée print
    Photograph: Andra Nelki

B.  FRAGMENTED BELL. 2006
    0.4 x 0.4 x 0.18 m
    Heat transfer printing on
    reclaimed garment
    Photograph: Andra Nelki

C.  VITAL ORGAN. 2001
    1.17 x 2.39 x 0.2 m Hand woven
    tapestry, cotton and nylon monofilament
    /brushed stainless steel tray
    Photographer: Christopher Tipping

What was the starting point for this new
body of work? When I went to Barcelona
and saw a wall of black Sol LeWitt drawings,
this was the start, the idea of working in a
series, each piece informing the next. I came
back from Barcelona and started sketching,
sampling and planning these pieces straight
away. They were related to images of the
Kent coastline that I am very familiar with;
the expanse of landscape, the surface of
beaches and white cliffs.

I was also interested in the scans and x-
rays of bone density, the fine lines and fragile
structures evident in bone disease. I played
with the stitching, backwards and forwards
over these squares, so each piece became
individual. As they developed, one after the
other, there was a sequence to them and
they related. Each one prompted the next. It
was a useful way to work.

Gradually two completely plain pieces
emerged, no obvious composition, no
distortion of shape, simply surface texture
and the effect of the discharging. The
simplicity of these pieces interested me. I
wanted to expand this idea of repetition with
slightly different tones that resonate together.

How did you decide on the sizes? The
maximum size of the screen and my print
table. I wanted these pieces to be just one
pull of the squeegee. It all happens in that
one movement. No embellishment, the
three layers stitched, washed, shrunk and

prepared then screen and discharged over
the top. This is how it is – just the cloth, the
stitch and the bleaching away of some of
the dye. That's all.

These squares are not distorted because
they are absolutely complete in themselves.
I think that I just want the simplicity of it
and if I can say something without having
to go back over it, then I feel I have got
somewhere. It can all be very simple. It
is fantastically risky to spend how ever
many hours stitching, and then everything
depends on that one pull of the squeegee.
There is an element of risk in it and
sometimes they do go wrong. It can be a
destructive process. I like putting myself on
the edge with that. I still love that feeling of
unwrapping it from the steamer. Wondering
if it has worked and watching the cloth
change when it is being washed.

Your work crosses over different areas of
practice… My work is quilted work – if it
needs a definition. It is three layers stitched
together, but that is as far as it goes. I have
actually made full-sized quilts in the past that
would fit a bed, if you wanted them too, and
I made them for sale. But this work doesn't
fit into the normal expectation of quilts. I am
both a printer and a stitcher – a result of my
education, which was embroidery followed
by print . My work is a result of the two
disciplines. My process is one of building,
slightly manic – the backwards and forwards
for me is like scribbling. I can scribble in
the sketchbook and get the same effect
in pencil, or I can scribble backwards and
forwards on the sewing machine that builds
up the same mark making, which is then
developed through the print.

METHODS OF MAKING
Diana Harrison is a quilter who,
while using traditional methods,
is challenging the expectation
of her genre, which is a shared
preoccupation for many of the
artists in this exhibition.

NARRATIVE OF MAKING
Surfaces provide both her starting
points (beaches, x-rays of bone
density, road surfaces) and the
outcome (the final surface of the
work). The processes of stitch and
print with which she achieves those
surfaces provide the narrative of the
work.

SUGGESTED LINKS
Surface narrative: see Masako Tate,
Katrin Pere.

Lesley Millar

DIANA HARRISON

PHASES (THREE SQUARES) (detail)
1.02 x 1.02 m (x 3)
Silk/cotton backing
Photograph: Damian Chapman
and Ian Forsyth

Do you see elements of narrative within your work? A personal narrative or perhaps the narrative of making? There is probably less obvious narrative in my work than with other textile work. I have always been concerned with process, materials and composition. Playing with the application of dyes, the quality of cloth, and then subsequently layering and thickening so the pieces have substance. It is important to me, I don't plan and plot everything out, but things evolve through experimentation. Sometimes the narratives in a piece come afterwards, when I look at it and realise what was happening in my life while I was making the work; sometimes it is the result of an event that needs marking in a visual, abstract way. They are always very personal to me.

I have been commuting most of my life, this has provided me with some very precious space, sitting in my car with nobody to distract me, it has become an important thinking time. I have photographed the roads, in the early hours of the morning I go out and stand on bridges or the middle of roundabouts to record them. Visually I love the roads, they started my working with curves – I like the patterning and the road markings and all the obvious signage that is painted on the roads.

And I like the actual surface and the tarmac. I like the colour going over the tarmac – when it gets worn out – it is fascinating. My long twisting pieces were an outcome of my road ideas, curves and travelling. Coming up and down the A3 relentlessly, it is a way of incorporating a part of my everyday life. I want to expand my work with shaped and draped pieces, exploiting the edges, and taking it out of the square, away from the picture. I have been working with distortion and stitching down one side of the cloth and allowing the form and the curves to dictate the shape.

What we are talking about is the importance of textile, the fabric, as the start and end points of your working process... I am coming back more and more to the cloth. I am using silk noile, which is almost like a calico – it is rough and ready, but drapes well and absorbs the dye beautifully because it is silk, but without the shiny surface. I always look at different materials and think what can they do for me? What can I make them do? The quality is essential, the feel of the piece as well as the look, so the visual and material are equally important to my work. ∎

WEBSITE STATEMENT EXTRACT
www.clothandculturenow.com

'English quilts, north-country plain or wide simple striped pieces have had a strong influence on my work, while I appreciate the tactile qualities and complexity of patchwork; it is the simplicity and economy of process and pattern that speak to me most.

My earliest interest in quilts arose from a visit to the Amish people in Pennsylvania... the quality, simplicity and colour made a lasting impression on my work.'

DIANA HARRISON

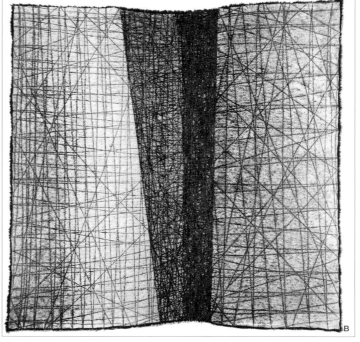

A. ROAD. 2007
0.24 x 2.4 m
Silk and cotton backing, half
stitched, cloth, double sided print
Photograph: David Westwood

B. DRAWINGS IN THREAD. 2006
0.6 x 0.63 m
Silk and cotton backing
Photograph: David Westwood

C. BACKWARDS AND FORWARDS. 2005
2.5 x 0.52 m
Silk and cotton backing
polyester thread
Photograph: David Westwood

■ Edited extracts from interview with Sue Lawty, Hebden Bridge, March 2007, with Lesley Millar

Stones, tiny stones, currently take a central role in your work, how do you relate them to your woven work? I've been looking at, drawing, photographing and generally playing with rock and stones forever really. I've found myself, almost unconsciously, selecting, organising and grouping them – progressively becoming tuned in to the subtle shifts in their shape and colour.

A while ago, alone on a beach in Wales, I had one of those revelation moments. It suddenly dawned on me that however much they looked the same, every single stone on this beach was different. And of course it followed that every stone in Wales, in Britain, in the world was different… and every grain of sand different, not just now, but always will be different. Even though, intellectually I already knew this, that was a moment of real understanding – completely felt, inside, internally. I experienced an immense sense of infinity, akin to the almost unimaginable time embodied in the structure of rock and the earth.

As an artist my work has become increasingly spare over the last ten years. I'm interested in how the rhythm and tensions of my making confer a kind of fingerprint to the work. Every single pass of weft over warp is a separate, tiny component which adds its own character to the final composition. It's this whole thing about unique individuality, individual marks, single elements, the correspondences with the nuances of difference I have observed in individual stones.

CALL AND RESPONSE: LEAD, LINEN, STONE, SHADOW (detail: LEAD)
2 x 2 m (x 4)
Lead, linen, stone, digital image
Photograph: Jerry Hardman-Jones

What gave you the idea of making four related works? I kept thinking of varying ways, alternative combinations, trying to come up with the idea, the definitive idea. I wanted to make a series that brought together all the materials I'd been working with, particularly the relationship between textile and stone. Both engender primal responses and are so steeped in a sense of the past. All my work has been about the land, about rock, structure and time.

The idea of working with shadow began with wanting to take the stone drawings off the wall, into space. I loved the idea of air around them, not being attached to a surface. One day, it was brilliant sunshine here in my studio, I put a piece of paper on the wall and took some photographs. I was so excited by the resulting distorted shadows, the visual strength of the ephemeral in contrast to the physical strength of the stone. I had the idea of stone/shadow, stone/shadow in repetition across a big wall or a moving light source making a billowing curtain of stone shadows. And then it became clear to me that I wanted to explore the whole nature of materiality – hard/soft, light/heavy, tangible/intangible – to make that ongoing dialogue evident in one body of work.

Where did the lead come from? I wanted to use raw materials from and of the ground – where does rock end and lead start? It's so elemental, solid and heavy (I just love that sense of dense weight) and yet malleable and textile.

These are imagined at quite a large scale – you really have scaled up in this work. There is a reason for this, not just that I want to do big work, it's much more about repetition. When I sample a thread I can think I understand it, but it's only over a greater area of weave that you notice the

METHODS OF MAKING
Sue Lawty is working with the most traditional form of art textile – high warp Gobelin tapestry, developing links between contemporary use of unconventional materials and traditional practice.

NARRATIVE OF MAKING
Lawty's time-based cultural and personal narrative is concerned with the substance of things, the nature of cloth, its structure and feel. She is exploring ideas of individuality and universality, a single thread within a piece of cloth, or a single stone on a beach made from millions of stones. The mapping of place and space, the structure of the landscape, the sense of time captured within that structure is paralleled in the structure of cloth and the sense of time captured with her tapestries, or challenged by the fleeting nature of light and shadow.

SUGGESTED LINKS
Tapestry: see Ieva Kumina, Lija Rage.

Lesley Millar

particular language that thread and structure impart, and can then begin to read the subtle shifts and changes across a surface. It's the same with stones. Through repetition the minutest nuances become visible.

I very much like the work of Robert Ryman, his sense of marking the subtle gradations of texture and tone, exploring the physicality of painting as an object. That is exactly what I want to do in my work. Ryman's own concerns lie in the visual pleasure of the painted surface and the artist's touch upon them. He says that when people see white paint they think that is the picture image. It's not. The white is just part of the structure of the painting. I feel increasingly that my work is about the basics of weaving – the process, the structure, the materials. The research that I have been engaged with has been with cloth, interlacement of warp and weft, the quality of thread, the way the cloth looks and feels.

For example, I love this tough, handspun hemp – its tight, scratchy hardness, and dense, stringy qualities. I'm not interested in prettiness. That's probably why I enjoy baskets – hard materials and structure. In old baskets, the structure becomes less visible, appearing and disappearing, concealed by age and use. In old, worn, textiles, where we get the reverse – the structure is revealed, the essential components of warp and weft made visible through age.

**The narrative of use and of making?**
Completely. I remember seeing a small dress, a Coptic dress, a child's garment, and I think because it was a child's garment, I immediately had the image of a child running around in it. It was darned just as I might mend my own children's clothes, so there was a real sense of wear and use in that cloth. It somehow became more pertinent and visible in my imagination.
All my work is also concerned with language. For many years I've been looking for ways of working with this notion of wearing out. It's about finding the appropriate language, finding the language for the materials that you are working with that has both integrity for me as artist and for the materials. Whether it's lead or linen, stone or shadow or any other material – to develop that language that is my journey. It's a journey and I just don't know where it's going to go. I feel it's like a spiral, getting nearer and nearer, tighter and tighter, closer to the core, but never really reaching it. ∎

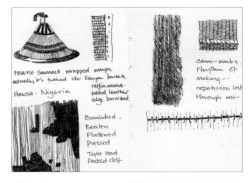

WEBSITE STATEMENT EXTRACT
www.clothandculturenow.com

'Throughout my creative life I have been drawn to textiles from times past, re-examining structure and exploring textile language. In the Bankfield Museum, Halifax, the Museum of Mankind (as was) in London and many others, I have pored over tapestry fragments from Peru and Coptic Egypt or raffia cloths from Zaire. These are obviously not of my ethnographic culture, but the more I research, the more I feel part of a rich woven tradition.'

SUE LAWTY

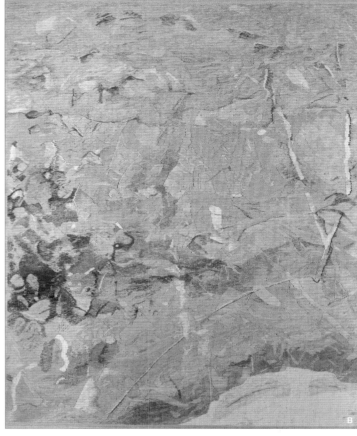

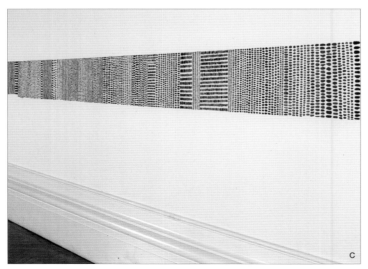

A. TERRA (detail). 2004
   0.70 x 2 m
   Woven tapestry, linen hemp silk wool
   Photograph: Peter Kelleher
   (courtesy V&A images, Victoria and
   Albert Museum, London)

B. ROCK TOUCH. 1996
   1.43 x 1.20 m
   Woven tapestry, raphia,
   linen, silk, cotton
   Photograph: Charlie Meecham

C. ORDER. 2005–2006
   0.4 x 6.17 m
   Site specific installation, V&A,
   natural stone on gallery wall
   Photograph: Jerry Hardman-Jones

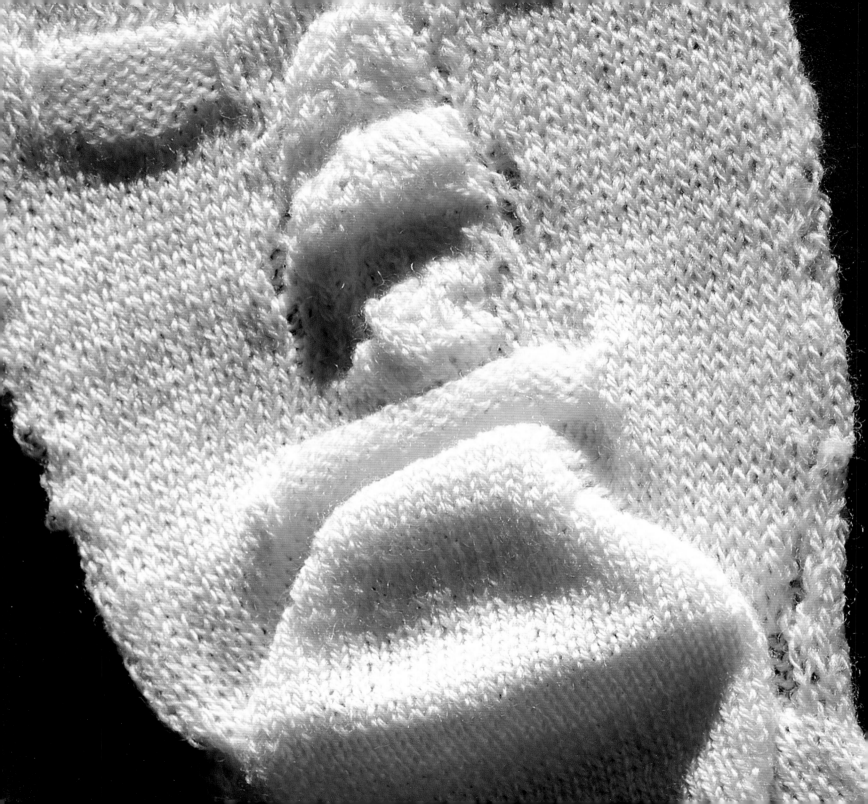

■ Edited extracts from interview with Freddie Robins, London, April 2007, with Lesley Millar

The knitted bodies in your new work look seamless, like cast-off skins... My work has a lot to do with perfection, which is probably more to do with me than the work – because I am real perfectionist. I have become increasingly interested in machines that have been developed to produce the perfect garment, time after time after time, without ever stopping. At the moment, I am working with the William Lee Innovation Centre at the University of Manchester and their Shima Seiki WholeGarment® machines that can knit 'in-the-round', creating a garment in one. This machine can knit a body, a complete skin, and just drop it on the ground. It is an innovation, but then there are sweaters in the Shetlands, which never come off the needles; they are knitted in the round, they grow up and have a yolk and then the sleeves grow off it.

The whole machine process takes just under two hours, which I watch and record. I have to work with a technician because I don't have the programming skills. This means that my aesthetic is being filtered not only through the machine, but also through the person controlling the machine. Therefore it is so important to work with someone who understands my aesthetic, to ensure the right quality.

The bodies even have faces – are the facial expressions important? I have been making some samples on my domestic machine, to see if I can create some other facial expressions. Also I have been trying on my domestic machine to knit how the Shima Seiki WholeGarment® machine works, working out how it is done, and then repeating it myself. Trying to figure it and put it into my own logic, I have been able to do it – because there isn't much that the Shima Seiki WholeGarment® machine can do that I can't do. In lots of my earlier pieces, for instance when I was doing my glove pieces which are all done on a machine, I got a pattern and knitted it to see how it was done. I then used that as my basis for rewriting and reworking how I want it to be done. I've always enjoyed looking at one way of doing things and then finding my own way of doing them.

My ideal is that the bodies would look more knitted, coarser. But it is not possible with this technology, which makes some things possible but it makes other things less possible – when you work with your hands you are much freer.

'Coarse' is an odd description, strangely unattractive... I had always stayed away from things that are attractive and pretty and decorative – because I was always trying to subvert. I have always liked going against the grain and being awkward and difficult. There has been a really huge emotional shift in me since I had my daughter and that has been apparent in my practice. I don't know if it is apparent to other people, but I can definitely see it. I find it very difficult to look at and think about some of the issues I was quite keen to embrace before, the bleaker and blacker things in life, which now I find very painful and quite often don't actually want to see them.

I think that my work is much more autobiographical than maybe I was fully aware.

THE PERFECT:ALEX (detail)
Installation
Wool
Photograph: Damian Chapman and Ian Forsyth

METHODS OF MAKING
For Freddie Robins there is overriding requirement for perfection in her approach to her work and in the work itself, a belief in the importance of skill as something to aspire to: skill enables perfection. This approach has led to her increasing involvement with new technologies.

NARRATIVE OF MAKING
Robins' constantly searches to express both a cultural and personal narrative through her own skill base. There is also a tension, an interest in 'coarseness', in things that have imperfection, an exploration of the truth that perfection can only be fully appreciated through imperfection.

SUGGESTED LINKS
Cultural and personal narrative: see Shelly Goldsmith, Eglė Ganda Bogdanienė.

Lesley Millar

There has always been a sense of connectedness in your work... I love connectedness and narrative, how things join together, the neatness is very satisfactory. I also really respond to the love invested in things. I have a huge collection of knitted toys, which really are the most hideous things – the complete lack of aesthetic understanding and lack of control of skill. That mismatch between so much energy invested into making something so gross. I don't know any children who like knitted toys – they don't feel nice. Misplaced love and misplaced energy, but it is about the doing, never wasting time and being useful.

As I have said, I am trying to create the perfect piece of work, yet I wonder why, or even if, that is desirable? I really like imperfection in others. It's a weird kind of double thing – in my own work I try and take any imperfection out of it so that it looks like it hasn't been made by hand.

I don't have unfinished work, I have got to resolve it. I can't have failure. I don't know if I am allowed to have failure. Like imperfection, that's for other people not for me.

Have you thought of working in any other medium? I have knowingly limited myself to knitting, kept myself just within that arena. When I left college I tried to do lots of different things because I did not want to be limited, but actually I really like those limitations. Having some ground rules. I am proud of my own skill – but if you don't practise it often enough it wavers, you forget bits and pieces, something I have become really aware of – that I am not as good as I was. I admire skill but I don't think I admire it just for the sake of it, rather as something to aspire to. Skill is a great confidence giver. The ability to make, to do something with your hands, is incredibly attractive. ■

WEBSITE STATEMENT EXTRACT
www.clothandculturenow.com

'My Godmother Pam… was like a second Mother to me and became my greatest inspiration. She was always making things, not frumpy, lumpy things that you hid in your wardrobe, but fashionable, desirable toys and clothes. She was a free spirit. She lived alone, was unmarried and just got on with her own thing. I associated textiles with her and therefore with freedom.'

FREDDIE ROBINS

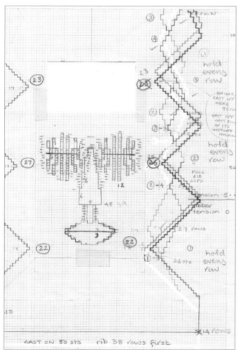
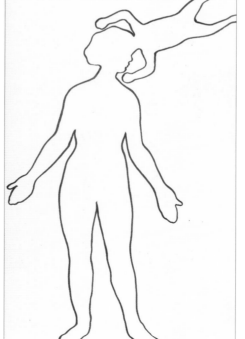

A. ANYWAY. 2002
1.62 x 3 x 3 m
Wool
Photograph: Douglas Atfield

B. HOW TO MAKE A PIECE OF WORK
WHEN YOU'RE TOO TIRED TO
MAKE DECISIONS. 2004
Dimensions variable
Wool, dress pin
Photograph: Ed Barber/Crafts Council

C. CRAFT KILLS. 2002
2 x 0.68 x 0.38 m
Wool, knitting needles
Photograph: Douglas Atfield

## MARE KELPMAN DOB 1958

**EDUCATION**
1990    MA Textiles, Estonian Academy of Arts, Tallinn

**RECENT EXHIBITIONS INCLUDE**
2005    Textile Contest, Tokyo, Japan
        Kaunas Art Biennial Textile 05, Kaunas, Lithuania
        Visions of Textile, International Exhibition of European Textile
        Network, Izmir, Turkey
        ReDesign Europe, Berlin Communication Museum, Germany
        Estonian Textile Art, Riga, Latvia: Pskov Kreml, Russia
2004    Internationale Design Biennale, St. Etienne, France
        Tradition and Innovation, 2nd European Textile and Fibre Art
        Triennial, Riga, Latvia
        Light.Things, Design Forum Finland, Helsinki, Finland.
        Estonian Embassy in Berlin, Germany
2003    Fibro, Estonian and Latvian Textile Art, Applied Art Museum,
        Riga, Latvia
        Crossing, Applied Art and Design Museum, Tallinn, Estonia (solo)

**AWARDS, COMMISSIONS AND COLLECTIONS**
05/06   Japan Textile Contest, Work with Superior Quality
2004    Textile Artist of the Year 2003 (award of Estonian Association of
        Textile Artists)

## KRISTA LEESI DOB 1966

**EDUCATION**
1993    Department of Textile Design, Estonian Academy of Arts

**RECENT EXHIBITIONS INCLUDE**
2007    Annual Exhibition of Estonian Artists Association Art of Living,
        Tallinn Art Hall
        My World: The New Subjectivity in Contemporary Design by
        British and Estonian Artists, Estonian Museum of Applied Art
        and Design
2006    Tallinn Applied Art Triennial Two Close Ones, Estonian Museum
        of Applied Art and Design
2005    An Archive, a retrospective summary of 25 years of existence of
        the Estonian Museum of Applied Art and Design
        International Textile Art Exhibition Textile 05, Kaunas, Lithuania
2003    International Textile Art Exhibition Right and Wrong Sides,
        Kaunas, Lithuania
        Estonian 3 Dimensional Art Notes, Szentendre, Hungary
        Contemporary Baltic / Sweden Textile exhibition Forever Young
        Stockholm, Sweden
        f-mail with Lylian Meister, Design Gallery, Tallinn
2001    Last word of Textile Art with Aune Taamal, Tallinn City
        Gallery

**AWARDS**
2007    Annual grant of Estonian Cultural Endowment
2006    Winning competition of Kesho Mawashi for Baruto (Estonian
        sumo wrestler) with Heino Prunsvelt
2005    25 best Estonian books of the year 2004. Honourable mention
2002    Cultural Award of Ministry of Culture
2001    Estonian Textile Artist of the Year
        Sleipnir grant for professional work in Sweden
1998    Krenholm Printed Textile Design Competition. 2nd Prize

## KATRIN PERE DOB 1952

**EDUCATION**
72-77   Estonian Arts Academy, Tallinn

**RECENT EXHIBITIONS INCLUDE**
2006    Big and Small. New Art Museum of Pärnu
2005    Estonian Textile Artists in Riga, Museum of Applied and
        Decorative Art
2004    Rose is a Rose is a Rose, ON-Group, Tallinn Art Hall
        Gallery, Estonia
2003    Tallinn Art Hall Gallery, Estonia (solo)
        Fibro, Riga Applied Art Museum, Latvia
        Handy Thing, Tallinn Art Hall, Estonia
2002    Masterpieces, Torino, Italy
1998    Roterman Salt Storage, Tallinn, Estonia (solo)
92-93   Flexible I. Bayreuth, Germany; Tilburg, Holland; Manchester, UK
92+98   International Tapestry Triennials, Lodz, Poland

**AWARDS**
2000    Scholarship Guest Studio Gmünd, Austria
1999    Annual Kristjan Raud Art Prize
1988    Award of City of Stuttgart, European Art and Craft, Germany
96+98   Textile Artist of the Year, Estonian Textile Artists' Association

**COLLECTIONS**
State Art Museum of Estonia
Estonian Museum of Applied Art and Design
Tallinn City Art Collection
Private collections in Europe, USA, Japan, Venezuela

## AUNE TAAMAL DOB 1963

**EDUCATION**
1993    Textile Department, Estonian Academy of Arts

**RECENT EXHIBITIONS INCLUDE**
2005    Kaunas Art Biennial, Lithuania
        Black, White and Colour, Estonian Museum of Applied Art and
        Design, Tallinn
        Textile-Improvisations, Estonian National Opera Gallery and
        Kuressaare Art Gallery, Tallinn (solo)
2003    Notes – 3Dimentional Estonian Art, Szentendre Art Mill, Hungary
01/04   European Textile Art Exhibition: Tradition & Innovation I, II, Riga
2001    The last word of Textile-Art, (with Krista Leesi) Tallinn Art Hall
        Gallery

**AWARDS**
2006    Best Textile of the Year, Estonia
2001    Estonian Textile Artist of the Year, 2nd Prize
1998    Printed Textile Design Competition in Estonia, 1st Prize

**COLLECTIONS**
Estonian Museum of Applied Art and Design

## KADRI VIIRES DOB 1964

**EDUCATION:**
2005    Postgraduate studies, Estonian Academy of Arts
1988    Textile Design, Estonian Academy of Arts
82-84   Industrial Design, Estonian Academy of Arts

**RECENT EXHIBITIONS INCLUDE**
2007    Art of Living, Tallinn Art Hall, Estonia
2006    Welcome to Love, Photographs from Ethiopia, Delicia Gallery,
        Tallinn, Estonia
2005    Estonian Textile Art, Baltic Cultural Centre Gdansk and Warsaw,
        Poland. Elegance of Ideas, Pskov Kremlin, Russia. Biennial
        exhibition Kurpfälziches Museum Textilsammelung Max Berk,
        Heidelberg, Germany
2004    XI International Lace and Contemporary Fibre Art Biennial,
        Brussels Belgium. Tradition & Innovation II, European Textile and
        Fiber Art Triennial, Arsenals Art Hall, Riga, Latvia
2003    3 Dimensional Estonian Art, Szentendre Art Centre, Hungary
        Handy Things, Tallinn Art Hall, Estonia. Light Textiles, Bureau of
        Nordic Council of Ministers in Stockholm, Sweden

**AWARDS**
94-07   Leader and supervisor of Finno-Ugric research program in
        Estonian Academy of Arts. Curator various exhibitions on Finno-
        Ugric Culture, Estonia, Hungary, Belgium, England, Latvia,
        Russia, Finland
2007    Estonian Cultural Endowment "Live and Shine"
2004    Estonian Cultural Endowment. XI International Lace Biennial and
        Contemporary Art in Belgium. Silver Prize

**GRANTS**
2006    Socrates/Erasmus
2004    MediaDesk. UNESCO Cultural Heritage
2003    Council of Ministries of Nordic Countries NORDEN
99, 05  Estonian National Culture Foundation
97-05   Estonian Students Fund in USA

**COLLECTIONS**
Estonian National Museum. Estonian Museum of Applied Art and Design.
Private collections in Estonia, Belgium, Sweden, Finland, Hungary

## HELENA HIETANEN DOB 1961

**EDUCATION**
06-07  Architecture of Light – education program for lighting design IADE / UIAH Helsinki
83-92  University of Industrial Arts UIAH, Helsinki
89-91  Drawing Department, Helsinki University

**RECENT EXHIBITIONS INCLUDE**
2006  3 levels, HoviArt Anttola, Mikkeli Finland together with Jaakko Niemelä. Genesis-unfinished, Candyland, Hammarby Artport, Stockholm and Galerie. Omotesando Tokyo, together with Jaakko Niemelä
2005  Taivaskone / Heaven machine, video-light installation, together with Jaakko Niemelä, Waino Alto Musem, Turku
       Cultures of Creativity, The Centennial Exhibition of the Nobel Prize, British Library, London and New York Hall of Science, New York
2003  Quietness, Finnish Art and Design, Ozone Center, Tokyo, Japan
2002  Beyond Paradise, Moderna Museet: Bangkok, Thailand; Kuala Lumpur, Malaysia; Shanghai, China.
       i8 galleri, Reykjavik, Iceland
1999  Les Champs de la Sculpture 2000, Paris, France
1997  Talvi, Barbican Centre, London, Great Britain
       Iluminazione, Venice Biennale, Venice, Italy
1996  Galerie Anhava, Helsinki, MUU Gallery, Helsinki
1993  Gallery Sculptor, Helsinki

**AWARDS, COMMISSIONS AND COLLECTIONS**
2004  Millennium Technology Award, design for the Award Statue,1st prize. Kuntien Eläkevakuutus new officebuilding, Kaisaniemi, Helsinki, 1st prize (with Jaakko Niemelä)
2002  3-lightwork and light plan for church of Tapiola, Espoo, Finland (together with light designer Tarja Ervasti)
01-06  Network lightwall and space devider at the Nobel Museums touring exhibition: Oslo, Seoul, Tokyo, Houston, Chicago, Kuala Lumpur, Firenze, New York, San Francisco, London, Bangalore, Singapore
2001  Network lightwalls permanently at the Nobel Museum, Stockholm, Sweden
1999  Finland State Prize

## AGNETA HOBIN DOB 1945

**EDUCATION:**
1971  University of Art and Design, Helsinki

**RECENT EXHIBITIONS INCLUDE:**
2007  Transparent, Fiskars Village
06-07  1:Infinity: Helsinki, Trondheim, Reykjavik
2005  Transformations: The Language of Craft, National Gallery of Australia, Canberra
       The Universe of Metal, Neue Messe, Munich, Germany
2004  Textile Artist of the Year, O-Gallery, Helsinki
2003  The Finnish Institute, Paris
2001  Nordic Award in Textiles, Borås Textile Museum, Sweden
2000  Norrut: Reykjavik, Bergen, Helsinki, Berlin, Kaunas
1998  Nature as Object, International Crafts Triennial, Art Gallery of Western Australia, Perth
1997  Winter, Barbican Centre, London

**AWARDS**
2005  The Bavarian State Prize, Munich, Germany
2004  Textile Artist of the Year, nomination by the Textile Artists Ascociation, Texo, Finland
2001  Torstrasse 140, Berlin-Mitte, Germany
       The Nordic Award in Textiles, Fokus Foundation, Sweden
1996  Stina Krook Foundation Award
1995  State long-term artist grant (15 years). State Prize Art and Design

**COMMISSIONS**
04-05  Etera Mutual Pension Insurance Co, Helsinki
1992  HAKA Co, Helsinki
1987  Supreme Court, Helsinki

**COLLECTIONS**
Finnish State Art Collection. President of Iceland. National Art Gallery of Australia, Canberra. Erik Anker Collection, Oslo, Norway. Fokus Foundation, Borås, Sweden. Design Museum, Helsinki

## OUTI MARTIKAINEN DOB 1962

**EDUCATION:**
1999  MA Textile Art and Design, University of Art and Design Helsinki
85-87  Vihti School of Arts and Crafts

**RECENT EXHIBITIONS INCLUDE**
2007  Under the Sun, Villa Roosa, Orimattila
       Points of View, Copper Smithy, Fiskars
       Galleri 5, Oulu
2006  The Window Gallery of the Office of Ornamo, Helsinki
       Textile Artists Texo 50th Anniversary Exhibition, Amos Anderson Art Museum, Helsinki
2005  Northern Fibre 6 – (Wo)man and Technology, Kerava Museum of Art
       Wetterhoff 120 Years Competition Exhibition, Hämeenlinna
2004  Forum Box, Helsinki
2000  Galleria Luisa delle Piane, Milan

**AWARDS**
2007  The Finnish Cultural Foundation
2006  The Textile Artist of the Year in Finland
       The Finnish Cultural Foundation, Uusimaa Fund
2005  Wetterhoff 120 years competition, Hämeenlinna, 1st Prize

**COMMISSIONS**
Design co-operation with SARC architects Ltd.
Finnish Pavilion, Expo2000, Hanover
KONE Building 2001, Espoo
Faculty of Medicine, University of Oulu 2004

**COLLECTIONS**
Art Collection of the State of Finland
Design Museum, Helsinki
Galleria Luisa delle Piane

## SILJA PURANEN DOB 1961

**EDUCATION**
1987  Textile Design, The Kuopio Institute for Art and Design

**RECENT EXHIBITIONS INCLUDE**
2007  Galleria Katariina, Helsinki, Finland
       La Galeria, Barcelona, Spain
       Tradition and Innovation, 3rd European Triennial Textile and Fibre Art, Riga, Latvia
       Zauber des Fadens – Fibre Art Today, Galerie Handwerk Munich, Germany
2006  Belgrade Cultural Centre Art Gallery, Serbia
       7th National Textile Triennial, Amos Anderson Art Museum, Helsinki, Finland
       Arttex Triennial of Textile, Liptovský Mikuláš Slovakia
2005  Visions in Textile, Izmir State Art and Sculpture Museum, Turkey
2004  Trame d'Autore, 4th Fiber Art Biennial, Chieri, Italy
       La Galeria, Barcelona, Spain

**AWARDS, COMMISSIONS AND COLLECTIONS**
2007  3rd European Triennial Textile and Fibre Art, Tradition and Innovation, Special Prize of the Riga City Council, Latvia
       The Museum of Contemporary Art Kiasma, Helsinki, Finland
       The Museum of Fine Arts and Lace, Calais, France
2006  Arttex, Trienále Textilu 2006, The Prize of the City Liptovský Mikuláš, Slovakia
2003  4th International Textile Art Exhibition, Kaunas, Lithuania. 3rd Prize
01-02  Kustaankartano Old People's Centre, Helsinki City Art Museum, Finland
2000  WCC-Europe Award for Contemporary Crafts

## KRISTIINA WIHERHEIMO DOB 1949

**EDUCATION**
1971  University of Art and Design, Helsinki

**RECENT EXHIBITIONS INCLUDE**
06-07  1:infinity, Helsinki, Trondheim, Reykjavik, joint exhibition with 6 artists
2005  Silence, Tampere, Finnish group exhibition
04-05  40/4 Design Event, Copenhagen, Cologne, Milan, Stockholm
2003  Behind the Chair, iD exhibition, Vaasa, Finland
2001  SE'01, Konstindustrimuseet, Copenhagen, Denmark
1997  Winter, Barbican Centre, London

**AWARDS**
2005  Public Display Grant for Visual Artists, The Arts Council of Finland
00-04  The Finnish State Grant for 5 years

**COMMISSIONS**
2001  Kone Corporation, Helsinki, Finland
       Sanitec Corporation, Helsinki, Finland
2000  Lärkan High School, auditorium curtain, Helsinki, Finland
1999  Danisco Finland Oy
1997  Kemijoki Oyj, Rovaniemi, Finland
1995  Espoo parish hall, Finland
1993  Finnish National Opera, iron curtain for the main stage

**COLLECTIONS**
Finnish State Art Collection
Pyynikinlinna Art Collections, Tampere, Finland
Vallila Interior Art Collections, Helsinki, Finland

## MERJA WINQVIST

**EDUCATION**
77-82  University of Industrial Arts, Helsinki

**RECENT EXHIBITIONS INCLUDE**
05-07  Paper & Meaning, Finland, Estonia, Denmark, Korea (touring)
05+07  Gallery Wiewinner, Osnabruck, Germany
2005  Gallery Lief, Los Angeles, USA
       Palace of Grand Duke Vladimir, St. Petersburg, Russia
2004  Gallery Lief, Los Angeles, USA
2003  Noorders, Brugge, Belgium
2002  Tondo Finlandese, La Spezia, Pisa, Bari, Genoa, Italy; Kisko, Finland
00+97  Gallery BAU, Helsinki, Finland
1999  Gallery Memphis, Rome, Italy
86+92  Gallery 25, Helsinki

**AWARDS, COMMISSIONS AND COLLECTIONS**
2007  Commission to The Caledonia Building, New York, USA
2003  Commission to The Laajasalo Church, Helsinki, Finland, Congregations of Helsinki Art Collections
       Textile Artist of the Year
1997  Commission to The Finnish Embassy, Dar es Salaam, Tanzania, Finnish State Collection of Art
1996  Design Competition of Savonlinna District, Finland. 1st Prize
1988  Commission to The Unitas Congress Centre, Helsinki, Art Collections of Nordea Bank
1987  Textile Art Competition of Union Bank of Finland. 1st Prize

## MASAE BAMBA DOB 1967

**EDUCATION**
1992    MFA Kyoto City University of Arts, Japan

**RECENT EXHIBITIONS INCLUDE**
2007    Textilkunst-Zauber des Fadens, Munich, Germany
2006    GalleryGallery, Kyoto, Japan
2006    [ex]Changing Tradition, Perth, Australia
2005    Triennial Higashihiroshima 2005, Higashi-Hiroshima Museum, Hiroshima
        Shibori [textile catalysts] Tama Art University Museum, Tokyo
        5th Triennial International Tapestry and Textile Art Exhibition Tournai, Tournai, Belgium
2004    GalleryGallery, Kyoto, Japan

## HIDEAKI KIZAKI DOB 1958

**EDUCATION**
1983    MA, Kanazawa College of Art

**RECENT EXHIBITIONS INCLUDE**
2007    Japan-Korea Textile Exhibition Musashino Art University Tokyo
        Diana Harrison Art Quilts Exhibition, Museum of Arts and Crafts Itami, Japan (support exhibit)
2006    Japan Textile Council Exhibition, 21st Century Museum of Contemporary Art, Kanazawa
2005    Japan Textile Council Exhibition, Contemporary Art Space, CASO Osaka
03-06   International Impact Art Festival, Kyoto
2003    KIZAKI Hideaki Art Works, GalleryGallery Kyoto
2002    KIZAKI Hideaki Art Works, GalleryGallery Kyoto

**AWARDS**
1996    Japan Contemporary Art and Crafts Exhibition technical prize, Tokyo
1984    Ishikawa Arts and Crafts Exhibition grand-prix, Japan

**COMMISSIONS AND COLLECTIONS**
2007    The 5th Cheongju International Craft Biennale 2007, in Korea, invited
2006    China Yunnan International Folk Arts and Crafts High-Level Forum and Arts and Crafts Exhibition, invited and collected
2005    Korea-Japan Textile Exhibition [Soft Forms] in Gallery Wooduk Seoul, invited and collected

## JUN MITSUHASHI DOB 1954

**EDUCATION**
1981    MA, Kyoto City University of Arts
1979    BA, Kyoto City University of Arts

**RECENT EXHIBITIONS INCLUDE**
2007    Some Rinpa, Some Seiryukan, Kyoto
        Japanese Suppleness Gjethuset, Gallery Spot, Denmark
2005    Gallery Konishi, Kyoto (solo)
        5th Triennial International Tapestry and Textile Art Exhibition, Tournai, Belgium
        15th Seiryu Dye Works Exhibition, Kyoto Municipal Museum of Art
2003    Tokyo international Forum (solo)
2001    Oriel 31 Davies Memorial Gallery, Wales (solo)
        Meeting Point, National Museum of Scotland (solo)

**COMMISSIONS**
Nara Tawaramoto Municipal Aogaki Library in Lifelong Study Center
Yamanashi Prefectural Central Hospital
Sumoto Civic Health and Welfare Center, Hyogo
Kumiyama Municipal Office, Kyoto

**COLLECTIONS**
Kyoto Prefecture
The National Museum of Art Osaka
Rias Ark Museum of Art, Miyagi

## SHOKO NOMURA DOB 1972

**EDUCATION**
1997    MFA, Kyoto City University of Arts
1995    BA, Kyoto Seika University of Arts

**RECENT EXHIBITIONS INCLUDE**
2007    LandscOpe-LANDeSCAPE, Gallery Art Site, Seian University of Art and Design
2006    GalleryGallery, Kyoto (solo)
        Worlds End Party, Gallery Art Site, Seian University of Art and Design
2005    5th Triennial International Tapestry and Textile Art Exhibition, Belgium
        Gallery Maronie, Kyoto (solo)
2004    Exhibition of Paper Works, Kyoto Art Center, Kyoto
        Women in Textile Art, 3rd International Biennial: Square-Carre-Cuadrado, Valencia-Venezuela
        GalleryGallery, Kyoto (solo)
2002    Mini-Textile International Contemporary Art Exhibition, Barcelona
        Encounters and Journeys, Craft ACT, Australia

**AWARDS**
2002    Scythia, 4th International Symposium & Exhibition on Textile Art, Ukraine. 1st Prize

## MASAAKI TATE DOB 1972

**EDUCATION**
1995    Osaka University of Arts

**RECENT EXHIBITIONS INCLUDE**
2007    Contemporary Dye Works Exhibition, Museum of Dye Works Seiryu, Kyoto
        Today's Art Textile Formation, Sembikiya Gallery, Tokyo
        Asia Fiber Art Exhibition, Urasoe City Art Museum, Okinawa
        Exchanging Tradition, Kyoto Art Center, Kyoto
2006    Asia Fiber Art Exhibition, Gwangju Art Museum, Korea
        Textile in Future Expression, 21st Century Museum of Contemporary Art, Kanazawa
        Exchanging Tradition, Southern Project Studio, Australia
        4th International Fiber Art Biennale, Suzhou Art & Design Technology Institute Art Gallery, China
2005    Seiryuten Some Exhibition, Kyoto Municipal Museum of Art, Kyoto
        Sembikiya Gallery, Tokyo (solo)

**AWARDS**
2002    Mihama Art Exhibition, 3rd Prize

**COLLECTIONS**
Museum of Dye Works Seiryu

## MITSUO TOYAZAKI DOB 1955

**EDUCATION**
1981    MFA, Tokyo University of Art, Japan

**RECENT EXHIBITIONS INCLUDE**
2006    Space Gion Konisi, Kyoto (solo)
        [ex]Changing Traditions Southern Project Studio, Australia
2005    5th International Textile Triennale Exhibition, Belgium
        Textile 05 Kaunas Art Biennale, Lithuania
2004    Tsuuzakigonomi Asahibeer Oyamazaki Museum, Kyoto
2003    Art of Fingertip Size, Gallery Keihu, Kyoto
2002    Sibukawa City Museum, Gumma (solo)

**AWARDS**
1994    4th International Textile Competition, Industrial Design Award, Kyoto
1991    In Our Hands: An International Competition, Nagoya, Grand Prix

**COLLECTIONS**
1998    Memories of the Flood: North Dakota Museum of Art, U.S.A

## DR ZANE BERZINA DOB 1971

### EDUCATION

00-05 Ph.D. at the London College of Fashion, University of the Arts London, UK
95-99 Institute for Experimental Fashion and Textile Design, Berlin University of the Arts, Germany
90-94 BA, Textile Department, Latvian Academy of Arts, Riga, Latvia

### RECENT EXHIBITIONS INCLUDE

2007 Our Cyborg Future? Discovery Museum, Newcastle
2006 Skin Stories II – Archaeology of Skin, Foreign Art Museum, Riga, Latvia (solo) (catalogue)
2005 Look at Me, National Portrait Gallery, London. Touch Me, Victoria & Albert Museum, Contemporary Space, London
2004 Designers' Saturday, Création Baumann, Langenthal, Switzerland Insane about the Membrane, Gallery – University of Brighton
2003 Skin Stories: Charting and Mapping the Skin, Fashion Space Gallery, University of the Arts London (solo)
Artists at Work: New Technology in Textile and Fibre Art, Textile Museum of Prato, Italy (catalogue)
2002 Adaptation – Contemporary Latvian Art Now, National Art Museum, Tallinn, Estonia.
International Biennial Design, Saint-Etienne, France (catalogue)

### AWARDS

07-09 AHRC (with Prof. J Jefferies) 'E-Static Shadows'. Constance Howard Resource and Research Centre in Textiles, Goldsmiths College
02-04 The Textile Institute Bursary
1999 Artist Grant from the Soros Center for Contemporary Art, Riga, Latvia
98-99 Scholarship from the Foundation Kulturkapitala Fonds in Latvia
1995 UIAH Scholarship, Finland
1995 CIMO – Nordic Council of Ministers Scholarship, Finland

### COMMISSIONS

04-06 Site Specific textile installations for a new office building Hessische Zentrale für Datenverarbeitung in Wiesbaden, Germany together with Stringl+Kramm Architects, Germany

## IEVA KRUMINA DOB 1964

### EDUCATION

92-93 MFA, Art Academy of Latvia
84-89 BFA, Art Academy of Latvia, Textile department

### RECENT EXHIBITIONS INCLUDE

2007 The 5th Cheongju International Craft Competition (Korea)
The 7th International Baltic Mini Textile Triennial, Gdynia, Poland Silk and porcelain (together with Aris Seglins)
Filare il Tempo International Miniature Textile exhibition, Como, Italy
12th International Triennial of Tapestry, Lodz, Poland
06-08 International Lace Biennial, Brussels, Belgium
2006 The Edge of the World, Gallery Maja, Liepaja, Latvia (solo)
Memories about the Garden, Gallery Apsida, Riga, Latvia (solo)
04-05 American Tapestry Biennial Five, Denver, USA
2004 From Lausanne to Beijing 3: Contemporary International Fibre Art, Shanghai, China

### AWARDS

2007 Special Prize, 5th Cheongju International Craft Competition, Korea Prize of the Public in International Lace Biennial (Heidelberg), Germany
2004 Prize of Distinction at the 6th International Baltic Mini Textile Triennial, Gdynia, Poland
2003 Riga, Latvian Book Art Competition. 1st Prize
1998 Competition Prize: Riga in Contemporary Art, Latvia

### COLLECTIONS

Latvian Art Fund
Latvian Applied Arts & Design Museum
Museum of The History and Navigation in Riga
Art Museum of Jurmala, (Latvia)
Commercial Bank of Riga
Private collections in Latvia, USA, Germany, Netherlands, United Kingdom

## UNA LAUKMANE DOB 1971

### EDUCATION

93-98 Textile Design, Department of Textiles, Art Academy of Latvia
89-91 Speciality of motion plastics producer, Moscow Culture Institute

### RECENT EXHIBITIONS INCLUDE

2006 The Diary, Agija Suna Gallery, Riga, Latvia
2005 Traveling exhibition: The mist falls, the dew falls, various cities, Sweden
2004 Forever Young, Baltic textile artists, Stockholm, Sweden
2003 World in the World, Arsenal Museum, Riga
2002 Connection, Museum of Applied Arts, Riga
Balance, St Peter's Church, Riga, Latvia

### AWARDS, COMMISSIONS AND COLLECTIONS

2005 Book design, Tales About Life of Children, (Annual Award for Golden Apple Tree)
2002 Textile illustrations to the book by I. Zandere, Inside and Outside, (Annual Award for Golden Apple Tree)
2004 Costume design, The Raven, Valmiera theatre, Latvia
2001 Interior design Nordic National Park
2000 Interior design Cafe Trio
1997 The Fifth Annual Exhibition, Opera, Soros Contemporary Art Centre, Riga

## LIJA RAGE DOB 1948

### EDUCATION

2003 MFA, Art Academy of Latvia
68-74 Textile Art Department, Latvian Academy of Art, Riga, Latvia

### RECENT EXHIBITIONS INCLUDE

2007 International Craft Biennale, Corey, USA
2006 Tallinn Applied Arts Triennial, Decorative and Applied Art Museum, Tallinn, Estonia
2004 Gallery Daugava (solo)
2003 International Fibre Art Competition exhibition, Kaunas, Lithuania
2002 Exhibition of Latvian Fibre art, Contemporary Art Museum, Liege, Belgium
2001 European Textile Art Exhibition, Exhibition Hall Arsenals, State Museum of Art, Riga, Latvia
2001 Gallery Daugava, Riga, Latvia (solo)
Riga Gallery, Riga, Latvia (solo)
1999 4th International Textile Art Biennial, Beauvais, France
1998 Baltic Patterns, Gallery Stairs & Co, London, England

### AWARDS

2007 Special Prize, 5th Cheongju International Craft Competition, Korea
1985 Grand prix, Baltic Applied Art Triennial, Tallinn, Estonia

### COLLECTIONS

Decorative + Applied Art Museum Riga, Latvia
Artists' Union of Latvia Art Collection, Riga, Latvia
Dortmund, modern art collection
Kristiansen University Art Collection, Norway
Private collections in Latvia, France, Germany, USA, Australia, Sweden and Russia

## PETERIS SIDARS DOB 1948

### EDUCATION

73-78 Department of Textile, Riga, Latvian Academy of Arts
64-72 Liepaja School, Department of Decorative Art and Interior Design, Latvia

### RECENT EXHIBITIONS INCLUDE

2007 No comments, Riga's Gallery, Latvia (solo)
2006 4th International Fibre Art Biennale Exhibition: From Lausanne to Beijing, Suzhou, China
International Tsai-mo Square Cloth Exhibition, Taichung Culture Centre, Taiwan
2005 Transience and Dissolution at Alingsas Art hall, Göteborg, Sweden
2004 10th International Lace Biennial, Contemporary Art, Brussels, Belgium
9th Tatun International Art Exhibition, Taichung, Taiwan
2003 Passions, Gallery of the Latvian Artists' Union, Riga, Latvia (solo)
IBM Zurich Research Laboratory, Switzerland (solo)
The European Textile Network exhibition Artists at Work, New Technology in Textile and Fibre Art, The Textile Museum of Prato, Italy
Wild Photographers, Communications Centre Factory of Dream, Riga

### AWARDS, COMMISSIONS AND COLLECTIONS

2004 Outstanding Prize of 3rd International Fibre Art Biennale Exhibition: From Lausanne to Beijing, Shanghai, China
Fine Art Prize of 9th Tatun International Art Exhibition, Taichung, Taiwan
2003 Annual Prize for innovative approach in visual art of the Culture Capital Foundation of Latvia
2002 Grant of Nordic Artists' Centre in Dale / Norway
Residency at the Cill Rialaig International Artists Retreat, Ballinskelligs, Co Kerry, Ireland
2001 Prize of Air Baltic
1999 Premium of annual exhibition: Autumn, Latvia
Grant of Ministry of Culture of the Republic of Latvia

## DZINTRA VILKS DOB 1948

### EDUCATION

2003 MFA, Art Academy of Latvia
73-78 Textile Art Design, Art Academy of Latvia

### RECENT EXHIBITIONS INCLUDE

2007 Exhibition Hall of Cesis, Cesis, Latvia (solo)
2006 Fibre Art and Textile, Exhibition Hall of Latvian Artists' Association;
2005 Expedition Agave, Exhibition Hall Melngalvju Nams, Riga, Latvia (solo)
2004 Group Exhibition, Exhibition Hall Bavaccano, Bolonga, Italy
Textile and Fibre from Latvia, Sevilla, Spain
2003 Gallery Daugava, Riga, Latvia (solo)
2002 Latvian Contemporary Art, The Central House of Artists, Moscow, Russia
Exhibition of Latvian Contemporary Art, Applied Art Museum of Liège, Belgium
2001 Palagio Di Parte Guelfa, Florence, Italy (solo)
Fibre Art Exhibition, UNESCO Centre, Paris, France

### COLLECTIONS

Decorative Applied Art Museum, Riga, Latvia
Artists' Union of Russia, Moscow
Latvian Embassy, Copenhagen, Denmark
Art Museum of Alborg, Denmark
Various private collections in: USA, Australia, Canada, Germany, Norway, Mexico, Italy, Russia, Finland, Latvia

## EGLĖ GANDA BOGDANIENĖ DOB 1962

**EDUCATION**

80-85 State Institute of Arts (now Vilnius Academy of Fine Arts), Textile Department, Graduated with honour diploma.

**RECENT EXHIBITIONS INCLUDE**

2004 Mark II, (with J. Vazalinskienė) Gallery Akademija, Vilnius
Penelope and Nausikaya. (with L. Oržekauskienė) Gallery Lutnia, Lodz, Poland
Day of Welcome. Killkenny, Ireland
In My very Own Shirt. The 1st bienale of Lithuanian Textile. Gallery Arka, Vilnius.
Diploma for Using New Techniques
One Gramme of Gold. Gallery Meno Niša, Vilnius.

2003 Forever Young. Baltic – Swedish textile exhibition. Gallery INFRA, Vasby, Sweden
Soft Meadow. Former Printing House, Vilnius

2002 Touchable Objects. Janina Monkute Marks Museum, Kedainiai, Lithuania

2001 10th International Triennale of Tapestry, The Central Museum of Textiles, Lodz, Poland

1996 Sweet Sight. Three Egles. (with E. Pukyte and E. Babilaite). Gallery Akademija, Vilnius

## SEVERIJA INČIRAUSKAITĖ-KRIAUNEVIČIENĖ DOB 1977

**EDUCATION**

2007 Awarded art licentiate
01-03 MA textile art, Vilnius Academy of Fine Arts, Lithuania
97-01 BA Textile art, Vilnius Academy of Fine Arts, Lithuania

**RECENT EXHIBITIONS INCLUDE**

2007 3+3 Junge Kunst Aus Drei Landern, Neues Kunsthaus Ahrenshoop, Ahrenshoop, Germany
Art For Sustainability, Abbekas Gallery, Abbekas, Sweden

2006 One Work Exhibition organised by the Lithuanian Artists' Association in the window of the Faculty of Arts, Vilnius College of Higher Education
4th Tallinn Applied Art Triennial 2006, Two Close Ones, Estonian Museum of Applied Art and Design, Tallinn, Estonia

06-05 Congratulations…, Vartai Gallery, Vilnius

2005 Beauty Should Live, Akademija gallery, Vilnius

2005 Contemporary textile art of Lithuania, Kornerpark Gallery, Berlin, Germany

2004 About Football, Softly and Femininely, Klaipeda Gallery

**AWARDS**

2003 3rd Prize of the Vilnius Academy of Fine Arts for her MA thesis.
Special prize at the international exhibition of textile, The Face and the Wrong Side

1999 2nd Prize of A. Tamošaitis, Honorary Professor of the Vilnius Academy of Fine Arts

## LINA JONIKĖ DOB 1969

**EDUCATION**

89-95 Kaunas Art Institute of Vilnius Art Academy
88-90 Private A. Aleksandravičius studio of anatomy painting

**RECENT EXHIBITIONS INCLUDE**

2006 Lithuanians Every Day Life, Gallery Sofa, Druskininkai, Lithuania.

2005 Textile Body, Domonic Rostworowski Gallery, Krakow, Poland.
New Lithuanian Textile, Museum of Decorative and Applied Arts, Riga, Latvia.
Junge Textilkunst aus Litauen, Gallery Körnerpark, Berlin, Germany
"Northern Fibre: (Wo)Man and Technologies" workshop, Tuusula, Finland.

2004 11th International Textile Triennial Lodz '04. Lodz, Poland.

2003 Textile and Me, Foreign Art Museum, Riga, Latvia

2002 Textile and Me, Kaunas Picture Gallery of National M. K. Čiurlionis Museum, Kaunas, Lithuania

2001 Lithuanian Country Star, Gallery of Textile Guild, Kaunas, Lithuania.

2000 World Wide Mobile Exhibition: Women in the World, White Columns Gallery, New York; Flint Art Institute, Michigan, USA; Brenau University, Alabama; Gaines Villa, Georgia; Delta Axis, Memphis, Tennessee.

**AWARDS**

2006 Lithuanian Textile Art Biennial Route. Vilnius, Lithuania, 2nd Prize

05-01 Excellence Award / First Grade Diploma 5th and 3rd international Kaunas Art Biennial Kaunas, Lithuania

2004 Best Foreign Artists Medal of Poland Artists' Association. 11th International Textile Triennial Lodz '04

1997 Excellence Award at 5th International Textile Competition. Kyoto, Japan.

**COLLECTIONS**

M. K. Čiurlionis Art Museum in Kaunas, Lithuania
Private collections in Denmark, Austria and Lithuania.

## AUSTE JURGELIONYTE DOB 1976

**EDUCATION**

99-01 MA (Art Textile), Vilnius Academy of Fine Arts, Lithuania
1999 Multimedia, Ecole Nationale Superieure des Beaux-Arts de Paris, France
95-99 BA (Art Textile), Vilnius Academy of Fine Arts, Lithuania

**RECENT EXHIBITIONS INCLUDE**

06-07 Litewskie Tkaniny Artystyczne, Warsaw, Poland

2006 …des mites au musée?!…, Le Musée du Feutre, Mouzon, France
Feast, St. Tomas Gallery, Rovinj, Croatia

2005 Track of Wool, "Vartai" Gallery, Vilnius, Lithuania

2003 Contemporary Baltic/Swedish Textile Exhibition "Forever Young" Gallery INFRA, Väsby, Sweden
Meeting Place, North-European Contemporary Art, Gothenburg (Sweden); Stavanger, Rogalands Art Centre (Norway); Helsinki, The Cable Factory (Finland); Vilnius, Former Printing House (Lithuania); Riga, The Museum Of Foreign Art (Latvia); Tallinn, Art Museum Of Estonia (Estonia); Södertälje, Art Hall (Sweden)
White Moths and 15 Men About Love, Meno Nisa Gallery, Vilnius, Lithuania
New generation 2003, Central House of Artists, Moscow, Russia

2002 Exhibition of the group White Moths and Panevezys Textile Artists, Civic Art Gallery, Panevezys, Lithuania

2000 Christmas Ravings of the Moths, Academy Gallery, Vilnius, Siauliai, Lithuania

**AWARDS**

2002 1st award to the artists'group "Baltos Kandys"("White Moths") for art installation "Paradoxal things" in the M. Valančius Street. Festival "Kaunas Days, Kaunas, Lithuania

2002 State grant awarded to promote arts and culture by the Ministry of Culture / Republic of Lithuania

1999 LVMH Awards for young artists in Paris ENSBA (Ecole Nationale Superieure des Beaux-Arts de Paris)

## LAIMA ORŽEKAUSKIENĖ DOB 1959

**EDUCATION**

78-85 Department of Textiles, Kaunas Art Institute of Vilnius Art Academy

**RECENT EXHIBITIONS INCLUDE**

2006 Parliament of Lithuania Republic, Lithuania (solo)
2005 International Textile Exhibition, Finland
2004 International Fibre Art Biennale, Shanghai, China
2003 Contemporary Lithuanian Textile, Stockholm, Sweden
2002 International Textile Exhibition "Garden of Peace", Venice, Italy

**AWARDS**

2005 National Award of Lithuania Republic (Winner of the Lithuania National Art prize of 2005).

2004 Outstanding honorable award. International Fibre Art Biennale, Shanghai, China.

2003 Grand Prix at International Textile Exhibition, Kaunas, Lithuania

01-02 Grand Prize from the Government of Lithuania

1999 Prize at International Textile Exhibition, Kaunas, Lithuania

1998 Diploma at International Textile Exhibitio, Kaunas, Lithuania

## LAURA PAVILONYTE DOB 1976

**EDUCATION**

2002 MA Art Textile, Vilnius Academy of Fine Arts, Lithuania
1999 BA Art Textile, Vilnius Academy of Fine Arts, Lithuania

**RECENT EXHIBITIONS INCLUDE**

2007 Fertile Felt, Museum Smallingerland Drachten, Netherlands

2006 ART'FAB / L'Art La Femme L'Europe, Saint-Tropez, France
Metaphysics of Spaces, Gallery Hobby, Tbilisi, Georgia;
Contemporary Art Center, Baku, Azerbaijan;
EU, Gateway, Tokyo, Japan

2005 Att varai i centrum, Krapperups Gallery, Hogan, Sweden
The 1st Quadriennale of Lithuanian contemporary fine arts, CAC, Vilnius
Track of Wool, Vartai Gallery, Vilnius, Lithuania

2004 Near is my Shirt, but Nearer is my Skin, "Arka" Gallery, Vilnius, Lithuania

2003 New generation 2003, Central House of Artists, Moscow, Russia
Grosse Kunst Ausstellung Dusseldorf NRW, Dusseldorf, Germany

**AWARDS, COMMISSIONS AND COLLECTIONS**

2006 Lithuanian Textile Biennial – Award of Professionalism; Arka Gallery, Vilnius, Lithuania

2005 Basanavičius state award for the best professional art debut of young artists

2003 Individual yearly state grant

2002 Individual yearly state grant
Avenue of Muses, Kaunas Days, 1st Prize

## MICHAEL BRENNAND-WOOD DOB 1952

**EDUCATION**
75-77   MA Textiles, Birmingham Polytechnic
72-75   BA (Hons) Textiles, Manchester Polytechnic

**RECENT EXHIBITIONS INCLUDE**
2007   A Field of Centres, Millennium Galleries, Sheffield (solo)
        Finding Lost Values, Cheongju International Craft
        Biennale, Korea.
        The Flower, Galerie Handwerk, Munich.
2006   Gilt Trips, Galerie Ra, Amsterdam (NL) (solo)
        Depth of Field, MAC Birmingham
2005   A Field of Centres, Harley Gallery, Ruthin Gallery, tour (solo)
        Transformations: the Language of Craft, National Gallery of
        Australia (AUS)
        Revealed, Castle Museum & Art Gallery, Nottingham
2004   Collect, The Victoria & Albert Museum, London
2003   The Kanazawa World Craft Forum, Invitational Exhibition (J)

**AWARDS**
2005   Visiting Professorship, Manchester Metropolitan University
2001   Arts and Humanities Research Board (AHRB) Fellowship in
        the Creative and Performing Arts in conjunction with the
        University of Ulster
2000   Year of the Artist, Eastern Arts Board, in conjunction with
        photographer James Austin

**COMMISSIONS**
2007   New Onocology Wing, Leeds.
2004   East Winter Garden, Canary Wharf Group PLC
2004   Royal Aberdeen, Childrens Hospital,

**COLLECTIONS**
21st Century Museum of Contemporary Art, Kanazawa (J)
Whitworth Art Gallery
National Gallery of Australia, Canberra (Aus)
www.brennand-wood.com

## MAXINE BRISTOW DOB 1962

**EDUCATION**
1985   MA Textiles, Manchester Metropolitan University
1984   BA (Hons) Fashion/Textiles (Embroidery), First Class Honours
        Manchester Metropolitan University

**RECENT EXHIBITIONS INCLUDE**
2007   Business as Usual, Angel Row Gallery
2006   Sensual Austerity, Hub: The National Centre for Craft and Design,
        Bolton Museum and Art Gallery
        Serial Repetition Grosvenor Museum, Chester.
2005   Revealed, Castle Museum & Art Gallery, Nottingham
        Hands Across the Border. Ruthin Craft Centre; The Hub, Sleaford;
        Mission Gallery, Swansea: The Black Swan Gallery, Frome.
04/05  Through the Surface, Collaborating Textile Artists from Britain
        and Japan. Brighton and Hove Museum and Art Gallery; The
        Sainsbury Centre for Visual Art, Norwich; Bankfield Museum,
        Huddersfield; Castle Museum & Art Gallery, Nottingham; Kyoto
        Museum of Modern Art, Kyoto.
2002   The Gaps Between, International Textile Biannual 2002. Ormeau
        Baths Gallery, Belfast.
        Jerwood Applied Arts Prize 2002: Textiles. Crafts Council Gallery,
        London and touring

**AWARDS**
2002   Shortlisted for the Jerwood Applied Arts Prize 2002: Textiles.
        Crafts Council, London.
2001   One of Four artists selected to represent Great Britain at The 10th
        International Triennial of Tapestry. Museum of Textiles,
        Lodz, Poland

**COLLECTIONS**
Crafts Council, London
Whitworth Art Gallery, Manchester
Castle Museum & Art Gallery, Nottingham, purchased by the
Contemporary Art Society Special Collection Scheme

## SHELLY GOLDSMITH DOB 1962

**EDUCATION**
85-87   MA Royal College of Art, London
82-85   BA (Hons) Degree West Surrey College of Art and Design

**RECENT EXHIBITIONS INCLUDE**
2007   Deep Inspirations, Jerwood Space, London
2006   Out of Place, The New Art Gallery, Walsall
        Penelope's Thread, Victoria and Albert Museum, London
        Depth of Field: conversations between photography and textiles,
        Mac, Birmingham and touring
2005   koko-ima/here-now, Gallery Kaze,Tokyo, Japan
        Revealed: Castle Museum & Art Gallery, Nottingham
2004   Japanese & British Art Now – A Review, Art Planning Room
        AOYAMA, Tokyo, Japan
2003   Kanazawa World Craft Forum, Korinbo Daiwa; Utatsuyama
        Workshop, Kanazawa Japan
2002   Jerwood Applied Arts Prize 2002: Textiles The Crafts Council
        Gallery, London and touring
2001   Ripened, Angel Row Gallery, Nottingham

**AWARDS**
2004   Arts Council of Great Britain: Grant to Individuals Award UK
        Trade and Investments research award
2002   Jerwood Applied Arts Prize 2002: Textiles
1998   British Council Travel Award
1994   The Parnel Prize, Royal Overseas League
1989   Artist Production Grant, Greater London Arts Maintenance and
        Equipment Grant, Crafts Council of Great Britain

**COMMISSIONS**
1997   Commission for The River and Rowing Museum, Henley. David
        Chipperfield Architects

**COLLECTIONS**
Castle Museum & Art Gallery, Nottingham, purchased by the
Contemporary Art Society Special Collection Scheme. The Crafts Council
of Great Britain. The Whitworth Museum and Gallery, Manchester. The
Victoria and Albert Museum, London

## DIANA HARRISON DOB 1950

**EDUCATION**
1973   MA Printed Textiles, Royal College of Art
1971   Dip AD Textiles/Fashion, First Class Honours,
        University of London

**RECENT EXHIBITIONS INCLUDE**
2007   Diana Harrison, GalleryGallery, Kyoto, Japan (solo)
        Diana Harrison Art Quilts, Museum of Arts and Crafts,
        Itami, Osaka
2006   The Festival of Quilts, Birmingham, UK
2005   Transformations, Crafts Study Centre, Farnham,
2004   Stitches in Time, Tullie House, Carlisle
2003   7th Quilt Nihon Exhibition, Tokyo (Toured)
2001   European Art Quilts, Netherlands, Denmark
2000   British Contemporary Quilts, Tokyo, Japan.
        Art of the Quilts, Shipley Arts Gallery, Gateshead.
        1st European Quilt Triennial, Textilmuseum,
        Max Berk, Germany

**AWARDS**
2005   Winner of Quilt 2005, The Festival of Quilts, Birmingham
2003   Silver Award 7th Quilt Nihon Exhibition, Tokyo
1999   Winner of Quilt 1999, awarded by Coates Crafts Ltd.

**COLLECTIONS**
Bankfield Museum, Halifax, Yorkshire
Crafts Council, London (3 pieces)
Victoria and Albert Museum, London
Crafts Study Centre, Farnham, Surrey
Museum of Modern Art, Kyoto, Japan (2 pieces)
Quilters Guild of the British Isles, Halifax, UK
International Quilt Study Center, University of Nebraska, USA

## SUE LAWTY DOB 1954

**EDUCATION**
73-76   BA (Hons) Furniture Design (First Class), Leeds Polytechnic

**RECENT EXHIBITIONS INCLUDE**
2008   Tapestry 2008: The Fine Art of Weaving, The Australian
        National University
2007   Touch Stroudwater International Textile Festival (catalogue)
05/06  Concealed–Discovered–Revealed: Artist in Residence,
        Gallery 101, Victoria & Albert Museum, London
2006   Beyond Weaving: International Art Textiles Flinn Gallery,
        Greenwich, USA (catalogue)
2004   Rock–Raphia–Linen–Lead, Bankfield Museum,
        Halifax (catalogue)
2002   International Textile Biannual Ormeau Baths Gallery, Belfast
        (catalogue)

**AWARDS**
2008   Hancock Fellow 2008, Victorian Tapestry Workshops, Australia
2002   Research and Development Bursary, Arts Council
1996   Bursary, Theo Moorman Charitable Trust

**COLLECTIONS AND COMMISSIONS**
Victoria & Albert Museum, London
Bankfield Museum, Halifax
British Embassy, Amman, Jordan (Foreign and
Commonwealth Office, London)
British High Commission, Ghana (Foreign and
Commonwealth Office, London)
Leeds Museums Collections, Leeds
St. Edmundsbury Cathedral, Bury St. Edmunds
World Beach Project (www.vam.ac.uk worldbeachproject),
V&A Online, 2007/8

## FREDDIE ROBINS DOB 1965

**EDUCATION**
87-89   MA (RCA), Constructed Textiles, Royal College of Art, London
84-87   BA (Hons), Constructed Textiles, Middlesex Polytechnic, London

**RECENT EXHIBITIONS INCLUDE**
2007   Body, Nobody, Somebody, West Norway Museum of Decorative
        Art Bergen, Norway (solo). The Perfect, Contemporary Applied
        Arts, London (solo). Radical Lace & Subversive Knitting, Museum
        of Arts & Design, New York and touring USA. Crimes of Omission,
        Institute of Contemporary Art, Philadelphia, USA
2005   Ceremony, Pump House Gallery, Battersea Park, London (co-
        curator and exhibitor). Revealed, Castle Museum & Art Gallery,
        Nottingham. Knit 2 Together: Concepts in Knitting, Crafts Council
        Gallery, London and touring (co-curator and exhibitor)
2004   Flexible 4: Identities, Whitworth Art Gallery, Manchester and
        touring internationally
2002   Cosy, Firstsite at the Minories Art Gallery, Colchester, touring (solo)
        Jerwood Applied Arts Prize 2002: Textiles, Crafts Council Gallery,
        London and touring.

**AWARDS**
2006   AHRC (Arts and Humanities Research Council) Small Grant for the
        Creative and Performing Arts
2003   Travel Award to Bangladesh, British Council
2002   Shortlisted for the Jerwood Applied Arts Prize 2002: Textiles
2001   London Arts Award
1998   Crafts Council Setting Up Award to produce new knitted work

**COMMISSIONS**
1999   Commissioned by inIVA (Institute of International Visual Art) to
        create a multimedia work for X-Space, their experimental web
        space. www.iniva.org/xspaceprojects/robins
98-99  Public Art Commission by the London Borough of Hackney for
        Shoreditch Library, London

**COLLECTIONS**
Victoria and Albert Museum, London. Crafts Council, London.
Castle Museum & Art Gallery, Nottingham, purchased by the
Contemporary Art. Society Special Collection Scheme. Aberdeen Art
Gallery, purchased by the Contemporary Art Society

# ACKNOWLEDGEMENTS

Most sincere and grateful thanks to the University College for the Creative Arts at Canterbury, Epsom, Farnham, Maidstone and Rochester for the continuing support for my work, with particular thanks to the Rector, Professor Elaine Thomas, and to Ian Dumelow, Head of College, Epsom. Very grateful thanks also to the Sainsbury Centre for Visual Arts, University of East Anglia, for the invitation to curate 'Cloth & Culture Now' and the huge amount of support supplied during the gestation and completion of the project – in particular, thanks to the Head of Collections and Exhibitions, Amanda Geitner, without whom the project could not have been realised. Thank you to the Embassies of Estonia, Finland, Japan, Latvia and Lithuania for their support and to the British Council in Estonia, Finland, Japan, Latvia and Lithuania. Special thanks to Keiko Kawashima Project Co-ordinator in Japan, and Astrida Berzina Project Co-ordinator in Latvia, who have given their knowledge, time and energy unreservedly, to Gerry Diebel and the team at Direct Design for the beautiful book and website, to photographers Toshiharu Kawabe, Damian Chapman and Ian Forsyth, and for Damian Chapman's overall photo editorship of the catalogue, and to John Pym for his patient and perceptive copy editing. Thank you to Astrida Berzina, Keiko Fujimoto, Jennifer Harris, Kai Lobjakas, Leena Svinhufvud and Virginija Vitkienė for their helpful and informative contributions to the catalogue, and to their diligent and sensitive translators. Thanks to Beatrijs Sterk and ETN for the pioneering mapping, in the 1990's, of textile practice in Estonia, Latvia and Lithuania, and to Dr. Frances Geesin who so generously shared her knowledge and contacts in Latvia and Estonia. My special thanks for their invaluable support to my research assistant Celia Pym, to Finance Officer at UCCA Epsom Peter Walshaw, to June Hill and to Bob White. And finally to all the artists who have given their time so generously in their interviews and in their extraordinary web statements, and for their wonderful work – thank you.

LESLEY MILLAR
Professor of Textile Culture
University College for the Creative Arts
at Canterbury, Epsom, Farnham,
Maidstone and Rochester